FISHING BASICS

8-1

FISHING BASICS

By Arthur L. Cone

WITHDRAWN

BLACK DOG
& LEVENTHAL
PUBLISHERS
NEW YORK

Published by
Black Dog & Leventhal Publishers, Inc.
151 W. 19th St.
New York, NY 10011

Distributed by
Workman Publishing Company
708 Broadway
New York, NY 10003

Manufactured in the United States of America

ISBN: 1-57912-021-0

h g f e d c b a

Cone, Arthur L.
Fishing basics : a prize catch for fresh and salt water anglers/
by Arthur L. Cone. New York : Black Dog & Leventhal. 1998.
ISBN 1-57912-021-0
I. Title.
98-11508
CIP

Book design by Jonette Jakobson

Table of Contents

FISHING
BASICS

Take a Look at Fishing

Why go fishing? Isn't this just another excuse for frittering away your time doing nothing? What challenge is there for an intelligent person to outwit a humble creature with a brain about the size of a pea? Is fishing moral? Aren't fish entitled to their lives, liberty, and pursuit of happiness without human intervention, especially in the name of sport? Wouldn't you save time and money by buying fish already cleaned and ready to cook at the corner market?

These are only a few of the questions people ask me about fishing! My answer to most of them is to point out that golf balls are inedible and then simply admit I go fishing because I like it. This poor logic saves—for fishing—much time I would otherwise waste in argument.

Actually, if the number of participants in a sport is any gauge, fishing needs no defense. It is here to stay. Governmental sources and the American Fishing Tackle Manufacturers Association estimate that 36,200,000 Americans go fishing. They both say that this number is increasing. According to the Department of the Interior, the sports catch of salt water game and food species now exceeds the commercial catch.

Pity the poor fish! Actually our piscine populations are doing better than ever. We seem as a nation to be emerging from the Industrial Revolution into the Recreational Revolution. With more leisure, more people are fishing. They want better fishing. And as long as politicians depend on votes for election, when the voters want better fishing, they'll get it.

Sports fishing now has its very own Bureau of Sport Fisheries and added help from the Bureau of Outdoor Recreation. Both of these are headquartered in Washington and report to the Secretary of the Interior. So many of the states are involved in fresh water fisheries research that the Bureau of Sports Fisheries has opened several research laboratories to study the life and habits of salt water game fish with the aim of discovering means to improve fishing in the ocean. All of this is part of the politician's response to 36,200,000 voters interested in better fishing.

This is just the start! To provide improved fishing in the Great Lakes region (about whose decline I could write a book) various states introduced salmon and steelhead trout from the Pacific coast.

Down south, Florida is experimenting with tilapia, a tropical panfish that eats algae and

Fishing for trout in fast moving water can often produce spectacular and virtually acrobatic results

other weeds instead of young fish. Other southern states are looking into peacock bass and assorted game fish from the Amazon basin with the aim of getting better fishing for Dixie. With money and research continually being poured into fishing, it's bound to improve even more in the future.

Of course, catching fish isn't all there is to fishing. Unlike some sports in which you compete against fellow humans, fishing is a matching of wits against nature. Therefore, it is often a humbling experience that builds character. As proof thereof, I submit the twelve Apostles, most of whom were fishermen.

Looking at it from another angle, fishing is one of the only extant sports where you can derive the satisfaction of killing and eating your opponent, or if you're in a Roman emperor frame of mind, you may magnanimously set him free to be caught again—as he probably will be.

Another good reason for going fishing is the scenery. You can see the world's finest, including a great deal that ordinary tourists never get to view. You can enjoy a good many glowing dawns missed by people who stay abed—but maybe they are more sensible. It's a matter of personal preference.

As indicated already, fish are edible. You may be prejudiced and dispute this, but doctors claim that fish are particularly good for humans, being all protein without those fatty acids that clog up arteries to the great benefit of the funeral-directing profession. Even if you currently loathe the idea of eating fish, be open-minded and give it a try after you catch a few of your own. Proper cooking could be helpful too.

One of the philosophical benefits of fishing is that it is timeless. Even if you fish every day—spring, summer, fall, and winter—you'll find each one different from those before and those that follow. When you're fishing you're in an ancient world that changes very little, even over centuries.

Here on land, we're living at the tail end of the age of mammals. The mammoth, the buffalo, the rest of the ice age animals are about gone. Only the caribou, far from civilization, still flow in herds across the tundra. In today's America, the open range is a far-off dream, vanished forever behind barbed wire. When you travel, you fly or stick to the highways. You can't wander at all.

Underwater, even in a small pond, little has changed since before the dinosaurs. Like buffalo on the plains before the Civil War, fish move about as they please. Many species go from winter grounds to summer grounds and back again in migrations that haven't changed one iota since long before the first air-breathing animal crawled out onto the sand.

Most fish (except for some tuna and others that have a body temperature) are cold-blooded animals that breathe underwater through gills, which work much as your lungs do with air. All fishes (except a few that have lost them in evolution) have two sets of paired fins, which developed into the arms and legs of land animals. The pectoral fins correspond to your arms. The ventral fins are the paired fins on the fish's stomach and correspond to your legs. Fish use these mainly for balancing. Their caudal fin—tail to you—is what really moves them. Fish also have dorsal fins on their backs and anal fins underneath and near the tail.

The most ancient fish around today are the sharks, rays, and lamprey eels. These really aren't even vertebrates, or true fishes, for they have cartilage instead of a bony spine. Next in age come the ganoids, which have hard, diamond-shaped scales. Fresh water gars of the southern United States are in this group.

The teleost, or bony, fishes are considered recent. However, most species are still millions of years older than any land animal. These are the fish that most of us hope to catch. Teleosts are in two groups: soft-rayed and spiny-rayed. The soft-rayed fishes are older and include most minnows, herrings, trout, pike, catfish, and carp. (Yes, catfish have spines, but they are classified as soft-rayed fishes related to the trout. Scientists can be a bit confusing at times.)

Spiny-rayed fishes include most of our more familiar food and game fish including the basses, perch, tuna, bluefish, swordfish, snappers, and many others. Codfish, cusk, flounder, halibut, and other flatfish belong in this group even though they have no spines. Makes one wonder just how rational an ichthyologist can be, doesn't it?

Fishing, then, is a sport that provides fun, food, relaxation, and scenery. It also presents an opportunity to exercise our skill, and we'll return to this a bit later on. It should be noted here that the investment necessary for any sport is important, although in fishing it isn't enough to hurt you badly. One minor expense I'll mention now is a fishing license. You need this in every state for fresh water fishing and in all states except from Delaware north on the Atlantic Seaboard (Maine and North Carolina may enact a saltwater license shortly)—for salt water fishing as well. These inexpensive licenses provide funds that are used to improve the fishing, so you get your money's worth. Get your license and a copy of your state's fishing regulations early in the game. They're available at most sporting-goods stores and from local municipal clerks.

I.

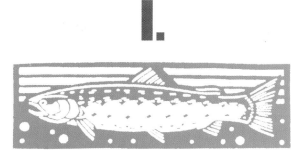

What You Can Choose From

Whether you're an athlete in tip-top physical condition or a person whose principal exercise is avoiding exertion, you can find a form of fishing that will appeal to you personally. Want me to prove it? Here goes.

Fresh Water Fishing

In rough general terms, we can divide all fresh water fishing, the world over, into three classes: panfishing, warm water game fishing, and cold water game fishing.

Panfishing involves small, easily caught fishes in a wide range of species. Most panfishing fans are happier with a lot of little fish than they would be with a few big ones. As most panfishing involves sitting still and watching a bobber, it takes practically no physical activity. Other advantages are that some form of panfishing is available almost everywhere, the equipment investment is small, and it's a great family sport for young and old.

Warm water game fishing includes the black basses, the pike family, and the pike-perch. These fish are available throughout the continental United States, and corresponding species are found around the world. Harder to find and catch than most panfish, warm water game fish will hit artificial lures. Selecting the right lure and casting it to the right spot is what makes this type of fishing interesting. Fishing for bass, pike, pickerel, muskie, and walleyes is typically American fishing involving quite a bit of skill and ingenuity. From the bayous of the South to the birch-bordered waterways of Canada, this is mostly lake fishing and probably 90 percent boat fishing.

Cold water game fishing primarily concerns the trout and salmon families. From Alaska to Tierra del Fuego, and Bergen to Capetown, this is the aristocratic form of fishing. In some areas only fly fishing is permitted. Aside from a few places where guides take you downriver in boats, trout and salmon fishing is mostly wading in fast-moving water. You have to be energetic to enjoy it. Magnificent mountain scenery is generally a part of the game, and

Sunrise on Piney Lake, Colorado

the colorful flies, the beautiful fish, and the interesting pools and riffles help make this type of fishing highly enjoyable. The only real disadvantage is the cost, which can include travel, expensive equipment, and guides (compulsory in some areas). Outside the United States high fees are often charged for trout- and salmon-fishing rights.

Salt Water Fishing

Salt water fishing opportunities include big-game fishing, party-boat fishing, surf-pier-jetty fishing, and bay-inlet-reef fishing.

Big-game fishing takes you out to sea to battle several species of tuna, marlin, sailfish, and swordfish, plus some of the gamier sharks like the mako. Except in a few areas such as Hawaii's Kona Coast and Newfoundland's Avalon Peninsula, you need a large cabin cruiser with special electronic gear. Until you really become expert, you'd better get a professional captain or charter a boat complete with crew. For anyone with muscle and plenty of money, this kind of fishing can provide fun and adventure around the world. Unless and until you're the skipper, you don't need to know much more about fishing than how to hold the rod and turn the reel handle. Locating fish, selecting and rigging baits and lures is handled by professionals. Good boat handling can be an essential part of landing a large fish and is sometimes a tougher job than holding the rod.

Party-boat fishing is available in all seacoast metropolitan areas. This type of fishing provides the advantage of a professional captain and crew on a seaworthy registered vessel at a small fraction of the cost of a private charter, for here you have a craft that will carry all comers, up to capacity, at a reasonable rate per passenger. Some ports offer half-day boats that provide a morning or afternoon of fishing at about two-thirds the daily rate.

Depending on season and location, party-boat fishing can offer anything from sinker-bouncing on the bottom for codfish and flounder to casting lures and bait for medium-sized game fish including bluefish, yellowtail, and albacore. In the Pacific Northwest some party boats troll for salmon with tremendous "cannonball" weights to keep the line under the passenger. Usually party boats going for the more active game species charge a higher fare and limit the number of passengers to ensure enough room for playing and landing big tough fish.

Advantages of party-boat fishing are convenience, economy, and the virtual certainty that a good catch will be made. Tackle and equipment is usually available aboard at a small rental. Bait is included in your fare. The mate will spend much of his free time coaching first-timers. Even with seasick pills, this is no sport for the weak-stomached or the socially snobbish. Regardless of how rough the ocean or how noisy the crowd, you're on for the ride once you leave the dock. Most regular party-boat anglers are good-hearted extroverts who really love the sport, and you'll likely find it a great experience.

Surf, pier, and jetty fishing concentrates on the many marine species that come right into the breakers to feed. There are dozens of these, and they vary in size and gameness from the northern blowfish that weighs six ounces and wiggles slightly to channel bass and salmon that will hit hard enough to almost pull you off your feet. Surf-casting is as close as your nearest beach (after bathing hours) and requires little investment in equipment unless you become a fanatic. However, like trout fishing, you'd better be in good condition before you start bucking the waves to toss nearly a half pound of lead and bait a hundred yards or so. Piers and jetties require less casting, although jetties can call for some very tricky foot-work. This type of fishing separates the real fishermen from the amateurs very quickly. The old hands catch about 90 percent of all surf-caught fish while putting forth about 10 per cent of the man hours. But it's fun even if you come home skunked.

Bay and inlet fishing is primarily a small-boat sport. It gives you a chance to get out to sea without fear of seasickness and catch flounder, porgy, weakfish, bluefish, Spanish mackerel, rock cod, white sea bass—nearly every shallow-water species. In southern waters you can get real excitement with tarpon, bonefish, and barracuda. This too is the only form of salt water fishing where fly casting is anything more than a stunt. The fly-rod enthusiast can do a good job with shallow-water game fish using streamers and other patterns that resemble small fish and shrimp.

Basic Factors
That Influence Angling Success

J ust like people, fish are concerned with eating, propagating, and staying alive. As a group, they're successful in these activities and have been for millions of years—since before the dinosaurs, as a matter of fact. If you're going to catch fish, you'd better decide to learn why fish bite and why they don't. Successful anglers are supposed to be able to "think like a fish." Actually, fish don't think much at all, and even an unthinking angler knows more about fish than the fish know about themselves.

Fish are not, however, just insensitive clods. They have feelings, much like people have. They have senses, which are adapted to life under water and therefore are somewhat different from yours. Because scent carries as well or even better in water than in air, most fish species have a sensitive sense of smell. All television viewers know that sharks can follow a blood trail for miles. But you've probably never realized that many predatory ocean species hunt by their noses, like hounds on a trail, or silent wolves. Chumming, which simply means attracting fish with ground-up oily menhaden, clams, shrimp, or other live bait, often makes for success where bluefish, tuna, yellowtail, or even flounder are loosely grouped over a wide expanse of water.

Many fresh water fish have good noses too. Catfish are especially noted for their olfactory prowess, and to tempt them nauseous mixtures of rotten blood and guts are brewed by Midwestern alchemists who honestly name their concoctions "stink baits." Going from the bottom to the top, cheese is so good a trout bait that it has been banned in some areas. An industry has been developed formulating attractants molded into plastic worms or designed to spray on plugs, flies and even spoons—primarily for bass. Yes, fish certainly use their noses, and an attractive odor—attractive to a fish, that is—can be a big help. This can work in reverse, however. Oil or grease on your hands can cost you action. Even insect repellent or suntan lotion is no help when getting fish to bite.

Clear, shallow water makes it easier to spot fish—but reflection from the sun can be a problem.

What about vision? Fish can see fairly well at short range. Because their eyes have a fixed pupil, which can't contract in bright light or expand in the dark, they tend to see best at dawn and dusk or on overcast days without glare. Light diffuses rapidly underwater, which makes an eye that can't accommodate to extremes in light less of a disadvantage to a water animal.

Trout anglers are always getting into bitter arguments as to how well fish can distinguish colors. As with most differences of opinion, the truth is some place between the two extremes. Color in flies and lures is important; but size, shape, and action are even more important. One point to remember is that any fishing lure should attract attention, but it shouldn't be so overpowering that it scares the fish. Salt water fish, by and large, are tough to dazzle; but in lakes, streams, and ponds you'd be better off staying away from chrome and nickel spoons and spinners on bright sunny days. Brass, copper, even black metal lures will get results when nickel is too shiny. Water color is a factor too. In cedar swamps where clear water looks like weak black coffee, you simply can't use too bright a lure. As a general rule of thumb, the more sophisticated the fish you're after the duller the lures you should use. Thus red and white, red and yellow, silver flash, and chrome are great for salt water, plus the Canadian Arctic and other places that see few fishermen. At the other end of the scale, black is the best lure color for sophisticated fish, even when fishing at night. Because yellow shows up better than white (that's why fog lights are amber), a yellow lure can bring results in muddy or turbid water when nothing else works.

Let's be realistic though and admit the a major reason for the wild proliferation of color combinations in fishing lures is that the tackle industry can sell more this way: the more colors that are available, the more will fishermen buy several different versions of the same plug to have an assortment. What an assortment! When you look at it sensibly, most surface-working plugs and poppers, except those that are all black, are white underneath. Whether they have frog spots, perch bars, silver shiners, or even imperial purple backs are usually inconsequential. The fish, beneath this gaiety, sees only the plug's white belly!

To repeat: Color is important in fishing lures, but less important than lure presentation and action. Every well-known lure, in every color combination made, will definitely catch fish. Try to steer a middle course and come fairly close to imitating nature, and experimentation will bring you the real answers for your own waters. It should be understood that, for a fish, motion rather than color brings the suggestion of a meal. Color is the supplement that can clinch the sale.

Fish are pretty good judges of motion, and the speed of a lure can be vital to success. Many salt water fish will ignore a slow-moving spoon or plug. Get it going fast enough and they'll swarm all over it. In fresh water the opposite is generally true, and the slower you fish with lures or bait, the better your results will be.

Hearing is a piscine forte. In addition to ears buried in the head, fish hear through nerves along the lateral line. Water, a dense medium, conducts sound better than air. See for yourself by grabbing a couple of rocks and knocking them together underwater while you're submerged.

Because fish are sensitive to sound, so-called sonic lures try to create an underwater statement of fish-attracting noise. As any bass specialist with popping bugs will tell you, fish will hit at the sound when they can't even see a lure. But it has to be just the right sound. This is why the experts who catch educated fish in hard-worked lakes put carpeting underfoot in their boats, install nylon bearings on their oarlocks, and never knock out a pipe, scrape a tackle box along the deck, or otherwise cause any vibration that will carry underwater. On the other hand, singing, talking, and listening to the radio are okay.

Fish can respond differently to sound than you might think. "Stoning the pool" (that is, tossing rocks into a stream filled with salmon) has been used to get them to show interest in a fly. This works with other fish too. A handful of small pebbles tossed into a pond will often attract sunfish and perch. When all else fails, try it and see. Or toss a boulder and feel better!

What about motors? Certainly fish can hear them, but whether or not they frighten them is something else again. Most salt water fish, particularly offshore species, seem attracted by a fast boat with a big wake. They'll come right up to the stern to grab a lure. One of the best striper anglers I know never turns his outboards off even in the shallows. Once again, fresh water can be another story, although my personal feeling is that the shadow of the boat flashing across the bottom in shallow water is more frightening to fish than the noise of the motor itself. As a rule however, the less noise and disturbance in fresh water fishing, the better. If you can't row or paddle, an electric motor run by a 12-volt battery is quiet enough.

Maybe they don't need it with a good sense of smell (can you taste with a head cold?), but fish seem to have little sense of taste at all. So don't worry about it. A largemouth bass obviously can't tell a pork-rind eel or a rubber worm from the genuine article.

Attracting fish is one thing. Frightening them is another. Except for the big, fast-moving offshore species, nearly all fish are afraid of shadows, especially fast-moving shadows. To them, a moving shadow is an osprey or a large fish looking for a meal. I think it's the shadows and wake rather than the motor noise that have ruined fishing in daylight hours on lakes where high-powered speedboats run more or less amuck. Shallow-water fish such as trout are so cognizant of danger from above that even the shadow of your rod will frighten them away. When standing on shore make certain that your own shadow doesn't fall on the water you're fishing.

Fish, just like other wild animals, are afraid of the unusual—the unfamiliar noise, the moving shadow. It's amazing that fish, living in a world where they're always somebody else's potential dinner, aren't even more jittery than they are. Bear this in mind. Generally, try to cast carefully without sloppy splashing. Wear dull or neutral-colored clothing. White T-shirts may be cool, but they're too visible to wear fishing.

All of nature is just one big schoolhouse. When you're fishing, you're at school. One of the charms of this sport is that no matter how much you know, you always pick up additional little bits of information that can make a so-so day into a success. It's the know-it-all who usually succeeds in getting skunked, like the guy I spotted up at Gananoque one bright sunny morning flinging a chrome-plated spoon so shiny it blinded me a mile away. Since I knew him, I suggested that maybe something smaller and duller would work better, and he exploded. But he didn't get a smell of a pike and came into camp complaining about the miserable fishing and ranting that the lake was fished out. Using small, dull-colored spoons and spinners, my wife and I had enjoyed a great morning. The lake wasn't fished out. But smart fish are more than a match for dumb fishermen.

Tides, Moon, and Fish Feeding Patterns

If you went without eating for several weeks, you'd probably be dead or wish you were. A month without food wouldn't seriously bother most fish. Because they are cold-blooded and don't burn energy to keep up their body temperature, fish have a very low metabolism. Therefore, they are rarely really hungry in the human sense. If they were, fishing would be too easy!

Why do fish bite? Hunger is part of it, naturally. In addition, there are varying motives of rage, curiosity, and the desire to kill. Also, jealously is a factor that explains why fish seem to bite all at once and quit all at once. A fish that sees another fish feeding will start feeding itself. One proof that hunger is really not too important is that when fish are really biting, their stomachs are full before you hook them. They need another minnow about as much as you'd need a fourth sirloin steak at a cookout. At times when fishing is poor, the fish you catch will be empty. According to human logic, this is when they should be feeding! Fish, then, need some stimulus besides hunger to put them in a feeding mood. This is where tides, moon, and weather come in.

Even if you've never seen the ocean, you know about high tide and low tide. If you live near the seacoast, you probably know that the time of high tide (and low tide) advances about an hour every day. Very few people, except Hawaiians, know that in mid-ocean high tide is always at noon and midnight, and low tide is always at sunrise and sunset. To explain this, just think of the ocean as a giant washtub filled with water. If you tilt it to one side or another, the level in the middle will stay the same even though the level at the sides of the tub will vary greatly. It's the same thing with the oceans. At mid-ocean, tides are caused mainly by the sun, which pulls the water away toward the horizon at sunrise and sunset and "releases" the water toward the middle at midday and midnight.

Especially in bays and estuaries, an outgoing tide brings bait fish, shrimp, and other food out of the shallows along shore into deeper water where fish can reach them. At the same time, the reduced volume of water tends to concentrate this food in a smaller area, and this eventually triggers a feeding reaction among the fish. Most surf casters prefer an incoming tide. This is because a flooding tide floats soft crabs and other fish goodies out of their burrows and again triggers a feeding reaction.

Because the moon, with help from the sun, creates the tides, the stage of the moon has an effect on the tidal range from high to low. So-called spring tides (no relation to the season) take place every twenty-eight days at full moon and are the highest tides of the month. Neap tides, at the dark of the moon, have the lowest tidal range. Because of all kinds of other complications, including the fact that full-moon periods are often accompanied by bad weather and a falling barometer, best fishing is usually at the neap-tide period of the month. And amid a wild flurry of theories about why it should be so, this holds true for fresh water fish who haven't known a tide since their remote ancestors left the sea hundreds of millions of years ago.

In an attempt to make some logic from all this, a fine sportsman and gentleman, John Alden Knight, spent years developing what he titled the Solunar Tables. These were the result of a great deal of experimentation during which he proved to himself that fish were apt to feed, for no apparent reason, at what would correspond to low tide in any locality, even in landlocked lakes thousands of miles from an ocean. Because tides can be forecast precisely from a lunar cycle, Mr. Knight figured out what he called the Solunar Periods in charts which could be utilized in any part of North America. Then, as you might guess, followed a wild orgy of name-calling by anglers who tried Mr. Knight's tables and swore by them, and others who simply swore at them.

My personal feeling is that Mr. Knight was on the right track and the only thing wrong with his theory is what knocks most generalizations out of the box: the fact that a generalization holds true only when other factors remain equal. Under set conditions of water level, sunlight, barometric pressure, and season, Solunar Tables and other charts based on phases of the moon will likely deliver the goods. On the other hand, local vagaries of wind and weather can certainly knock them into a cocked hat. This is why I leave the theories to the theorists and follow the simple philosophy of going fishing every chance I get!

I know, however, that the moon does affect fishing and so does the barometer. A barometer is simply an instrument that measures atmospheric pressure expressed in inches of mercury. Modern barometers work on coiled metal springs and are called aneroid barometers, but they still read in inches of mercury. A rising barometer shows improving or good weather and good fishing. A continuing steady high barometer over a period of days brings poor fishing. Low barometric pressure is a poor sign, and a quickly falling barometer makes fishing hopeless. Because the barometer usually rises as much as twenty-four hours before rain ends, some of the best fishing is on rainy overcast days on a slowly rising atmospheric pressure.

Wind direction can also be a tip-off to fishing conditions. Possibly because they accompany a high barometric pressure, light westerly winds usually bring good fishing. In some areas an east or south wind is an indication that fishing will be poor. Violent winds from any direction are bad for fishing in lakes and large bays, with the exception that landlocked salmon seem to prefer a gale that pours oxygen into the water. On the ocean, wind can make it too rough to fish, but ocean fish don't seem to mind unless the barometer is sliding. An approaching storm that sends big, quiet, oily-smooth ground swells across the sea brings fishing to an abrupt halt. Even if you find fish on a depth recorder they simply refuse to bite.

No doubt about it, during most of the year dawn and dusk are the best hours of the day for fishing. As we've seen, fish see better at those times. Additionally, boat traffic is usually light then too. On the other hand, in very cold water, midday can sometimes warm things up enough so fish start feeding. What about night fishing? Depends on what you're fishing for. Down on the Gulf Coast, fishing by flares at night for sea trout is a great sport. Farther north, some species such as walleyes in fresh water and frostfish in salt water prefer to feed at night. Others, including yellow perch and most of the pike family, go to bed early.

Obviously, water conditions will influence fishing. As a rule in lake fishing, low water beats high water. Low water concentrates the fish and bait in a smaller area, and this kicks off feeding sprees. Stream fishing is usually best on normal water levels and on a slight rise following a rain. In every kind of fishing, extreme water conditions, whether high and muddy or too low and clear, will present the angler with head-scratching problems. The problems of high, muddy water are obvious. Gin-clear water, especially in a dead calm, makes fish supersensitive to every disturbance. Even the shadow of a leader will frighten them.

A new school of thinking has developed that revolves around water temperature and the thermocline, which is the point where warm surface water and cold deep water meet as opposing layers. This is the point that fish like best, according to these pundits. Thermometers have their place in fishing, but the folks who rig out with special gear to find the exact depth of the thermocline seem as far out to me as those who worry about the exact shade of the hackles on an Iron Blue Dun. Why make a simple thing like fishing so difficult?

Have we established anything in this chapter? Here's a list of hints to paste in your fishing hat.

1. Fish can see, hear and smell.

2. Fish are attracted by color and motion as long as it's natural.

3. Fish are frightened by too much flash, too much noise and fast moving shadows.

4. Dark of the moon is generally a better fishing time than full moon.

5. Outgoing tide is often best in bays and estuaries.

6. Incoming tide is usually best in the ocean.

7. Fish on a rising barometer. Stay home on a falling or low barometer.

8. Dawn and dusk are good times to be fishing (also for coffee and cocktails if they're not biting).

9. In a lake, low water beats high water. In a stream, medium or slowly rising water is best.

10. Extremes of wind, mud, clarity of water, give poor results.

11. Fish don't necessarily bite because they're hungry. Try and figure out why they are biting and you'll get them.

III.

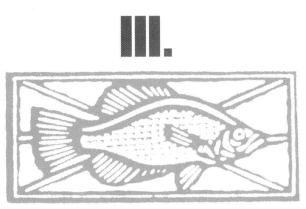

Panfishing—Action for Everyone

Description of Panfish Species

Panfish of one sort or another are found nearly everywhere in fresh water clean enough to support fish life. Since panfishing is far and away the most popular form of fresh water angling, it makes sense to start with it.

Why is panfishing popular? First of all, it offers plenty of action. Secondly, there's little need to worry about bag and size limits in most states. Most important, while fishing for major game species is often a solitary activity, panfishing is great sport for groups of all ages. These fish aren't very shy. They bite readily. Some of them are an epicure's delight. What they lack in individual poundage they make up for in brilliant color and dashing spirit.

By definition, a panfish will fit in a frying pan. Since this obviously includes a wide variety of species, some of them with little in common except size, or lack of it, I've divided them into six groups. So come along and take a look at the most common, most popular, and most easily caught fish in the United States.

Sunfishes

There are well over a dozen species of these small-mouthed, usually brightly colored, fish. There are northern species and southern species. There are sunfish that can live in water too acid for most other fish. There are others that demand very special conditions. Because few panfishermen are scientists, sunfish are called by all sorts of regional names such as pumpkinseed, perch, bream, and shellcracker.

Bluegill Sunfish

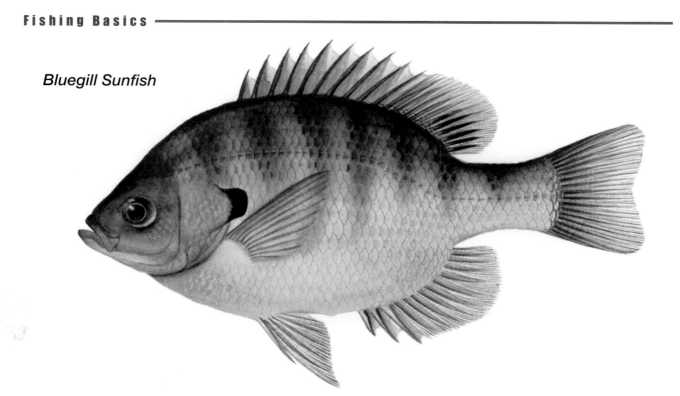

Sunfish range in size from the pygmy sunfish, a beautiful black and white fish that rarely gets over an inch in length, to the bluegill sunfish, which often weighs a pound or more, and the Sacramento perch, which can weigh nearly ten pounds.

Regardless of species or geography, all sunfish are similar. As a group, they live in very shallow water close to shore. While water weeds, lilies, and fallen trees are part of their environment, sunfish generally live in the open.

Sunfish are among the very few fishes that build nests and care for their eggs and new-born young. Because the male sunfish is quite a fighter and eager to defend his brood from any intrusion, sunfish are ridiculously easy to catch during spawning. In southern states, catches of a couple of hundred bream a day are made in early spring when the fish are nesting on their spawning beds. Before you throw up your hands in horror at this poor conservation practice, let's note that it doesn't seem to hurt the sunfish supply at all. Actually, a basic problem with sunfish management is that they tend to overpopulate their environment with the result that more and more fish competing for a limited and static quantity of food results in stunted growth.

Most sunnies have small mouths, yet they're easy to take on bait. Little earthworms, catalpa worms, caterpillars, grubs of all kinds, grasshoppers, even doughballs, all will take sunfish. Sunfish are good fly-rod fish too. Small wet flies on size 10 hooks are the ticket. Tiny rubber spiders, fly-rod pork rind strips, and little fly-rod popping bugs round out the list of useful artificials. Catching sunfish on your fly rod is a good way to get ready for bigger game. And all species are excellent eating, especially when skinned before cooking.

Sunfish Relatives—Little Bigger League Division I

In this division are those species that are shaped like a sunfish but come in larger sizes. It includes the white and black crappies, rock bass, and warmouth. All of these have much larger mouths than the sunfishes. In suitable environment they will all grow to fair size, with the record black crappie (also known as calico bass and strawberry bass) well over five pounds.

Similar in habits, the two crappie species, white in the south and black in the north, are generally found in huge schools. Primarily minnow feeders, they hang off weed beds, sunken brush, and lily pads where small fish hide. Most crappie fishermen use a cane pole, bobber, size 4 hook, and live shiner bait hooked through the back, just behind the dorsal fin. However, these fish will hit small spoons and spinners with a mighty sock, and in the spring, before the big schools drop off into deep water, fly casters do very well with white streamer flies fished on a sinking line.

Rock bass and warmouth, both also known as redeye and bream, are cousins and look it. Rock bass are a northern fish that prefers clean lakes and slow streams with plenty of rocky edges. Warmouth are more at home in weedy, muddy southern rivers. Both species have big mouths, short tempers, and a militant attitude that leads them to attack big bass plugs. However, small shiners, earthworms, grasshoppers, and tiny frogs are the sure way of getting them. Small spoons and spinners will also score as will fly-rod streamers.

Neither the crappies nor the rock basses are noted for fighting zeal. They hit with a wallop and then resistance ceases. They aren't nearly as good eating as the sunfishes either, unless you like fish fairly mushy.

Yellow Perch, White Perch, White Bass, Yellow Bass— Little Bigger League Division II

Yellow Perch

White Bass

By size and basic habits these four species belong in the Little Bigger League. I put them in a separate division because none of them are related to or resemble a sunfish, and also because they are basically deep-water fish rather than the shallow-water species we've been discussing. Aside from the yellow perch, these are members of the sea bass family. You may have heard of landlocked salmon, so landlocked sea bass shouldn't be a total surprise. (In Central America, there are landlocked fresh water sharks and sting rays.)

Yellow perch are an easygoing fish that get along well nearly everywhere. Extremely prolific and active year-round, they'll quickly eliminate trout and other species of game fish if given the chance. In defense of the yellow perch, he's good-looking, fun to catch, and among the best eating fish anywhere. Like the crappies, yellow perch are usually found in large schools. These range anywhere from shallow water to depths of nearly one hundred feet.

Since most perch are about eight inches long, small shiners are the best bait, with worms the runner-up. They'll also take very small spoons and spinners eagerly.

White perch are a marine species found in landlocked lakes from Maine to Maryland. White bass and yellow bass are midwestern and southern species that bear the stripes of their distant striped bass cousin. All three species average about a pound or less in weight, prefer deep water, live in large schools, and feed mostly on minnows. Because they rarely show on the surface, these three species may be plentiful but hard to locate and catch. Small lifelike shiners are the preferred bait everywhere, but worms and tiny frogs will catch fish too. Small spoons and spinners built to run deep are the only artificials worth using. While all these fish are excellent eating and great fun to catch, getting them to hit can present a tougher challenge than with most other panfish. Species in the sea bass group often go for long periods without feeding. If fish can be considered moody, this gang of relatives is positively morose.

Carp, Suckers, Chub, and Shiners

While unpopular here, these and their relations are the big panfish species in most of Europe. In parts of France and England, fishing contests with thousands of competitors are based on species in this group. More ancient by far than the spiny-rayed fish we've been discussing, carp and their relatives have a single, short, spineless dorsal fin, large scales, and small mouths. Actually, a carp stretches our definition of a panfish since a good-sized

Common Shiner

one will weigh twenty pounds.

Carp, suckers, and their tribe are animated vacuum cleaners that scour the bottom looking for food. Best rig for them consists of a saltwater three-way swivel to which is connected your line, a small sinker, and a four-foot leader of light monofilament. At the end of this leader goes a size 6 Eagleclaw hook. Best baits are small earthworms, kernels of canned corn, small doughballs, or cornmeal balls. Most successful carp and sucker anglers bait their fishing grounds in advance either with doughballs or cooked oatmeal. The following evening they go out, cast into the baited area, and wait. This is very quiet, patient fishing, and because you can prop your rod on a forked stick and do something else, it goes well with family picnics. Keep an eye on your rod or else a big carp will have it out in the middle of the lake! Best idea is to leave your reel on the click. Then you can listen for a bite.

Chub and shiners, some species of which reach over a foot in length, are found in the same general type water as sunfish. Various chub species occupy the sunfish niche in northern lakes too cold for sunfish growth. Others live in trout streams and give anglers fits. They'll take a fly, a tiny spinner, anything a trout will. They're not as pretty as a trout, and they

Yellow Bullhead Catfish

certainly don't taste like a trout, so fishermen complain about them. Big shiners, known as roach in many areas, are a favorite of small boys. They go for sunfish baits with wild abandon and fight like tiny tarpon.

Unless you have the equipment and finesse and recipes of a fine European cook, none of the species in this section will do anything good to your taste buds. Suckers from cold water in early spring aren't too bad, but without special treatment all these fish will remind you of toothpicks fried in sawdust.

Bullhead Catfish

There are a few related species of bullhead, but unless you're an ichthyologist you won't care. They're all small, easy to catch, not a bit finicky, great eating, and provide a lot of recreation for people who work all day. (Bullheads bite best after dark.) With huge mouths and a keen sense of smell, bullheads scavenge the bottom. Small bits of smelly cheese and pieces of frankfurter, the garlicky the better, are very successful baits. As an added attraction, punch a couple of holes in each end of a can of dog food and lower it to the bottom alongside your lines. In some Maine lakes, bullheads have pink meat just like a trout. Regardless of whether their flesh is pink, all bullheads are delicious, and this, with panfish, is the name of the game, isn't it?

Best bullhead rig again uses a three-way swivel. Use a short leader or by the time you feel the fish he'll have your hook partly digested! Important thing is to put your bait on the bottom and leave it there. In very shallow ponds you can catch bullheads with a bobber adjusted so that the hook is on the bottom.

Unhooking a bullhead can be a real problem for novice anglers. Best idea is to use eyed hooks tied to leader material. When a fish swallows the hook, simply cut it off and tie on another. You'll recover all "lost" hooks when you clean the fish, and meanwhile you'll save time, temper, and trouble.

Panfishing Techniques

Bait fishing

Long before Whittier immortalized the "barefoot boy with cheek of tan," the long cane pole—equipped with line, bobber, and hook—was the standard method of taking most panfish. Man may have left the horse and buggy era for outer space, but the cane pole is just as good as it ever was. Actually, with modern fiberglass poles, plastic bobbers, and improved fishhooks, it's better than ever.

Whether you use a cane pole or modern spinning gear, the business end of your outfit is about the same. Use hooks in size 6 or 8 for sunfish, sizes 2 and 4 for both divisions of the Little Bigger League. A split BB shot will keep your bait under the bobber where it belongs. Best bobber you can use is the skinniest you can get. Big fat bobbers are good for salt water fish only, or maybe for giant catfish. Little thin bobbers give you high visibility when you have a bite; they offer little resistance in the water and make hooking a fish much easier.

The crux of float-fishing is the distance between hook and bobber. Generally, something between two and four feet is right, and since the exact depth can be important, sneak a peak at other local anglers and copy them.

A basic point to remember is that shallow-water panfish stay within a few feet of shore and around such cover as tree stumps, beds of weeds, and lily pads. Clusters of poles or pilings are also good.

An expert bobber angler can often tell the species and size of the fish before setting the hook. Small panfish take little nips at the bait. Larger fish such as the perch and crappies will pick up your bait and run with it. The time to strike is when they have gone about a yard. If your bobber moves very slowly and deliberately away just under the surface, you could have a really good-sized bass or pickerel.

In more than six feet of water, a bobber becomes impractical. Take it off and add another split shot or two so that you can reach bottom. Even with spinning tackle this will add enough weight so you can cast thirty feet or so. Unless you're fishing for carp or bullheads, the best idea is to cast, let your bait sink to the bottom, and retrieve as slowly as possible, an inch at a time. When you feel something tugging, stop reeling. As the fish starts to swim away you can usually hook him.

We'll discuss the actual baiting of the hook a little later. For now, the big thing to emphasize is that bait, to be effective, should look natural. A worm hooked lightly through the head or collar, leaving a long tail to wiggle, will get more response than one bunched on a hook. When float-fishing with a bobber, you can hook a minnow through the back so he'll hang horizontally in the water. When you take off the float and retrieve him near the bottom, hook him through both lips, otherwise you pull him along sideways, and fish don't swim like that.

As we've mentioned before, movement—as long as it is natural—attracts fish. It's a good idea therefore not to let your bait sit forever in one place. Don't jerk it along but move it slowly and gently if there's no current to move it for you.

Fish of all species move about with time of day and time of year. Therefore, if one spot doesn't pay off, move along and try another. However, even eager biters like the sunfishes don't feed all day every day.

While we're discussing bait fishing generally, let's mention that the effectiveness of different bait on panfish can change with the season. Basically, this means that worms work best in early spring when water is high and muddy, minnows are good through most of the summer and fall, and grasshoppers start being very effective in late summer.

Spinning and Bait Casting for Panfish

Leaving aside sunfish with very small mouths, and bottom feeders that take only bait, the Little Bigger League can be caught on most small spoons and spinners. A No. 2 Colorado spinner with a couple of small earthworms draped over the treble hooks so that the ends flutter will often out-fish bait. If worms are in short supply, substitute a tiny bit of pork rind. All panfish lures should be in so-called trout sizes.

Fly Fishing for Panfish

Small wet flies on size 8, 10, and 12 hooks are effective with sunfish and most other panfish. The best patterns are Black Gnat, Western Bee, and McGinty. Nearly any pattern with yellow or orange in it will take panfish. Larger sunfish will hit a small-bass popping bug or artificial grasshopper on the surface. When in shallow water, members of the Little Bigger League will whack at streamer flies with great enthusiasm. Any streamer with plenty of white or yellow will produce results; those similar to Black Ghost and Parmachenee Belle are usually good. These should be tied on a No. 6 hook.

Both flies and lures should be fished in the same kind of places as you would use bait. A slow retrieve, just fast enough to get action from a spoon or spinner, is generally best. Flies should be worked deep and slowly, and surface lures should be twitched rather than yanked along.

IV.

Warm Water Game Fish— America's Favorites

I t's been well established by now that trout and salmon on the one hand, and civilization on the other, are mutually exclusive. If you have one, you can't have very much of the other. The march of the dam builders across America and the siltation caused by agriculture and lumbering have long worked to turn deep clear brooks into shallow weedy streams and to make lakes of rivers. Thus the salmonoid fishes have been pushed back from much of their original range into areas where the soil is too poor for farming, the hills too steep for lumbering, and the streams too small to be dammed for power. Suburban trout fishing, in most of America, is put-and-take fishing, with stocking on the same basis as the planting of pheasants on a game preserve.

It's an ill wind that blows no good, yet the factors that have all but exterminated trout and salmon have opened up great new areas to the so-called warm water game fish. Dams have created new fishing opportunities, notably in the Southeast and in such states as Kansas, Nebraska, and the Dakotas, where almost no fishing existed before. The basses, pikes, and other species including the walleye and the catfishes, have never had it so good. Neither have the fellows who fish for them.

What is a warm water game fish anyway? Everything is relative, but the best definition is that this is a fish that can live and reproduce and be happy in an environment where a trout would turn belly-up and die. And just like the panfish we've glanced at already, warm water game fish can easily be divided into family groups. The first and foremost of these, at least in North America, are the so-called black basses.

The Black Basses

When Shakespeare wrote, "A rose by any other name would smell as sweet," he could have had the black bass in mind. None of the four species and six subspecies of black bass are black! To make things even more confusing, in some parts of the United States black bass are called trout—even green trout! Had Lewis Carroll been a bass fisherman, Alice in Wonderland and the Mad Hatter would certainly have gone angling for green trout, with the Cheshire Cat along to explain why a green trout wasn't a trout at all. Can't you just see the Red Queen, armed with a tuna outfit and a big hookless marlin teaser for a lure, screaming "Off with his lead!" at her hapless guide?

Originally found only in North America, the green, brown, striped, and spotted black bass are as American as apple pie, and our favorite game fish. Before the Civil War all species were fairly well limited to the Mississippi River drainage and down through Georgia and Alabama into Florida. Thanks mostly to volunteers, who carried small bass in pails on locomotives, and to fish and game departments of long ago, bass are found today from sea to sea and Canada to Central America. They have been introduced into waters all over the world, especially in Europe.

Much of today's fishing equipment was developed in the United States strictly for bass. The short casting-rod, the plug, the crankbait, the multiplying reel, the popping lure, were all invented by bass fishermen.

The four species of black bass are:

Largemouth Bass—widely distributed and biggest in size.

Smallmouth Bass—best game fish and with widest world distribution.

Spotted Bass—a little known species that is intermediate between largemouth and smallmouth basses.

Redeye Bass—smallest in size and distribution, this colorful fish resembles the smallmouth and lives only in streams of a few southern states.

Because the habits of these varying species are quite different from one another, we'd better take a quick look at each separately.

Largemouth Bass

It's easy to see why he got this name, for a big largemouth has a maw like a bucket. This is the only bass whose mouth extends back past the eye. Because he is especially at home in

Largemouth Bass

warm weedy shallows, he is found in nearly every state of the Union and most Canadian provinces. As you go south, the largemouth gets bigger and bigger until you reach Florida and find occasional twenty-five-pounders. (Technically these monsters are Florida bass, a largemouth sub-species, but they are largemouths for all practical purposes.) Cuba is known to have enormous bass, but at present these fish are safe from anglers—if not from netters. Mexico would have great bass fishing too, except that largemouths are netted commercially on a year-round basis. Toward the north, largemouth territory ends at about the Belgrade Lakes in Maine and Gananoque Lake and the Rideau Lakes in southern Ontario.

Most largemouth bass are dark bottle-green on the back, shading down to a white stomach. Young fish have a black longitudinal line that breaks up into a chain of dark splotches as the bass grows.

A lover of weedy, warm water (he'll take 85 degrees or more) filled with lily pads and bulrushes, the largemouth feeds on frogs, sunfish, minnows, and everything else he can swallow. Bats, birds, mice, chipmunks, ducklings, turtles, even snakes, have been found in largemouth stomachs.

Yet for all his big mouth, the largemouth bass can stay out of trouble. Very smart—for a fish, that is!—he learns quickly from experience, and many so-called "fished-out" lakes are filled with largemouths laughing at unskilled anglers. While not in the same league with the smallmouth as a scrapper, the largemouth is heavy and strong and will often take a pretty fair jump. He's also quite an expert at wrapping lines around the underwater snags, lily pads, and stumps which usually abound in his territory.

Plastic worms and weedless spoons with pork rind probably account for more captured largemouth bass than any other lures. Surface plugs, bugs, and poppers are especially good at dawn and dusk. Best live baits are frogs, minnows, and worms, in about the order named.

Trim and streamlined as compared with the often paunchy largemouth, the smallmouth does best in deep cold lakes and rocky streams. He spawns when the water gets about 60 degrees in the shallows, and if it never gets over 65 degrees, he'll be quite happy. Because of this preference for cool water, the smallmouth is really found near the surface only at spring and fall. In midsummer, he stays deep, in sixty feet of water or more.

More finicky than the largemouth, the smallmouth dines mainly on minnows, with an occasional frog, crawfish, or hellgrammite as a snack. In a stream, he'll feed on insects like a trout; and because he can stand water up to 80 degrees, which a trout can't, he's especially well adapted to rivers that run cold most of the year but become low and warm in midsummer.

The original small mouth range was mostly the upper Mississippi Valley and east into the Great Lakes. From there he's been transplanted with great success into Maine, New Brunswick, Ontario, and even Oklahoma, and west to the Pacific. Bass in the Potomac, Susquehanna, Delaware, and other eastern rivers were brought in by piscine Johnny Appleseed types after the Civil War. TVA lakes in the Southeast produce monster small-mouths of up to twelve pounds, but much of the most enjoyable fishing for these bronze-backs is in rivers. Float trips, for smallmouths, especially in the Ozarks, have become almost an institution.

Because of his liking for rocks and ledges, the smallmouth is often found in the same lakes with largemouth bass, with one species in the marshy shallows and the other offshore around rocky islands. There's no problem telling them apart either. A smallmouth bass is a dark bronze-colored fish with broken vertical stripes in a sort of light tiger pattern. He's never colored green in the yellow-green sense of a largemouth.

Touted by Dr. James A. Henshall, a noted angler-author of the last century, as "inch for inch and pound for pound the gamest fish that swims," the smallmouth never stops trying to live up to this reputation. Although he averages less in size than a largemouth, about three-quarters of a pound as against the largemouth's one-and-a-half pounds, he'll out-jump, outrun, and outstay his bigger relative by a giant margin. In midsummer, it is almost impossible to land a good-sized smallmouth in many lakes. Hooked on the bottom, he'll be up, four feet out of the water, and off, before the angler can get his line tight.

In the spring, around spawning time, smallmouths go for surface bugs with gusto. A little later they'll swat small plugs, and a fly-and-spinner combination is always good. In deep water, they'll attack wobbling spoons, diving plugs, and, of course, bait. Nightcrawlers, hellgrammites, minnows, and very small live frogs are all good when fished deep. In the fall, smallmouths tend to come back up near the surface in large schools. If (and it's "iffy") you can locate a school, your wrist and arm can get worn out! Wherever found, the small-mouth is a great fish, and like the largemouth, he can be quite ornery. I understand that smallmouths were successfully stocked in lakes in Switzerland, but are now practically impossible to catch in that country.

Spotted Bass

This bass was thought to be a cross between largemouth and smallmouth until 1927, when he received recognition as a separate species. It is quite possible that this was the original parent stock of all black bass species and that it was pushed back into its present restricted area by the glaciers.

Spotted bass are found primarily in Kentucky and Tennessee and down into the northern Alabama hill country. They look more like a largemouth in general green coloring, but have dark spots below the lateral line and a smaller mouth. While they breed in shallow water much like the largemouth, they prefer colder water than the smallmouth and are caught at depths of over one-hundred feet in the TVA reservoirs. Very popular throughout their range, they are caught by much the same methods used for smallmouth bass. In rivers, the smallmouths are in the rocky runs, the largemouths in the lazy backwaters, and the spotted bass in long deep pools with good current flow.

Redeye Bass

You know the old saying about how nature abhors a vacuum. Here's an example. The redeye bass, closely related to the smallmouth, lives where brook trout would if they could stand the summers. Its main range is in the hill country of northern Alabama and northwestern Georgia but it is found in clear, fast-running streams down into Florida and up into Tennessee. So much a stream fish that it will only spawn in running water, the redeye is the smallest and least known of the four major bass species. Its vertical markings are more distinct than those of a smallmouth, and where the smallmouth has orange fins and a general orange eye and cast, the redeye has red fins and a red eye. Because it behaves like a trout but lives where trout can't, this bass should be much sought after for streams that have become too warm in the summer to support trout. A self-sustaining population of redeye bass would certainly be better than put-and-take trout stocking.

Living almost entirely in streams, the redeye bass feeds on minnows and insects much like a trout. Best lures are wet and streamer flies in trout sizes, with worms, small minnows, and grasshoppers among the best baits.

The Pike Family

Perhaps you noticed that the four main members of the blackbass family had quite distinctive habits. Among the pikes, this just isn't so. Generally speaking, pike, pickerel, and muskellunge act as though they were the same fish. The differences are due more to the

Northern Pike

size of the species than any variation in habits. Aside from muskellunge, which are temperamental prima donnas, pike are generally easier to catch than bass.

Northern Pike

A true cosmopolitan, the northern pike—pike for short—has circumpolar distribution around the Northern Hemisphere. He lives in the British Isles and across Europe through Siberia and on into Alaska and Canada, where he ranges east into Quebec but is not found in the Maritime Provinces. While he prefers a cool climate, pike are found south into Italy and in the American Midwest.

It's easy to tell a pike from any other fish. He is long and lean, with reddish fins and tail. His duckbilled mouth is equipped with a ferocious set of teeth that are sharp as needles and point backward down his throat. Fortunately, he has weak jaw muscles and can't snap like a barracuda, though he doesn't need to. When he closes that mouth on a small fish, his prey has only one way to go: into the pike's stomach.

The best and easiest way to tell a northern pike from other members of his family is that this fish always has rows of spots, usually white or lemon-yellow, on a dark bronze background. It is interesting to note that in Siberia there is a photographic negative of the northern pike. Called Esox reicherti by scientists, and who knows what by Siberians and Manchurians, this is a silvery fish with two rows of dark spots. Judging from a picture in—of all places—the magazine Business Week, fishing for these reverse-colored pike is sensational. Someday, I'd like to get over there and catch a big pike of another color.

Interestingly enough, the pike's worldwide distribution is thought to be caused by the simple fact that fresh water is lighter and floats on salt water. Thus, when the Ice Age ended, and the glaciers melted around the Arctic Circle, the pike could migrate in the resulting torrents of ice water and could even cross open ocean on the melting ice. (They can stand salt water up to a point; the Swedes catch pike commercially in the brackish Gulf of Bothnia.)

A pike is a reasonably efficient converter of small fish into big pike. He'll eat an occasional frog or duckling, but his main interest is fish, and a good-sized pike will swallow a chub weighing a pound or more. Pike can, therefore, reach large economy sizes, with fish that weight forty pounds and over being landed annually, especially in Canada. In most waters in the United States, however, a ten-pounder is about maximum.

Very interesting fish to catch, pike have definite personalities that vary from fish to fish. This shows up in their fighting qualities, which can range from the magnificent down to practically zero, depending on Mr. Pike's current mood of the moment. A favorite pike trick is to strike a lure savagely and then be led like a lamb to slaughter until he is nearly at the boat. Then, he'll take a look around, not like what he sees, and uncork an underwater record for the 100-yard dash, sometimes away from the boat, sometimes directly at and under it and out the other side. At this point, a lot of anglers have lost rods, lines, and tempers.

Another pike trick, usually used when all seems lost, is to lie flat and apparently beaten at the surface and then rotate like an electric drill and wrap himself up in the line. A mighty surge of the tail then busts the line wrapped around it, and Mr. Pike glides calmly off with a baleful look of hatred in his protruding eyes. Anglers consider this a dirty trick, but if you could save your life by playing dirty, wouldn't you? Besides which, who slipped a hook into whose lunch?

In spite of all this cunning behavior after being hooked, pike are still usually suckers for anything that looks like chowtime down below. Hardware, meaning spoons and spinners, has been effective for centuries. Plugs are often excellent. Catching pike on surface baits is a bit tricky, but a well-worked pork chunk is something else again. You can catch pike on a big streamer fly, and while trout buffs may sneer, a five-pound pike will give quite a bit more action on a fly road than a one-pound trout.

You'll find pike in the same type of water in which you find largemouth bass. Shallow bays with plenty of water lilies and weeds are ideal when there are a few old logs or rocks in the water. If you can't find weedbeds, look for drowned trees and stumpage. But always look for weeds and weedbeds. They are so much a part of pike fishing that Izaak Walton solemnly wrote that pike were spontaneously generated from pickerel weed!

Eastern Pickerel

Historically speaking, east and south of the Appalachians there are no pike. This area, from Nova Scotia through Florida and west into Texas, is the home of the eastern pickerel, also called chain pickerel. Easily distinguished from the pike by his markings, the pickerel is generally light green with a reticulated pattern of black markings that always includes a distinct black line through each eye. Pickerel from different waters have slightly different coloration, but even the darkest—nearly as dark as a pike, and found in New Jersey cedar swamps—have the chainlike pattern on their sides instead of a pike's light spots.

Largest of the pickerels, the eastern pickerel usually ranges in size from about fourteen to twenty inches. Anything over two feet is a good fish, and although a five-pounder is very unusual, the accepted world's record, caught by a New Jersey Boy Scout, weighed a bit over nine pounds.

Members of the pike family generally decrease in size toward the south, while members of the bass family increase in size. Therefore, the largest pickerel should be in Maine, New Brunswick, and Nova Scotia, at the northern end of their range. My experience would indicate that they are, and when I retire, I'll go to Maine and set a new record, which should be easy. Pickerel weighing better than ten pounds are caught in Maine as a matter of course, but in a state filled with landlocked salmon and trout, bass are looked down upon, and pickerel are considered as practically trash, which is a shame, at least in my book.

As you go south, pickerel are slightly smaller but more appreciated. By the time you reach New Jersey, Maryland, and Delaware, you find that anglers are making special fishing trips solely to catch pickerel. They have a good time too, because pickerel fishing is fun.

While pickerel can't really compete with their big relatives, the pike, both fish are found side by side in some waters, and some interbreeding takes place. I doubt that this cross is really fertile. If it were, you would have a good fish with the size of the pike and the fighting qualities of the pickerel. For when it comes to fight, there's just no comparison. A pickerel will outfight a pike twice his size and make a largemouth bass double his weight look lazy.

In addition to fighting ability, pickerel can live in acid cedar-swamp drainage where other fish can't survive. It thus is the only game fish in some areas. The only other fish life in such waters is the tiny pygmy sunfish, one of the few American natives to become popular with the tropical-fish set.

Today, in most of its range, the pickerel is found together with the largemouth bass, and the same lures and baits that take one will take the other. However, pickerel are especially fond of spinners, small wobbling spoons with pork rind, and pork chunks worked through the lily pads. He'll take surface lures and streamer flies with a rush.

An eager biter, the pickerel is too hungry for his own good. Unlike the bass family, pickerel can be just about fished out of a pond or stream. For this reason, really first-rate pickerel fishing is getting difficult to find near big cities. But with this fish gaining in popularity, he's sure to be around for a long time to come.

Muskellunge

Giant of the pike family, the muskie ranges up to seventy pounds or more in weight. His original range was in the upper Mississippi and Ohio River drainages plus the Great Lakes and St. Lawrence River. Some scientists think that this was originally a marine form of pike that got stranded in the upper Mississippi basin in the last Ice Age. Fossils of muskellunge have been found in the southern United States and in Europe. The nearest to a muskie in the Eurasian land mass today is the dark spotted Esox reicherti of Siberia already mentioned.

Muskellunge

This Asian fish has the habits of a pike, however, and is much too easily caught to be classed with the muskies.

There are three color forms of muskellunge: greenish with dark "tiger" stripes, silvery with dark spots, and clear green with no stripes or spots. The tiger-muskie variety is found to the north, in Ontario, Manitoba, and Saskatchewan, and from there southerly into Lake of the Woods, Minnesota, and Wisconsin. The spotted form is the muskie of the Great Lakes region; and the Thousand Acre Shoals in the St. Lawrence River between Watertown, New York, and Kingston, Ontario, has produced some record fish. Lake Chautauqua in western New York State is reputed as the home of the clear-colored muskie, but this greenish fish is now found all the way south into North Carolina and Tennessee.

Solitary by nature, muskies want plenty of room. Although found in some West Virginia rivers that are simply big creeks, the muskellunge does best in the big lakes and river systems with plenty of natural food and ample cover. While muskie habitat suits pike fine, and northern pike are a prime scourge of the muskie angler, muskies are usually found around points of land, near tangles of fallen trees and such like lairs, generally in or near weedbeds.

In most fishing, a couple of casts in a likely spot is enough and you move on. Muskie fishermen, however, concentrate on areas where muskies are likely to be, and will keep casting until they get a hit. Just tossing a plug and retrieving it eventually gets the fish annoyed enough to strike. Unlike other members of the pike and pickerel clan, muskies will bite at night. This gives muskie addicts twenty-four hours a day to fish, and some of them try to fish all of these.

"Upon what food doth this our Caesar feed, that he is grown so great?" For the muskie, the answer is mostly other fish. Muskies, however, are also noted for their appetite for chipmunks, squirrels, and ducklings, and while the ASPCA could well object, chipmunks are still used for bait in some areas of the north.

Standard procedure in many areas still is to cast a two pound chub or sucker and retrieve slowly. Plugs and spoons in large economy sizes have long since come into their own, and casting and trolling these probably catches more muskellunge than bait of any kind. It's strictly stunt fishing, but when everything jells you can take muskies with a big streamer fly; the fly-rod record comes from the St. Lawrence River.

Because muskellunge do tend to keep panfish under population control, and because anglers love to try and take them, their range is being rapidly extended into all waters that the biologists feel will support them. Today they are found right down the Alleghenies into the TVA Lakes and west to the Dakotas. As they are usually extremely selective feeders and difficult to catch, fishing pressure has little effect on muskie populations, and muskellunge fishing in Pennsylvania can be equal to that in Ontario.

The same people who make a fetish of the striper in salt water do the same with the muskie in fresh water. Catching a trophy fish becomes nearly a religion; and sleep, job, and family all come a distant second.

Walleye

This fish and its nearly identical cousin, the sauger, have a nearly infinite variety of names. Blue pike, yellow pike, sand pike, river salmon, jack salmon, pickerel, walleyed pike, are a few of the most common. Despite all the pike and pickerel innuendo the walleye is a perch, a big-toothed, predacious perch. Aside from size, his distinguishing characteristic is his large eyes from which the name walleye derives.

A nearly identical species to the walleye is distributed throughout northern Europe and Asia, so this fish may be considered to have world-wide distribution. His original North American range was in the Great Lakes and their rivers and therefore down the Mississippi valley and up the Tennessee, the Ohio, and other streams throughout the Midwestern and South Central States. His range has been greatly increased by man, and walleyes are now found from Maine through Minnesota, south to Louisiana, and north to central Canada.

Extremely prolific and wonderful eating, you may have eaten him without even knowing it, for walleye under the name of pike is a prime ingredient of commercial gefüllte fish and

Walleye

other mid-European fish delicacies.

The walleye resembles a large yellow perch except for color, which can vary from a sort of yellow-ochre nearly to brick-red and even into a sort of yellow-blue and a dark blue that is almost like a dull navy blue. Unlike the perch, he has no stripes or bars but has instead sort of a freckled effect above the dull white underneath.

Ounce for ounce and inch for inch, the walleye, especially when caught in lakes during midsummer, is probably the dullest game fish that swims. More than once I've reeled in a weed-snagged plug to find that instead of vegetation I'd hooked a good-sized walleye. River walleyes and saugers, however, are quite different in temperament and will give a much better account of themselves.

Much like the yellow perch, walleyes congregate in huge schools, which seldom if ever come near the surface. A deep-water fish in all seasons, they can be very difficult to locate without an electronic fishfinder or a really good knowledge of the lake or river you are fishing.

In lakes, most walleye fishing consists of anchoring over a reef and livebaiting with minnows. Trolling with a spinner-and-worm combination is another standard method, and a spinner-lamprey eel combo is considered especially effective in the Delaware River above Port Jervis. The walleye, however, will hit nearly any bass lure that can be fished deep enough, and the familiar Dardevle wobbling spoon and deep-sinking-and-diving plugs will take plenty of walleyes.

River fishing for walleyes is a tougher proposition. The fish are not schooled to the extent they are in a lake, and since there is no surface sign of their presence, river walleye fishing is mainly blind casting, bait fishing, or trolling in areas where they are known to hang out.

Once you hook a walleye, you have the makings of a meal. In many waters they average about three pounds, and plenty of monsters up to twelve and fifteen pounds are caught each year. Because of a hatchery mistake many years ago, walleyes were stocked instead of landlocked salmon in Great Pond, Belgrade Lakes, Maine. These fish aren't caught often but are usually over seven pounds. Even in rivers, these "jack salmon" will run well over a pound, and six- and seven-pounders are commonplace.

Most walleye fishing is reminiscent of salt water bottom fishing, and if you enjoy bottom-bouncing for cod, flounder, ling-cod, red snapper, or whatever, you'll feel at home with the walleye. Best of all, as a table fish he's hard to beat. The best description is "Delicious!"

The Catfishes

There may be some difference of opinion as to whether catfish are really game fish; however, they are quite important to a large body of fishermen. Some towns in the Deep South have even been known to select a pretty girl to be Catfish Queen.

Ancient in lineage and varied in appearance and habits, catfishes are found around the world. There are fresh water and marine species. These are important food fishes in Asia and Africa and have possibly reached their ultimate development in South America where

Channel Catfish

there are species of all shapes and sizes, including armored catfish, electric catfish, even parasitic catfish that attack bathers.

In North America the major catfish species are the flathead catfish, the blue catfish, and the channel catfish. Of these, the channel cat, a silvery fish with dark spots and a forked tail, is the most attractive. Because he hits readily in midsummer, when other fish snooze in the heat, channel cats have been widely stocked in recent years. They are as big a hit in New Jersey as they are in Texas, and the outlook for the popularity of this clean-water-loving catfish is optimistic.

The blue and flathead catfish are at home in the muddy waters of the Deep South, especially in the lower Mississippi Valley, where they range from Alabama west to Texas. Big catfish are even caught far up the Rio Grande near El Paso, which shows they are tough hombres. The tailwaters of Pickwick Dam, Tennessee, which is near the conjunction of Alabama, Mississippi, and Tennessee, are especially noted for monster catfish. Giant blue and flathead cats up to forty pounds and more are caught on live herring and chunks of other bait. The Mississippi River from Cairo to the Gulf, and far on up the Missouri, Ohio, and other major tributaries, is catfish water. Salt water gear is generally used for these monsters, so that a large amount of surf-casting equipment is sold in landlocked mid-America.

Since catfish are bottom dwellers with a terrific sense of smell, it's usually necessary to get a bait down to them. Heavy sinkers are a part of fishing for the big cats. And the best fishing method is simply to anchor your bait on bottom and leave it there until Mr. Catfish comes along.

While live minnows, frogs, and worms are good bait for the clean-channel catfish, the muddy-water catfish will also go readily for all kinds of blood-and-stink baits. Stink bait are wild concoctions formed by leaving fresh water mussels or chicken guts, or both, in a sealed glass jar in the hot sun for a few days. When you feel this concoction is ripe enough to use, you open the jar. Although the aroma could make weaklings pass out cold, catfish seem to enjoy it. If you're smart, you'll leave stink baits to people with dead olfactory nerves. Of course, you can make a milder form of stink bait with a bit of Limburger cheese mixed with bread dough, and this will do as well as the more hairy-chested variety. When I tell you that congealed clots of blood from a slaughter house are looked on by catfishers as dandy bait too, you're probably going to be quite willing to leave this whiskered tribe alone. However, they are the nearest thing to big-game fishing that much of mid-America gets, and amazingly good eating too. Through Arkansas, Missouri, Louisiana, and many other states, a blue cat of sixty pounds or better gets your picture—with fish—in the local newspaper. And they come even bigger than that! There are tales of man-eating catfish seven feet long.

Carp and Company

While the phrase "carp and catfish" has a nice ring about it and conjures up the image of an older guy in dowdy clothes sitting on a camp chair by a sandy shore behind a row of fishing rods resting on forked sticks, the fact of the matter is that carp are a lot tougher to catch than catfish. A catfish is a stomach-motivated fellow. If he were human you'd think of him as the type of person who digs his grave with his teeth. Carp enjoy eating too. But they are epicures rather than gluttons.

Carp and their close cousins, the goldfish, are imports to America; and like the English sparrow and starling in the bird world, their reception has been rather mixed. Feeding almost entirely on aquatic vegetation and minute crustaceans, carp tend to root on the bottom of a lake like pigs, muddying the waters and causing silt to settle on and kill the eggs of other fish. Thus they destroy habitat and kill off competition at one and the same time. This doesn't win them many friends. In many areas of shallow ponds and streams that contain little native-fish life, however, they definitely provide interesting sport.

About the only similarity between carp fishing and catfishing is that both are done on the bottom. But while a catfish will eagerly bite on a hook tied to a tarred rope, carp are really finicky. A single kernel of canned corn, a tiny earthworm, a small doughball, are carp baits. Use these with a No. 6 hook, about the same size you'd catch sunfish with, and a long fine

Carp

monofilament leader of at least a yard, and you'll catch carp, or at least hook them.

While most carp run less than five pounds in weight, I've heard authentic reports and seen photos of seventy-pounders. And don't let anyone tell you that a carp won't put up a scrap. Having caught plenty of both, I think a carp fights exactly like a striped bass. A fifteen-pound carp on a bait casting or spinning outfit will test your ability as an angler, make no mistake about it!

Goldfish, which are usually golden-tinted green descendants of the five-and-ten-cent-store aquarium fish, are very common in some areas. While they can't be compared to a small-mouth bass, goldfish are better than nothing. You catch them just as you would carp. And you'll find that wild goldfish often reach five pounds in weight. A basic trouble with carp and goldfish is that unless you have a cookbook filled with European recipes, eating them is something less than pure pleasure. Dry and bony, they taste like sawdust unless you know some culinary trade secrets.

Buffalo, the North American equivalent of the carp, are found in major river systems and the Great Lakes. They and a whole group of chubs and suckers can be caught with carp-fishing methods. All of these fish are edible—if you are very hungry.

Fresh water drum are found south and west from Lake Champlain. This landlocked species of a salt water family is a bottom feeder and better eating than the soft-rayed fish we've mentioned previously. You can tell a drum because he has a double dorsal fin instead of the short single dorsal of the cyprinoid fishes mentioned above.

Another landlocked representative of a marine family is the ling, or lawyer or cusk, depending on what you want to call him. Not a warm water fish at all, he lives in cold deep lakes and ventures into the shallows only in wintertime. This interesting fish is a double for salt water ling, or red hake, and an authentic member of the cod family. From Maine to

Minnesota, he's in a lot more lakes than most people would imagine. The best time to catch him is in the summertime at night, and the best place is any reef in at least sixty to eighty feet of water. You should use catfish tackle, as a ling may run up to thirty pounds or more. When you land one, you'll see a slimy mud-colored animal with a beautiful black-and-gold spot on each side near the tail. A moonless night on a Maine or Adirondack or Michigan lake can get you ling steaks for frying, and they are certainly good, very much like codfish.

One remark to make about all these bottom-feeding fish, including the catfishes already mentioned, is that baiting your fishing grounds pays off. A few cans of dog food with holes punched top and bottom, a bucket of doughballs, even sardine cans punched with an ice pick, or a weighted sack full of feed corn, will draw carp, catfish, buffalo, drum and ling from all over the place. In most areas, this is legal. If you're in any doubt, call your local fish and game representative and check.

These aren't all the fish you could catch in troutless areas by any means. But we have covered most of them, omitting only such nuisances and menaces as garfish, bowfins, and mud puppies.

V.

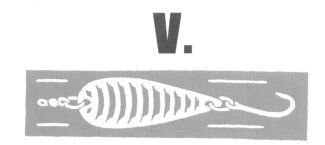

Spinning and Bait Casting Lures for Warm Water Game Fish

Spinning and bait casting lures may be considered identical, except perhaps in size. The five basic types of lures used with spinning and bait casting tackle are plugs; spoons; spinners; jigs; and rubber, pork-rind, and plastic lures; all of these come in a dazzling variety of sizes, shapes, and finishes.

Plugs or Crankbaits

These are wooden or plastic lures, either hard or soft, usually designed to resemble a small fish. Years ago, they were made by hand from clothespins, or whittled into shape from a chunk of wood. Originally designed to catch largemouth bass, they've been developed into excellent lures for a wide variety of fish active in both fresh and salt water. They come in several varieties: poppers, surface agitators, shallow wobblers, sinkers, and divers. Poppers have a concave face that creates a glug noise when the plug is jerked forward. Surface agitators have propellers, metal plates, or a revolving head that create a disturbance when reeled along the surface. Shallow wobblers have a built-in swimming action when reeled. They generally run from a foot to four feet under water. Sinkers may or may not have a swimming action, or propellers. They are built to sink and are used in deep water impossible to reach with a floating lure. Diving plugs are constructed so that they plane downward when reeled and can actually be trolled deeper than sinking plugs.

Standard size for a bait casting plug is $5/8$ ounce; spinning size is $3/8$ ounce. Crankbaits, however, come in weights varying from $1/4$ ounce to 2 ounces and more, with the big sizes very popular for muskies and salt water fishing.

Fishing with plugs generally consists of casting into likely spots and then retrieving. But plugs are great trolling lures too, and even some of the surface- and shallow-working models can be trolled deep with a wire line or a lead drail (a trolling sinker).

What size plugs to buy? It depends on what you're fishing for. Bass plug sizes get bigger toward the southern United States, where monster largemouths are found, and smaller toward the north, where bass are both smaller and sophisticated. The $^3/_8$ ounce spinning size plug is probably the best all-around size for everything except pike and muskellunge.

Plug colors are quite wild. You can get color schemes that imitate nearly anything, including frogs, tadpoles, shiners, perch, sunfish, crawfish, and even baby ducklings. There are any number of imaginary patterns too, including white with red head; white with red, blue, and green polka dots; black with a white skeleton effect; rainbow; and so forth. All of these will catch fish. An extremely popular lure today is a scale-finish plastic minnow that has been metal plated so that it really shines. These come in gold, silver, copper, and other finishes, with various-colored backs.

The more heavily fished the lake or river, the better the conservative plug patterns work. Dull colors, such as all black or all red, with frog and perch markings, are good under these conditions. (Although not considered so by us earth-bound specimens, red as a color by itself is very dull under water.) Relatively unfished waters call for high visibility, and you can break out the red-and-white and metal-finish plugs with equanimity.

Of course, other factors enter in. Very low clear water and mid-day fishing call for dull-colored plugs. Dawn and dusk and off-color water usually demand brighter colors. Regardless of where you fish or what you fish for, solid black is always a prime color at night. Yellow gets results in turbid water. Before the metal-finish plugs, rainbow was a prime color for the pike family. It still is, but the shiny metallics are good, especially on very dull days.

There are dozens of plug manufacturers, and each marker has his own specialties and finishes. Because selling fishing lures is a business, all this variety serves to move plugs off

Plug

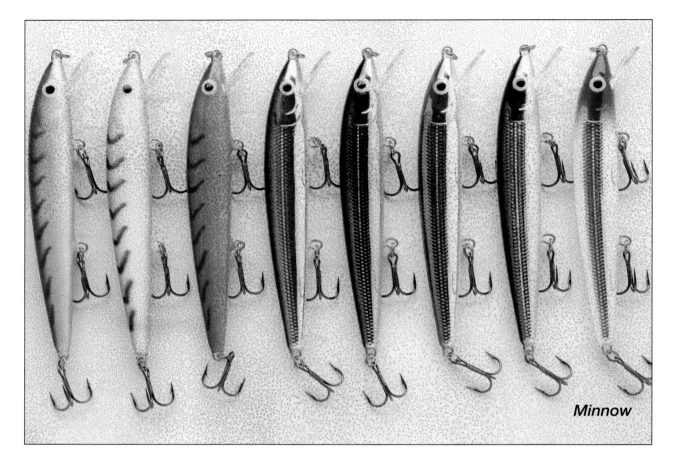

Minnow

the dealer's shelf as well as catch fish. For 90 percent fresh water plug-casting for game fish, you can get by with something like the following assortment:

1 popping plug—black

1 surface agitator or injured minnow—perch or frog markings

2 swimming plugs—one metallic, one dull scale finish

1 sinking plug—white with red head

1 diving plug—yellow or white with red head

The best idea is to check with your local sporting-goods store and your local fish and game conservation officer, and find out what lures they recommend. Generally, they'll advise an advertised product by a well-known manufacturer. These are the lures that have stood the test of years and you can buy them with confidence.

Spoons

The origin of the spoon is in Europe and is lost in antiquity. Cut the handle off a household spoon of any size, drill a hole in one end for attaching a hook and at the other for fastening your line, and you'll get an attractive wobbling motion when you move it through the water. Spoons aren't all shaped like spoon bowls any more. But they all are curved pieces of metal that wobble when retrieved and reflect flashes of light like a swimming minnow.

Spoons come in an infinite variety of sizes, shapes, and finishes, but the so-called spinning size, which weights $3/8$ ounce like the spinning plug, is about right for most fishing. Copper, brass, and painted spoons usually work better than nickel and chrome spoons on bright days in clear water. Shiny chrome plate is especially good on dark or rainy days and in dark or muddy water. Pearl is a good neutral finish for nearly all conditions, and while mother-of-pearl spoons are a bit fragile, they have a sheen and attractiveness that works. South Seas natives have used pearly flashers to attract fish for thousands of years.

Most spoons today are engineered to ride upright in the water with their broad surface vertical or nearly so; however, there are very effective spoons that lie flat in the water so that the hook is always pointing up, thereby making them invulnerable to weeds. With a pork-rind tail or a rubber skirt, these are excellent lures in weedy areas when fishing the lily pads. They can be skittered right over logs and other floating debris.

Spoons have become very specialized over the years. Some are weighted for casting, others are ultralight in construction and used for trolling only. There are spoons with treble hooks and spoons with single weedless hooks. Avoid spoons with double hooks, as this particular kind of hook results in many lost fish. Check with a local expert if you want, but generally speaking you can get by with the following spoons:

2 weedless, hook-upright wobblers—one nickel, one brass in "bass" size

1 casting wobbling spoon—brass on one side, red and white on the other side

1 pearl wobbler

Spinners

Pierce a teaspoon bowl at one end and attach a yoke so it can rotate around a wire shaft. The result is a spinner. Like spoons and plugs, spinners come in sizes, shapes, weights, and colors that are nearly infinite. The longer the spinner blade in proportion to its width, the closer to the shaft it revolves; the broader the spinner blade, the farther from the shaft it revolves. The extremes are the long, narrow willow-leaf spinner and the nearly round Colorado spinner. Both catch fish.

Just as with spoons, you'll find spinners in nickel, chrome, brass, copper, white, black, and with polka dots and stripes. There are plain, enameled, and painted finishes. Some spinners

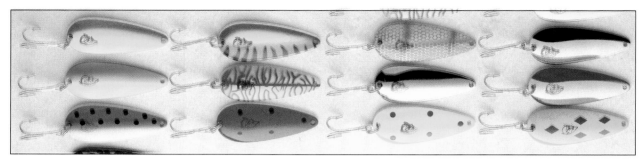

Spoons

have a hammered pattern and some have a combination effect of copper and nickel, or red and silver. Most spinners are sold with a feathered treble hook at the business end; however, the June-Bug spinner nearly always comes with a long-shanked single hook and is used with worms, a minnow, a frog, or pork rind.

You could fill a tackle box with nothing but spinners and catch plenty of fish—at least in fresh water. For some reason, salt water fish usually prefer wobbling spoons by a wide margin.

In most waters, dull spinners, including copper, brass, pearl, and even black bring best results. Gold and silver are good on dull days and in dark water. The intense flash produced by too bright a spinner seems to frighten fish more than it attracts them, and probably the single most effective spinner made has a very dull, unpolished blade.

Spinners come in all sizes, of course, and there are a variety of weighted spinners for easy casting. My advice is to go small in spinner size. Big spinners are primarily for virgin waters, except in very special lures used for deep-water trout trolling. Here are some spinner suggestions:

2-3/8 ounce spinners for casting —1 nickel, 1 brass or copper

2 small Colorado-type spinners—with size $^1/_0$ hook*

2 small spinners—single or double blades for trolling —1 nickel, 1 brass, with feathered hooks

1 June-Bug spinner, with size $^2/_0$ hook

One big advantage of spinners is that besides being an attractive lure by themselves, they are often used to give more appeal to bait. Some rigs for deep-water trolling feature a dozen or more spinner blades of various sizes. This large assortment of hardware is followed by a single small hook baited with a worm, minnow, or slice of fish.

On a smaller scale, many stream fishermen use a tiny spinner as an attractor for worms.

*Hook sizes start at 1 and go down to size 22, which is the smallest size. Hooks may be larger than a size 1, however, and these are shown by a /0 after the number; 12/0 is about the largest hook made.

This spinner-worm combination is extremely effective. The Colorado spinner with a couple of small earthworms hooked by their heads on the treble hooks is one of the best pickerel, bass, and panfish gadgets anywhere. It will take fish when nothing else works. The combination of a June-Bug spinner and a nightcrawler is a standard walleye lure that works well on bass and pickerel. You can't go wrong with either or both of these spinner-worm combinations.

Spinnerbaits

You wouldn't think that any self-respecting game fish would attack such a thing. Yet, spinnerbaits are extremely effective and a mainstay of bass tournament entrants. I had one kicking around my tackle box unused, until one day, on a lake filled with uncooperative bass, I looked at it and asked myself "Why not?". My next cast resulted in a good fish. Someone may have missed a profitable patent with this basic lure that appeals to bass, pike, pickerel and muskellunge. In small sizes, it will get you perch, rockbass and bluegills.

A spinnerbait is two wire arms of an incomplete triangle. The upper, hookless arm, offers one or more (usually two or three) spinner blades in a wide range of sizes and colors. the ones along the shaft may spin wile a terminal blade wobbles erratically. The lower arm is bare until it terminates in an upward facing hook, or sometimes an artificial minnow. This hook is generally covered by a deer hair or plastic skirt to which may be added a plastic

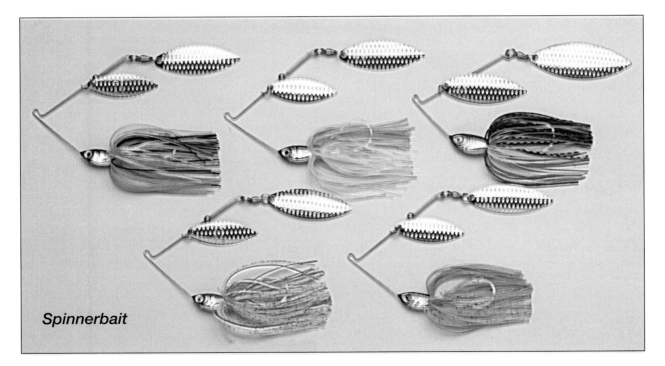

Spinnerbait

worm or porkrind strip of any color.

This entire rig, attached to your line or leader at the apex of its arms, can be skittered just beneath the surface, bumped along the bottom, reeled fast or slow, or allowed to hesitate and sink. Reasonably heavy, it is easy to cast—and being nearly weedless, is ideal around heavy grass and Lilypads. Why does it work? My best guess is that a game fish perceives it as a small group of minnows pursued by a small predator. the so-called buzzbait is similar. The main difference there is that spinner blades are modified to create maximum surface disturbance. It seems to be a dinner gong that lures fish up from rocks, weedbeds and other cover.

Jigs

Jigs

These are a recent addition to the family of fresh water lures. They were developed for salt water fishing and used in catching game fish on the bottom of deep water. A jig typically consists of a single hook molded in a metal head, with feathers or hair tied to the hook. This is thus the end result of the weighted streamer fly. (Oddly enough, although seldom if ever fished with a fly rod, jigs are worked like a fly.) A big advantage of a jig is that it is designed to ride with the hook upright and this makes it nearly weedless in lakes with weeds on or near the bottom.

For most fresh water use, $1/4$ ounce and $3/8$ ounce jigs are best. Black, red, white, and yellow are favorite colors. To use a jig you cast into fairly deep water, let the jig settle to the bottom, and retrieve slowly with little jiggles of the rod tip. Or you can lift the jig off the bottom, let it settle, and reel in the slack, repeating until the lure is at the boat. You can drift slowly along in a boat gently working your jig along the bottom and covering a large area of water.

Jigs are designed for use on gravel or rocky bottoms with little vegetation. In floating weed beds, you'll be constantly fouled up. These lures are especially effective in midsummer, when fish have left the shallows for deeper and cooler water.

In salt water fishing, jigs are often used with a piece of pork rind or marine worm. In fresh water fishing, a nightcrawler makes an attractive addition to most jigs.

Rubber, Pork-Rind, and Plastic Lures

While used with other lures, these are really a family all by themselves. They go beyond the general rough imitative concept of a plug or spoon and provide an exact imitation, including motion, of a natural bait. The basic difference between these lures and live bait is that they must be given movement by the angler. Again, this family of lures is often scented.

Like other animals, fish are very alert to movement. A rubber worm or a pork-rind frog gets results by moving like the genuine article. These pork-rind frogs, or pork chunks, are among the oldest lures. Used with a weedless hook, they are cast right into lily pads and other underwater jungles and retrieved on the surface with the rod tip held high. You can keep them up on top even with a fairly slow retrieve, and a twitch-and-reel effect gives the swimming-frog movement real substance.

These pork chunks come in bottles and are either off-white or colored. I don't think color makes much difference. It's the action you can give this lure that is going to pay off. In special cases these pork chunks are sunk with split shot and worked right on the bottom, though you still have to give them the swimming-frog motion.

Pork-rind strips are used with a spinner, spoon, or jig to give added action. They give a live creepy-crawly motion that the pike family in particular finds hard to resist.

Rubber and plastic worms and pork-rind eels are basically all worm imitations. They are used with just enough lead to get them down near the bottom. Then they are worked along

Worms

very slowly, which gives them a chance to wiggle and squirm. These worms and eels should be hooked only through the head.

This type of lure can also be used as an adjunct to a jig. But the important thing is to move them slowly. Black and red are favorite colors, but orange, lilac, and many other hues are available, and you might get a kick out of catching a fish on a magenta worm imitation.

Not as successful as the frogs and worms are the imitation crawfish, hellgrammites, etc. The problem is that these creatures move with actions that are difficult to duplicate. (You can, however, do a wonderful job on the fly rod with an imitation cricket.)

Over the years there have been hundreds of attempts to develop a plastic minnow that will both look real and act naturally. Unfortunately, a lure that is too minnow-like in appearance loses the action of the less imitative plug, which is the best minnow imitation that can be successfully used.

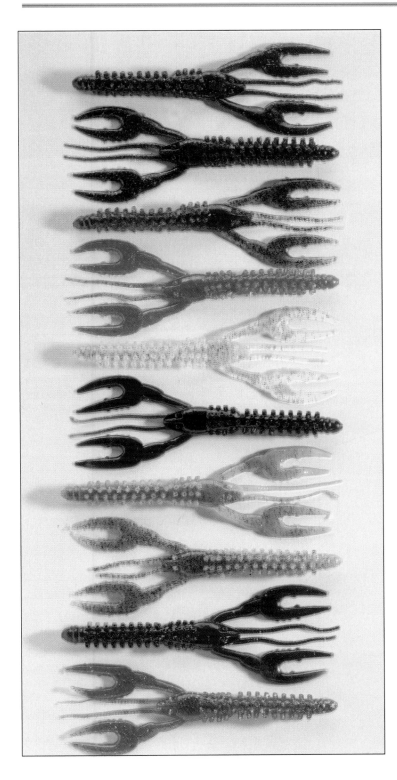

Caterpillar crayfish

Plastic and rubber lures come in literally hundreds of shapes, colors and scents. They are designed to imitate various animals, amphibians and bugs, including:

Caterpillars
Grubs
Worms
Lizards
Salamanders
Frogs
Crayfish
Grasshoppers
Water bugs
And many, many more.

Take a look around the edges of your lake or stream and see what kind of bugs and amphibians are lurking around in the grass, in the mud and under rocks—then choose a lure that resembles what's around you.

VI.

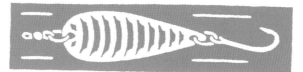

Spinning and Bait Casting Techniques for Warm Water Game Fish

As we have seen, spinning and bait casting lures are virtually identical except that the standard bait casting lure weighs $5/8$ ounce, and the standard spinning lure weighs $3/8$ ounce. (A light bait casting outfit will handle spinning lures, and nearly any spinning outfit will handle bait casting lures.)

It's reasonable to suppose that to catch fish on lures, you must first know where they are. And there are two glittering generalities to cover this:

Fish tend to stay in comparatively shallow water in spring and fall. (This is because sunlight keeps the shallows warmer.)

Fish tend to go deep in midsummer and midwinter. (In summer the shallows get too hot; in winter they get too cold.)

Generalities, however, aren't specific enough to be of much practical use. Just as human population is concentrated in cities instead of being spread out evenly all over the countryside, the piscine population of any body of water is concentrated in a few specific areas which provide food, shelter, protection from enemies, and generally comfortable temperatures. Here are some of those areas:

So when you go fishing, you look for inlets, outlets, fallen logs, dead brush, stumps, lily pads and weedbeds, rocks, shoals, and reefs. Most of these you're going to find fairly near the shoreline of the average lake or pond, and in most lakes, the majority of warm water game species will be found at varying depths of water within a distance of fifty feet from the shore. Unless there are offshore islands, reefs, and shoals, the center of a lake usually is a very poor place to find basses, and the pike family. Without a map, fishfinder or both, you'll obviously have a tough time locating reefs under many feet of water. One shortcut for finding them is to look for a chain of islands. The ridge that forms these islands usually continues underwater as a reef or shoal.

Fishing with lures actually takes two forms, trolling and casting. Trolling, the older of the two, consists of using the movement of the boat to pull the lure along a course that general-

1. Inlets and outlets of lakes are good because the current brings food, and there are generally weeds, deep holes, or rocks that are useful for purposes of hiding.

2. Fallen trees, dead brush, and stumps are decomposing and therefore feeding microscopic plant and animal life. This starts a food chain that attracts progressively larger fish and gives them a hiding place as well.

3. Lily and weedbeds also provide a nursery for paramecium and other one-celled animal life that attract tiny fish, which, in turn, attract larger fish. By their very nature water lilies and waterweeds provide hiding places.

4. Because rocks at or near the surface get a coating of algae that attracts small fish to nibble, shallow rocky areas are usually good fishing. (Crevices provide hiding places.)

5. Shoals and reefs, which are usually raised ledges in the lake bottom, attract fish because even though they may be too deep for algae growth, they provide homes for crawfish, fresh water mussels, and some specialized larval forms of insects (depending on water depth). Big fish tend to congregate around the end of points, waiting for food from either direction. On the other hand, a flat sand or mud bottom, without weed covering, usually has very little life of any kind. (This can be different in salt water where specialized fish like the flounders can hide in mud or sand and feed on minute crustacea.)

ly runs parallel with the shoreline. In casting, the lure is tossed toward a specific objective: a fallen stump, a hole between a couple of rocks, an opening in a thick bed of lily pads, and then retrieved at a speed determined by time of year, species sought and even time of day.

Trolling

The art of pulling a lure along behind a boat is so old that it is virtually lost in antiquity. Until about the middle of the last century there were no reels available for casting (fly casting does not require a reel), and all lures heavier than the fly could be used only by trolling or by an ancient form of fishing known as skittering, which employs a very long pole as much as twenty feet in length with a line of about equal length. The lure is simply tossed out to the end of the line and then retrieved by working the pole.

Whether you are fishing for bass, pike, pickerel, muskie, or walleye, trolling simply consists of snapping an appropriate lure on the terminal end of your line, getting it overboard, starting the boat, and letting out enough line to suit conditions. The major factors to consider in trolling are the depth of the water, the length of line, the type of lure, and the speed of the boat. This form of fishing is a good way to explore a body of water. You'll cover a good deal of water in a comparatively short period of time, and by noticing the spots where you get fish, you can return to them for more intensive casting.

Spoons and spinners, especially the fluted spinners with feathered hooks, are time-honored trolling lures. Wobbling plugs, the type that dive when pulled and float when at rest, are also excellent, especially on bright days when the flash of metal can frighten fish. Take your choice, or if one doesn't work, switch to the other. Under extremely weedy conditions, troll a weedless spoon with pork rind and hope for the best.

Where should you troll? The best bet is usually about twenty to forty feet from the shoreline. This is usually along the drop-off point from shallow to deep water. If you can see weedbeds or underwater rocks, stay just outside them. If there are islands and rocky ledges and points, troll alongside these too.

The amount of line to let out is a real problem. With casting equipment, I generally take a good healthy cast astern, let out a few additional feet of line for good measures, and start there. If I start hooking bottom, I know I'm too deep and reel in some line. If nothing happens at all, I either switch lures or let out more line so I'll be fishing deeper. Because fish have few brains, they aren't very logical, and there really are no hard and fast rules which always apply.

How fast should you troll? The best answer to this is usually the slowest speed at which you can get real action out of your lure. Until very recently, all trolling was a matter of rowing or paddling, which meant that you could vary between slow rowing or fast rowing. Today, with outboard motors, the speed variation has changed a great deal. Before you start fishing, toss out a few feet of line and look at your lure. Speed up until it is spinning or wobbling or whatever else it should do. That's the speed at which to start fishing.

If you get no action at slow speed, move it up a bit. Once you start going faster than a good rowing pace, however, be sure to switch from metal lures to a plug. Fast-trolled spoons and spinners will twist your line badly and result in quite a mess. Plugs will never revolve and therefore cannot twist. By bringing your spoon in and watching it in the water, you can pretty well set the maximum speed you can hit without twisting. Some spoons, especially those designed for salt water trolling, can be pulled along nearly as fast as a plug. Fast trolling at eight to ten miles per hour sometimes brings results when conventional slow trolling fails. If you try this, start out with a short line, just behind the wake, and lengthen gradually until you get hits, or quit!

It used to be thought that outboard motors frightened fish. Today it is fairly well established that the waves and turbidity caused by high-speed operation are what causes trouble, and that an outboard running slowly is no more scary to fish life than the noise of rowing. There's even a school of thought that the outboard sound attracts fish attention, and when they see your lure following, they are alert and pounce on it.

Personally, I'm not wild about slow trolling with a gasoline outboard. It's too much of a spark-plug fouling operation. Also, while gas power may not scare fish, I'm not convinced that it helps fishing. The new electric outboards run on an automobile battery, are noiseless and efficient, and the battery can be recharged from your house current.

I haven't mentioned weather in connection with trolling. One advantage of this form of fishing is that you can troll in winds too stiff for casting. In fact, trolling for landlocked salmon is often best in a stiff gale.

These basic trolling methods will work for most warm water species we've been discussing. If you're especially after walleyes, or even smallmouths in southern lakes, you should move out much farther from shore and use a quick-sinking line which will lower your lure without need for much additional weight.

Casting

This second form of fishing with lures is to trolling as a rifle is to a shotgun. Trolling covers large areas of water of which only a portion is prime fish habitat. By casting, you can pinpoint your target and keep your lure working where it will do the most good. The big advantage of trolling is that in a relatively short time it will give you an overall idea as to where you'll find fish in any particular body of water. Casting is the means by which you can cash in on information gained while trolling. Additionally, you can cast in areas, thick weedbeds for example, where a troller would get hopelessly bogged down.

Casting lures successfully takes some practice and experience just like golf, tennis, or any other sport requiring coordination. The best way to develop this is to simply pick out a target and cast at it. This can be the end of a fallen log, a rock sticking out of the water, just about anything. It really doesn't make too much difference whether you hit your target right on. If you place your lure within a foot either way you're probably better than 90 percent of today's average anglers.

Because you're aiming at a target, which is usually right on the shoreline, you're bound to occasionally miss and get hung up. Everybody does this, so just relax and retrieve your lure from the stick or tree it's hooked on. Luck runs both ways, and you'll also find yourself accidentally dropping a lure into a tiny pocket you didn't see and couldn't have hit if you had. Your fishing buddy will probably exclaim "Great cast!" with wonder and amazement. But remember the old motto—Never Complain, Never Explain—and shrug slightly as if bored at being reminded of your skill.

One big advantage of casting for warm water game fish is that you can approach in dead silence. Especially when fishing for educated largemouth bass, many experts ship oars and pick up a canoe paddle to eliminate any oarlock squeak that can be transmitted underwater. Fish lying in shallow water realize they are more exposed to enemies and are much more conscious of any strange sound. By eliminating boat noise, casters take fish that trollers can't get near. Notice I said boat noise. Singing, talking, laughing, and yelling can't get underwater to frighten fish. Feet scuffed on the floor of a boat, pipes knocked out on the gunwales, a tackle box picked up and dropped with a thump, are examples of the kind of noise that telegraphs "Trouble" below the surface.

If you're standing up to cast, clothing color is especially important to fishing success. White shirts are just about the kiss of death on a bright day in clear water. When I see a fellow with a soft white hat fishing in a white T-shirt labeled Camp Schmuck, I don't even need to ask him how the fish are biting. For him they aren't—unless you count panfish, which usually get so used to people that nothing bothers them.

Decisions, decisions, decisions! If you think selecting a trolling lure was tough, for casting it can be nearly impossible. You could literally buy a trunkful of casting lures; however, as we've already mentioned, a small but select group is all you really need.

Surface lures are the most fun to use. You see all the action, including the strike. These usually work best at dawn and dusk except on very dull gray days. If there's a brisk wind and lots of wavelets, forget surface lures entirely.

Generally speaking, the hotter and brighter the day, the deeper you have to fish. As you get south this depth increases markedly. Up near the Canadian border probably 90 per cent of pike and 80 per cent of bass are caught in water of fifteen feet or less. Down in Alabama, you may have to get into sixty feet or more of water to catch smallmouths and spotted bass. This simply means that as the sun comes up, you put on shallow-working plugs, sinking plugs, and finally diving plugs. As it goes down, you reverse the process.

Properly weighted spoons, spinners and spinnerbaits are effective casting lures too. They are especially good for pike, pickerel, and muskellunge, while plugs seem to have the edge with the basses.

Jigs and rubber or plastic worms fished right on the bottom are summertime casting lures supreme. They are especially good where the shoreline falls off fairly sharply into deep water and they can be inched down the slope. Rubber worms are distinctive in one respect. They are the only lure with which you don't want to immediately hook the fish. Because they are soft, fish will suck them in like a real worm. And because worms usually are only hooked in the head, you won't get the fish if you yank at the first touch. With any other lure, either trolling or casting, you should strike (this doesn't mean yank) at every hit. As soon as he closes his mouth on a plug, spoon, or spinner, a fish dimly realizes it isn't edible and wants to get rid of it. You've got to set the hooks before he succeeds.

Casters will argue the advantages and disadvantages of plastic shiner finishes, frog color, and red and white until the cows come home—or even all night long. Just as in trolling, however, black is the best color for night fishing, red and white or red and yellow for dull days, murky water, or poor light, and dull or natural finishes the rest of the time.

What do you do if all the fish seem concentrated in a giant bed of weeds that comes just about up to the surface of the water? The answers are either a weedless spoon, with or without pork rind, a spinnerbait or a pork-chunk frog on a weedless hook. Both of these should be worked fast and either on, or just under, the surface.

Wooly spinners

Fly Fishing for Warm Water Game Fish

Most people associate fly fishing with a stream and trout, but fly casting for bass, pickerel, and even pike is not only possible but a very effective means of fishing. Granted, the bigger the lure the bigger the fish, and you aren't quite as apt to hook a monster with the fly rod as you are with the casting rod. It's probably more fun fishing with a fly rod, however, and those fish you do catch will make up in fight all they may lack in size. (Actually, they'll run not much smaller than those caught on casting tackle but will give a better account of themselves—and without a mouthful of hardware.)

Because bass, pickerel, and northern pike are not eaters of small insects once they reach legal size, fly-rod lures for these fish are quite different in most cases from the traditional trout fly. Here are the fly-rod lures for warm water game fish:

1. Feather minnows. These generally have a wood or cork head and a feather body. They are retrieved along the surface in a series of quick jerks, or sometimes very slowly. They come in a wide range of colors from black to white and everything in between. All black, yellow, white, and various combinations with red are good. The action of the lure is more important than the color.

2. Deer-hair frogs, bugs, mice, and grasshoppers. Because they are constructed of deer hair, which is hollow and contains air, these little lures are light and float high in the water. Generally they work best when moved very slowly, with lots of long pauses.

3. Bass bugs. These are wood, cork, or plastic creations, with a few feathers or hairs added for ornament. Usually they have a flat or concave face that makes them gurgle or pop when given a quick flick. Normally these perform best when left alone for a long time after casting, then popped gently and left alone again. Like the deer-hair lures, these should be worked very slowly.

4. Streamer flies and bucktails. These are flies tied with long wings to imitate a minnow. Bucktails are simply streamers with a hair, instead of a feather, wing. Since they are underwater lures, streamers should be soaked before using. Retrieved in a series of uneven jerks and pauses, they create an uncanny effect of a swimming minnow. Both streamers and bucktails come in an infinite variety of patterns. For warm water fish, the flashy patterns, with plenty of red, white, and yellow work best. Gold- or silver-tinsel bodies are a plus. Some streamers are tied with marabou feathers, and these should be handled very gingerly, as the creeping feathers themselves will provide the action.

5. Wet flies. Similar to trout flies but gaudier, patterns like Scarlet Ibis (all red), Yellow Sally (all yellow), and Parmachenee Belle (yellow, red, and white) will catch bass. They were formerly used a good deal for smallmouths in streams and fished just like trout flies. Today these patterns are mostly trolled along with a small spinner to add flash.

6. Dry flies. On rare occasions in early spring, smallmouths in northern lakes will rise to dry flies. Frankly, you don't need them and will seldom use them even if you have them. Best patterns would include the White, Grizzly, and Royal Wulff, named after their inventor, Lee Wulff.

In actual practice, fly fishing in a lake or pond for bass, pike, or pickerel is exactly like casting spinning or bait casting lures. You aim for stumps, rocks, fallen trees, and so forth. Because fly-rod lures are almost weightless, they hit the water with a tiny plop that won't frighten the most sophisticated fish. Therefore, they'll take bass in situations where plugs and hardware draw a blank. If you expect to go trouting, it's a good idea to practice your casting and rod-handling technique on bass and pickerel too.

No matter what you're after, you'll find that surface lures do best at dawn and dusk and on very quiet overcast days. During midday, stick to streamers and bucktails.

If you're specifically fishing for pike or pickerel, speed up your retrieve. The pike family prefers a lure that swims actively. For bass, on the other hand, you normally can't be too slow except with streamers, which tend to sink when not worked, and wood-headed feather minnows, which should be moved at a fair pace.

Stream fishing is mostly for smallmouths, and streamers and bucktails are probably the most effective lures. Fish the heads and tails of pools and the rocky riffles connecting pools. Cast across-stream and let your streamer float down and around. When it is directly downstream, retrieve with a series of short jerks like a minnow trying to get back upstream.

Fly fishing is especially effective with largemouth bass, but also works fine with smallmouths in early spring, when they are in shallow water. Pickerel fishing with a fly rod is fine sport too, but when you get to northern pike things get a bit sticky, as they tend to stay in fairly deep water during hot weather. Fly fishing for walleyes is impractical, since they are deepwater feeders. Muskellunge have been caught on streamers, but this is really stunt fishing.

Live Bait Techniques for Warm Water Game Fish

Cane-pole fishing with a bobber is only one aspect of bait fishing. When you consider that fish are attracted by motion, you wonder why a dead minnow floating quietly under a bobber gets any notice at all. It does, and some very successful fishermen plunk their minnow bucket into the water and their backsides onto a camp chair as they commune with nature and the contents of a thermos jug—all the while keeping a watchful eye on their bobbers. Fellows like this use as many rods as the law allows, and in some states this can be a half-dozen. My personal feeling is that conventional bobber-fishing is a very ineffective means of using bait, except for panfish, or possibly catfish and carp in very shallow water. When you're after large predatory fish, you should be covering a good deal of water, and sitting on the shore is a poor way to accomplish this.

The most successful all-around way of using bait is to work it like a very slow moving

---

Two effective ways to use a bobber:

1. When fishing over weedbeds where the weeds come to within about four feet of the surface, you can drift along in a boat and use the bobber to keep your bait just over the weeds. By drifting you'll cover a good-sized piece of water, and on a breezy day this can be very effective.
2. Without a boat, simply keep working along the shoreline and casting your bobber into likely places. In other words, hunt the fish instead of waiting for them to come to you.

In short, a bobber has many limitations, and among these is its complete failure in any kind of a current. (Your bait comes to the surface.)

lure with just enough weight so you can cast effectively. Add a split shot or two about a foot up the line from your hook. Then hook a minnow about four inches long through both lips. Cast him gently toward a fallen log, a stump, a rock, or any other target that could harbor fish life. Let the minnow sink a bit and then very slowly reel him in. As a variation, raise your rod tip about a foot, lower it, and take in slack. When you can't catch fish this way, you can be sure they aren't biting. Big nightcrawlers will work as well as minnows when hooked lightly through the head, but you'll get more attention from sunnies and perch than you may want. You can fish this way even in heavy weeds, providing you use a weedless hook and keep your bait moving close to the surface.

This no-bobber-just-enough-sinker-to-get-it-down-and-then-move-it-slowly fishing method is ideal for spinning and very light bait casting gear. You can even strip-cast bait with a fly rod, but you'll miss the delicate touch you get with a light spinning line.

Another advantage of this style of bait fishing is that it works equally well in deep and shallow water. When fishing for smallmouths or walleyes, simply let your bait sink to the bottom. Then let out a bit of line and drift or row slowly along moving your rod tip occasionally. You'll snag a few rocks, but you'll catch fish too.

The biggest bait fishing problem for the inexperienced angler is knowing when to set the hook. Too late is as bad as too soon. With bass and walleyes you'll get a series of light tugs, after which the fish will probably start running off with the bait. Let him go about a foot and then strike. The pike family is much tougher. If you fail to hook a fish and suspect that pike or pickerel are biting, flip the bail on your reel to release the line and let the fish run several yards after the preliminary tugs. He'll then probably stop for a moment and then take off on a second run. That's the time to nab him.

Dawn and dusk fishing with live frogs on the surface is practically a sport in itself. Using weedless hooks, you hook the frog, which should be about six inches from head to extended feet, through both lips. Then cast him out in a jungle of lily pads or surface weeds and let him swim around. If you're squeamish about live frogs, dead ones are almost as effective. Cast them out, adding a split shot to sink them a trifle in the water, and retrieve by alternately pumping the rod and reeling to create the illusion of a swimming frog. With dead frogs, you can use a so-called frog harness for added hooking power. Whether the frog is live or dead, let the bass carry it off, turn it around, and start to swallow. At this point, he'll take off on a good run, and you can hook him.

While we've discussed bait fishing methods primarily as they apply to lakes and streams, the same ideas work equally well in rivers. The important thing to recognize in stream fishing is that you want your bait bouncing along just off the bottom. This means enough split shot or small sinkers to sink it without anchoring it. Cast across-current, let your line swing on down, and then retrieve very slowly, maybe with a bit of rod movement to add a lifelike appearance.

It's a mistake to consider that bait fishing is any less sporting than using lures. It often requires much more skill to hook a fish on bait, whereas with most lures nearly every fish will hook himself. In this day and age, a major problem in using bait is obtaining it in the first place. If you can find frogs, minnows, or nightcrawlers, give them a good try. You won't regret it.

Father and son, searching for trout on the East Fork of the Wind River, Wyoming.

VII.

Cold Water Game Fish—
The Sportsman's Prize

I t sounds a bit absurd, here on the brink of the twenty-first century, but there are still many places around the globe where fishing for salmon, and sometimes for trout, requires either good social connections or a well-stuffed wallet, or both. Outside the United States, fish and game are usually considered to be the property of the landowner, and fishing means that you either must own or lease a stretch of stream or the right to fish in a lake. In parts of Canada, notably Quebec and New Brunswick, individuals and corporations control nearly all the salmon fishing in major rivers. And many rivers, even in Patagonia, are owned by families very jealous of their trout and salmon prerogatives.

In medieval times, when a man's clothes, type of home, and business were determined by his station in life, stag hunting was a sport for nobles only, and salmon belonged to the king. Today, you and I can wear what we please, go where we want, and rise in business or the professions regardless of our forefathers' occupations. A certain aura still clings to trout and salmon fishing, however, and many trout anglers are social snobs who look down their aristocratic noses at bass and pike fishermen.

What's the cause of all this nonsense?

First of all, the various trouts and salmons are extremely good-looking fish. A brook trout resembles a masterpiece of jeweled enamelware, and a fresh-run Atlantic salmon gives the appearance of having been dipped in silver. It's almost redundant to say it, but these fish eat as good as they look. They put up a good, but possibly overrated, fight. The real clincher that sets them aside is simply the environment in which they are caught.

These cold water game fish can't stand pollution, or mud, or even warm water. All it takes is a few hours of high summer temperatures to turn a trout stream into a former trout stream. Because they are fussy about their environment, trout and salmon are usually found among the most beautiful scenery on earth. Spruce-covered mountains, tinkling

, snow-capped peaks in the distance, are all part of the picture. And while you
out from commercial hatcheries and stock them in a neighborhood swimming
ds to catch, this is a far cry from genuine trout fishing.
t and salmon lend themselves very well to artificial reproduction. It's difficult to
commercially, but trout are extremely easy. Because fertilized trout eggs and
t are easy to ship, the various species have been spread all over the globe. New
ustralia, Argentina, Chile, and even the White Highlands of Rhodesia have
out fishing. Salmon, especially Atlantic salmon, are more difficult to work with,
coast species have been introduced into the Great Lakes with the hope that
up the tributary rivers and spawn.
art of the mystique of cold water game fish is their willingness to take a fly. Fly
e of those sports that looks terribly hard but is actually pretty easy, and fun too.
that trout and salmon fishing brings up a mental picture of tremendously
fishing requiring a degree in Latin and another in etymology is enough to put it on
superior plane. But don't let them "snow" you. Trout in a mountain river are a lot less
sophisticated than largemouth bass in a weed-choked pond.
We'll take a brief look now at the various trout and salmon and their relatives.

Brook Trout

While any trout that lives in a brook could be called a brook trout, this name is usually
given only to the eastern brook trout of North America. To make things more confusing,
this fish isn't a trout at all, but a char. We can let the ichthyologists haggle over why a trout
is a char, but I'll point out that char have bright spots and markings on a dark ground,
while trout have dark spots and markings on a lighter ground.

Brook trout

Char or trout, the eastern brook trout is one of the world's most beautiful fish. Glowing with red and sky-blue spots, blazing with salmon-colored fins edged in white, he is truly gorgeous. The original range of this fish was along the Appalachian mountains from Newfoundland and Nova Scotia to Georgia and eastward, water conditions permitting, to the sea. Because the brookie requires the coldest, cleanest water of any trout found south of the Fiftieth Parallel, a lot of his original range has been lost to pollution and siltation. He has been widely introduced in suitable waters all over the world, however, and brook trout are probably more plentiful today than ever.

Brook trout, like most other fish, range in size depending on where they are found. Tiny streams in Maine, Nova Scotia, and Pennsylvania produce native trout that rarely get over six inches in length. In major rivers and large lakes, the same fish will reach six or seven pounds or more.

Like the proverb, "beautiful but dumb," brook trout are just that. Many states stock them early in the season just to give the license buyers something they are sure to yank in easily on opening day. In addition to worms, they can be caught on salmon eggs, bits of cheese, and even kernels of corn. Naturally, they'll take a fly, with nymphs and wet flies especially effective. This is not a dry fly fish to the extent the brown trout is.

Arctic Char

This close relative of the brook trout is found in circumpolar distribution from Norway to Alaska and to Labrador. A staple food of the Eskimos, this fish has especially brilliant spawning colors. He's usually caught on spinning tackle and spoons, but will take a streamer fly if you can get one to him.

While few of us think about it today, the Ice Age had a big effect on our fish distribution. The North American glaciers evidently split the arctic char population in half. Those fish that were south of the ice are believed to be the ancestors of the blueback trout and Sunapee trout found in Quebec and New England today in very small numbers.

A closely related char is the Dolly Varden trout, or bull trout, of the Rocky Mountains and west coast. For years this fish was reputed to be a big destroyer of salmon eggs, and a one-cent-a-tail bounty in Alaska was only recently repealed. (One of the arguments for repeal was that tails of young salmon were being turned in and collected on too!) The western equivalent of the eastern brook trout, the Dolly Varden is almost identical with the brookie but less brightly colored. If it were prettier, it would be more popular instead of being considered a sort of wallflower of the family.

All species of char (and trout) live well in salt water, and sea-run fish, known as salters or sea trout, have regular salmon-like runs in areas where the ocean stays cold all summer. For some unexplained reason, some brookies in a stream will move to salt water, and others will stay behind; those that go live in the sea will turn silvery, reverting to their regular colors after a few weeks in fresh water. The controlling factor on sea-run brook trout is whether they can reach the sea directly without having to pass through a warm water barrier. Therefore, where cold rivers run directly to a cold ocean in Maine and the Maritimes, salters are common. About the farthest south they are caught is Connecticut, with a few stragglers around Long Island and northern New Jersey. Because these sea-run brookies are caught on a spawning run, anglers look for them each year about the same time of year, which can range from April in Connecticut to July in Newfoundland and Labrador.

Brown Trout

This is the trout of Izaak Walton's tales and the only trout species found widely in Europe. From Italy to Norway, and from the British Isles to Siberia, brown trout are found in mountain streams, rivers, lakes, and salt water estuaries. Just as the brook trout is the salter of northeastern North America, the brown trout is the sea trout of northwestern Europe.

Much smarter and tougher to fool than the brookie, the brown trout can stand warmer

Brown trout

water temperatures. In fact, he can live nearly anywhere a smallmouth bass can. He was introduced into the United States after the Civil War, when it became apparent that lumbering and farming with their attendant silt and warming waters would make native brook trout fishing a thing of the past. Even today there is good fishing for brown trout in the Catskills, within a couple of hours drive from New York City.

In large bodies of water, the brown trout is a silvery fish with black spots and is often mistaken for a landlocked salmon. It takes a real expert to tell them apart; the best clue is that spots on the brown trout are round, while those on the salmon are X-shaped. In small streams and rivers, the brownie is a yellow-brown fish with black and red spots.

Brown trout are really the fly caster's dream fish. They delight in feeding on May flies and other tiny floating insects and will rise to a dry fly much more readily than other trout. Of course, big brown trout become fish-eating cannibals and will readily consume smaller trout without a twinge of conscience. Brown trout of nearly forty pounds have been recorded, and you can't expect a fish even half that size to be content with midges. But it's the smaller fish of six inches to three pounds or so that have really sparked interest in fly casting everywhere brown trout are found. Their range today is tremendous, as they have been introduced on every continent. In North America they are found in streams and lakes from Maine south to Tennessee and Alabama and west into Michigan, Wisconsin, and the Dakotas. Cold tailraces of Ozark dams have brought brown trout fishing into Missouri and Arkansas, where they share the spotlight with the more easily caught rainbow.

Rainbow Trout

If brook trout are school dropouts, and brown trout are Ph.D's, then rainbow trout are the happy medium. Originally native to the Pacific coastal drainage, this handsome fish with the broad red slash down each side has, together with the brown trout, been introduced everywhere. Like the brownie, he can stand warmer water than the brook trout, and like both of them, be likes to go to sea and come back as a steelhead, minus the red slash but with plenty of fighting poundage under a silver skin. Rainbows, especially the migrant steelheads, are the biggest jumpers and toughest fighters in the trout family.

The biggest problem with most planted rainbows is their tendency to drop downstream into salt water and only return at spawning time. Unlike brown trout, which will stay anywhere food and water conditions are adequate, rainbows are continually on the move. This is fine in big cold water river systems plunging right into the ocean, but other stream stocking of rainbows makes for good fishing for only a few days, until the fish move on. Rainbows do quite well in lakes that remain reasonably cool in the summer, and some of the biggest rainbow ever, the so-called Kamloops trout, come from Lake Pend Oreille in Idaho, where they feed on Kokanee salmon and sometimes weigh forty pounds and more.

Because they are good-looking, good eating, and easier to catch than brown trout, rainbows are very popular with fishermen. Even New Jersey, the most densely populated state in the Union, has spent a good deal of time and effort on rainbows, including an attempt to turn the Manasquan River, a shallow, silty, polluted stream, into a haven for steelheads.

Like brown trout, rainbows will go for wet and dry flies, streamers, and small spoons and spinners. Steelhead fishing for the big salt water migrants that return to Pacific-coast rivers to spawn is a specialty in itself. Many rivers have a winter run, and all kinds of special baits are used, including salmon eggs and so-called fluorescent bobbers, which resemble salmon egg clusters. From Alaska and British Columbia down to San Francisco, steelhead anglers cheerfully brave potential drowning and freezing and feel it worth all the effort and then some.

Cutthroat Trout

He looks like the victim, not the villain, with a red slash across the throat that may run up

Cutthroat trout

onto his cheeks on either side. This is the native trout of the Rocky Mountains from Alaska to Arizona. Closely related to the rainbow, he is much less migratory and very likely less flexible in water-temperature requirements. Unfortunately, cutthroats do not compete successfully with other fish, and attempts to introduce them out of their native range have not met with much success. For put-and-take stocking, this relatively non-migrant trout should still be a good bet. He is found from the Rockies down to the Pacific, although he tends to interbreed with, and become lost in, a heavy rainbow population.

Good fly-rod fish, cutthroats hit dry and wet patterns and are caught on just about the same lures as rainbows and browns. In river systems with all three species, you can catch all three from the same section of stream.

Occasionally, cutthroat trout get down to the sea and form small sea-run populations. Basically, however, this fish does best at altitudes of five thousand feet and over, which tends to show that the cutthroat, rather than the rainbow, could be the ancestral form of the golden trout.

Golden Trout

Whether or not the golden trout is more beautiful than the brook trout depends on whether you go for the flamboyant or the subtle. A dazzling picture in gold and red, with black spots and blue parr marks, golden trout were originally found only in the headwaters of the Kern River and its tributary, Volcano Creek, in California. Most scientists feel they are a high-altitude sub-species of rainbow trout, but who cares?

Because goldens simply don't exist at low altitudes, you have to get up in the mountains near Sequoia National Park to fish for them, at least in their native home. A great deal of effort has gone into transplanting golden trout into suitable high mountain lakes and streams in California, Wyoming, and Idaho. If you're interested in catching goldens, you have to either hike or use a pack train to get to the best fishing.

Because insect life is minimal in the icy waters where they reside, most goldens are caught on tiny wobbling spoons rather than flies. They will hit wet flies and streamers and even dry flies on occasion, but their basic food is mostly made up of tiny shrimp.

Golden trout fishing takes place amid the most spectacular scenery on the North American continent, and the biggest fish come from crystal clear ponds in high mountain valleys. Because fishing pressure in most golden trout areas obviously remains light, the fish are not too sophisticated. But unless they are feeding, it can be very difficult to get them to bite.

Lake Trout

Any trout that lives in a lake could be called a lake trout, although this is actually the name of a separate species that is more closely related to the chars than to the actual trout family itself. Like the chars, lake trout have light spots or markings on a dark ground and typically have lemon-yellow spots on an olive-green background. They also differ from other trout in having a forked tail that is unmistakable.

Called togue in Maine and grey trout in Quebec, lakers are widely distributed in northern North America, with related species found in Siberia. North of the Arctic Circle, where water temperatures never get over 40 degrees, lake trout are in both rivers and lakes. As

Lake trout

you get south, and stream temperatures rise, this species is found only in large lakes deep enough and therefore cold enough for them to survive the summers.

Up until about twenty years ago, lake trout were an important commercial fish, especially in the Great Lakes. But when the sea lamprey (an animal that attaches itself to other fish and sucks their juices, weakening or killing them in a sort of vampire fashion) reached the lakes through the Welland Canal, it practically exterminated this fish. Only after tremendous effort in research and money has the lamprey been brought under control, and now there is a possibility that Great Lakes lake trout may be restored.

Except just at ice-out in the spring and before freeze-up in the fall, lake trout fishing south of the arctic regions has little in common with other trout angling. Most lakers are caught by deep trolling with wire lines and/or heavy lead drails, which make them slightly less than a sporting proposition. When at the surface, they will attack wobbling spoons and even streamer flies with enthusiasm and give a good account of themselves.

Wonderful table fish, lake trout come in large economy sizes, with forty and fifty pounds not impossible and a possible weight limit of one hundred pounds or even more. In waters that can be reached by automobile, they usually average five to ten pounds, with a twenty-pounder considered a good fish. As you get north the fish are bigger and bigger. Twenty pounds is a good average fish in Canada's Northwest Territories.

Grayling

Closely related to the trouts, this is an arctic fish whose closely related species have circumpolar distribution. Grayling are found in the British Isles, Scandinavia, and eastward to Alaska and Canada. There are still some Montana grayling in the Rocky Mountain states, but the Michigan grayling was exterminated by the loggers in Michigan, Wisconsin and Minnesota, as erosion following deforestation choked the streams and created shallow, warm water conditions that this species couldn't take. There are still plenty of grayling in Alberta, British Columbia, Northwest Territories, and Alaska. Found in both lakes and streams, they feed heavily on insects and insect larvae, which makes them a natural for the fly caster.

Grayling are small fish (a two-pounder is big and a three-pounder a giant) and are especially noted for their large, colorful dorsal fin, and small, almost suckerlike mouth. Good to eat and fun to catch, these Ice Age fish could be in trouble eventually. Meanwhile, their hard-to-reach habitat gives them protection.

Smelt

Equally at home in fresh water and salt water, the delicious smelt is sought as food by man and fish. Dark green above and light beneath, with a silvery stripe down each side, the smelt's adipose fin, a small fatty fin on the back near the tail, shows its close relationship to the trout, grayling, and salmon. Found in deep, cold lakes and salt water bays in winter, smelt run up streams to spawn in early spring. This brings out a dip-net brigade at night in parts of Michigan and Wisconsin, where smelt are caught by the bucket.

For tricky hook-and-line fishing, it's tough to beat catching smelt in the summer in eighty feet of water. The new ultralight spinning tackle is a real help here, as you have to feel the slightest nibble. All you need are a couple of small earthworms cut into tiny pieces and a No. 8 trout hook plus a split buck-shot. If you can find a reef where smelt hang out, you can

Smelt

have a ball, and your catch is equally good fried for yourself or as bait for lake trout and landlocked salmon.

North of New York City, smelt run into some of the salt water estuaries in winter and are called frostfish. Because this is cold weather and cold water, they're caught with a cane pole and bobber, like sunfish. A bit of worm or raw shrimp from the supermarket will do the trick here.

Used as live bait or trolled in deep water with a big spinner, smelt are excellent bait. In addition to lakers and landlocks, you're apt to pick up an occasional big walleye, eastern pickerel, or northern pike, for practically everything that likes to eat small fish loves smelt.

Whitefish

A distant relative of the trout and salmon family, the whitefish presents a generally silvery appearance. He isn't called whitefish so much because of his exterior, but because the flesh of fresh whitefish is exceptionally snow-white. With a range that spans the continent from Maine to the Pacific, whitefish of closely related species are found in most large lakes, and mountain whitefish are caught in cold Rocky Mountain streams from Idaho north to Alaska. Whitefish are almost as international as trout and salmon, with very closely related varieties living in northern Europe and Asia as well as North America. Wherever found they have much the same habits and are regarded as a valuable commercial food fish.

With a forked tail as evidence of fighting ability, and weight that can run up to ten pounds or more, whitefish are still first-rate game fish. Back in the late 1800's and early twentieth century, when whitefish were a prime target of sports anglers in the Adirondacks, buoys would be anchored over deep-water reefs, and the areas around these would be baited with corn or doughballs to attract the whitefish. Hooks were baited with worms, cornmeal balls, or tiny pieces of fish.

Until the fish is hooked, whitefish angling is almost exactly like fishing for smelt. Both are small-mouthed species, residents of deep water, very delicate biters, and difficult to hook. All similarity ends there, however. Because of the whitefish's small, soft mouth and determined spirit, hooking a whitefish and landing him are not necessarily the same thing. While maybe not quite as strong as a landlocked salmon, whitefish will run, jump, and go through a full bag of tricks before giving up. Stream-living species will hit a wet fly fished close to the bottom, and lake whitefish in northern Canada are caught on dry flies during the May fly hatching period.

The lack of greater sports fishing interest in whitefish today probably reflects the general active tenor of our times. Most sportsmen today want to cast and troll and generally keep moving and be doing something. Whitefishing was popular in the Diamond Jim Brady era, when many sportsmen were overstuffed executives who preferred to do their fishing sitting down in a boat with a guide to bait grounds and hook, row back and forth from the landing, and handle the catch from landing net to kitchen door.

With commercial netting banned in most lakes an rivers that contain them, there's a great deal of good whitefishing to be had.

Atlantic Salmon

The king of fishes and the fish of kings is a good description of this fellow. He's probably the most expensive fish in the world to catch on hook and line (if you eliminate black marlin and other marine giants for which you first have to purchase a yacht).

Atlantic salmon

At one time the Atlantic salmon's range was from the Delaware River north to Labrador plus the George and other rivers flowing into Hudson Bay. He was also found in Iceland, Scandinavia, Britain, and down the coast of Europe to Spain. Dams and pollution have today greatly restricted the salmon. Maine is valiantly trying to restore runs in once wonderful salmon rivers, but for first-rate fishing on the east coast of North America, you have to go to the Miramichi River in New Brunswick. This is the most southerly mainland stream having a top salmon run. Northern New Brunswick, Quebec, Labrador, Newfoundland, and Nova Scotia offer good fishing if your timing is right. Iceland has more salmon rivers than a man could fish in a lifetime; Norway is fabulous; Great Britain fair; France and Germany are practically a lost cause due to pollution; Spain has some salmon rivers.

Why, with five species of salmon on our Pacific coast, is the Atlantic salmon so highly regarded? The major reason is that this is the only salmon that affords any sport when caught in fresh water. By the time Pacific salmon leave the ocean to spawn, they are so far along toward spawning and death that catching them is about as much fun as pulling in an old boot, and they won't hit anyway. Thus, the Pacific salmon are salt water game fish, and only the Atlantic salmon is a fresh water game fish and in a class by himself.

Atlantic salmon generally reach a river months before spawning and may spend weeks in fresh water before they lose their silvery color and fighting ability. Because they don't completely collapse physically in spawning, as Pacific salmon do, Atlantic salmon may spawn twice or even three times before finally dying.

Salmon fishing is expensive for many reasons. For most people, it is far away, and the travel is costly. Salmon tackle and flies are expensive too, and in North America flies are the only legal lure for Atlantic salmon. Then, as mentioned previously, most of the best salmon rivers, especially in New Brunswick, Quebec, and Europe, are privately owned. Worst of all, salmon are unpredictable in that fishing for them is governed by water conditions over which the angler has no control. Salmon come upstream on rising water, but too much rain brings muddy water that knocks fishing right over the head. When you have to time a trip so that you're fishing two days after a heavy rainfall or one day after a light rainfall, you'd better have a friendly oracle. The only way to beat this is to camp at your salmon river for a month figuring that in this time you'll get a few days of good fishing. Thus, you have to take time off from work, travel a long way, pay high fees for top fishing, and stay around a long time to catch salmon. Is it worth it? Well, figure that if it weren't, the price would come down.

For inexpensive salmon fishing that can be good at times, the best place to go is Nova Scotia. Guides aren't required (they are everywhere else except Maine), and a license is very inexpensive. The St. Mary's and Margaree rivers are small enough to wade and offer some dandy trout fishing in addition to salmon.

The next least expensive alternative, especially in terms of results, is to fly to Norway and fish the less expensive rivers, like the Sand River, which are as good or better than the best in North America. By the time you get through with guides and lodging and fees, it's cheaper to go to Norway than the Restigouche in New Brunswick.

While only fly casting for salmon is allowed in North America, from Iceland east plenty of salmon fishermen fling spoons, worms, prawns (shrimp), and all kinds of bait and hardware into the water. They all catch fish, yet fly casting is probably the most effective salmon-fishing method and certainly the most fun.

Because salmon bite from curiosity or annoyance rather than hunger, salmon-flies include just about everything that anyone who ever lies awake nights has thought of to put in a fly. Feathers of guinea fowl, peacock, crow, wood duck, and even hair from a moose (it works)

Coho salmon

are combined with tinsel, silk, wool, and junglecock eyes (these are feathers, so relax) to make a salmon-fly. It's no wonder that these bits of fluff are expensive.

Is all this salmon-fly nonsense really necessary? All I can answer is that in Newfoundland, the locals use a bit of moose hair for body and wings and catch salmon. Lee Wulff, a famous salmon angler, caught salmon very successfully on simple patterns he invented. If you're far from home on a costly vacation, you might as well use whatever the locals use because they wouldn't use it if it didn't work. On the other hand, if you can stick around the area for a while, it could pay to experiment. Just because one thing works doesn't mean that another fly, lure, or bait won't work much better. This applies, of course, to all kinds of fishing.

You should realize that you don't have to be an expert fly caster to catch Atlantic salmon. Unlike trout, who are very nervous and fidgety, salmon have to be more or less bothered and teased into striking. Plenty of salmon have been hooked by little old ladies who simply held a fly rod so that the fly moved around in the water with the current while the guide poled the boat to maneuver it into position. The basic qualities you need for salmon fishing are money and patience. In most places you'll fish with a guide or gillie who can easily teach you everything else in an hour.

Pacific Salmon

As mentioned, the five Pacific species, of which the Coho, or silver salmon, and the Chinook, or king salmon, are top game fish, are really salt water rather than fresh water species. Nobody except someone who likes rotting fish will bother with them in fresh water. There is a single exception: the Kokanee.

Kokanee Salmon

The tiny Kokanee salmon is a landlocked dwarf form (an eighteen-incher is a giant) of the sockeye salmon, one of the five Pacific species referred to above. He has several characteristics that have made him extremely popular with fisheries people and with anglers too. For one thing, he doesn't compete with other fish for food. Kokanee salmon feed mostly on daphnia, the tiny water-fleas you buy in pet shops to feed tropical aquarium fish. Kokanee also have the virtue of being easily controlled. Except in lakes with suitable tributaries for spawning, Kokanee will die off in about three years. This means they will provide fishing during an interval in which other species are being developed, without competing for food at any time. A delicious salmon to eat, the little Kokanee isn't too hard to catch once you learn how. The best method in most lakes is deep trolling with a tiny spinner or glass bead followed by a No. 8 single hook baited with a very small earthworm.

Landlocked Salmon and Ouananiche

About the only difference between these two fish is that the former is found in New England and the latter in Quebec and the Maritimes. They bear the same relationship to the Atlantic salmon as the Kokanee salmon bears to the Pacific sockeye salmon. For all practical purposes landlocks and Ouananiche are not only the same fish but so closely related to Atlantic salmon that it is hard to make much of a distinction. The primary difference is that landlocks live in large cold lakes and never migrate to the sea. As a matter of fact, they also live in rivers such as the St. Croix and Penobscot, and it is possible that if the polluted mouths of these streams were cleaned up, these landlocks would revert to their ancestral form.

Although much smaller than Atlantic salmon (a three-pound landlocked salmon is a good fish), this is a tremendous game fish with all the dash and zing of his salt water relative. The best time to catch him is shortly after ice-out in the spring. That's when he's up on the surface chasing smelt around the mouths of brooks and ready to hit a streamer fly. Both fly casting and trolling big streamers on a fly rod will catch salmon at this time of year. As surface water warms, he sinks down to lower levels, although brisk windy days that pour oxygen into the surface water may bring him up within twenty feet or less so that he may be caught by casting and trolling spinning lures on regulation tackle. For much of the

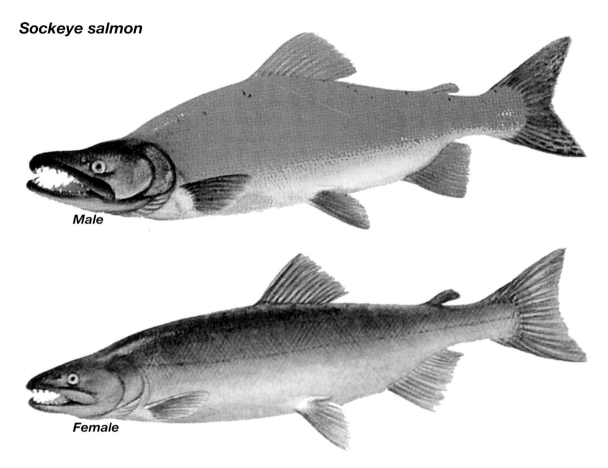

Sockeye salmon

Male

Female

summer, however, catching landlocks is the same business of wire lines and heavy lead drails that has been mentioned in connection with lake trout. In rivers, and sometimes in lakes, landlocks will take regular wet and dry trout and salmon flies, and this type of angling is specially popular with sportsmen who don't want to weight the fish down with a mouthful of hardware.

Landlocked salmon have been very successfully introduced into some Argentine rivers and lakes; according to people who have made the trip, it's worth it if only because Latin American landlocks can weigh twenty pounds.

Landlocked and Atlantic salmon, along with brook trout, are the status fish of northeastern North America. Mentioning that you're going to Maine for ice-out fishing for landlocks has about the same effect on some anglers as hinting that you've been invited to a private dinner at the White House. This is all quite silly—sort of on the same level as a polo player snubbing a tennis player. Trout and salmon are beautiful fish and fun to catch, but so are plenty of other species, and when it comes down to actual fight, plenty of salt water species will tow the entire salmon family around backwards.

VIII.

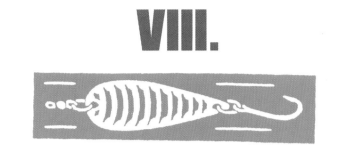

Basic Spinning and Bait Casting
Techniques for Cold Water Game Fish

What, you don't have to catch trout on a fly? That's right, trout will take a good many other lures, including spoons, spinners, and even tiny plugs, imitation grasshoppers, and so forth.

Since we've already discussed spoons and spinners in relation to bass and pike fishing, we can briefly say that for trout in most of North America and Europe, the small spinning-size wobbling spoons, about an inch or so in length and weighted for casting, are highly effective. So are little spinners, particularly the Mepps spinner, which has a dull silver blade and a squirrel tail-hair treble hook. Whether or not you prefer spinning or bait casting gear is irrelevant. Both will do the job. Because spinning functions so well with light lures, it is especially popular south of the Canadian border. Up where big lake trout live, bait casting tackle is used to cast and troll big wobbling spoons of the same size you'd use for northern pike. There are various details to remember about spoons and spinners as related to specific fishing situations.

Rivers

While spinning tackle is great for worm-dunking in tiny brooks, you can't use spoons and spinners in anything much less than fifty feet or so wide. Trout are easily alarmed in shallow water, and hardware splashing over their heads would simply frighten them away.

Spinning tackle is made to order for fishing a good-sized river, however, especially one with a head of water. Fish are lazy, just like some people, and in a roaring torrent they're too smart to buck the current. Instead, they lie behind rocks, or go right down to the bottom, where the flow is always comparatively slight and further reduced by obstructions. The best way to find trout in such a place is to use a lure heavy enough to sink down to them, and a feathery fly hardly qualifies here. With spinning gear, you can cast much farther than with a fly rod and reach water that otherwise would either be completely out of range, or that you'd have to risk drowning to get near. These are some of the reasons why steelhead anglers from Alaska south generally fish with spinning tackle. Another reason is that spinning gear can be handled with gloves on during the winter and early spring steelhead runs, and this lets you fish without freezing your hands off. It may not sound like much, but the combination of icy water and freezing winds can really make your hands uncomfortable to the point where you are miserable.

Spinning tackle is thus especially effective in big rivers with a good current flow. Hardware will also out-fish flies in turbid or muddy water because it is bigger and has more visible flash.

Under low-water conditions, especially with crystal-clear streams, conventional spinning lures are useless. Modern ultralight outfits, with a one-pound test line that can handle a $1/8$ ounce lure, can be used then, but fly fishing is easier. For best results, fish with spinning tackle in high dirty water, and use the fly rod in low clear water. This applies to trout and steelhead everywhere, plus Atlantic salmon in Europe, where spinning gear may legally be used.

Incidentally, many states today have set aside fly fishing -only stretches where only fly casting is permitted. If you prefer spinning tackle, stay out of these unless you want to explain to the judge that you were only fooling. These fly-only stretches are always explained and pointed out in the little booklet that comes with your fishing license. They are also usually marked with signs near the water.

River fishing with spinning lures calls for casting across and slightly upstream, drifting the lure down on a tight line, and then retrieving. Sometimes, especially in a torrent, it pays to cast nearly upstream so that your lure can sink on slack line and bounce along the bottom. A steelhead bobber, which is a globular lure imitating a cluster of salmon eggs, is often fished this way.

Long deep runs and pools are the best spots to use spinning tackle in a river. Rapids and shallow, fast riffles will get you completely hung up in the rocks and assorted waterlogged timber, and you'll lose more lures than it's worth. You'll lose them in pools too but not nearly to the same extent. As in fly casting, the head and tail of a pool are normally more productive than the middle. These are the areas used by feeding fish waiting for the current to bring something delicious to them.

Lakes

With the exception of deep trolling, spinning and bait casting tackle in a lake are handled as when fishing for smallmouth bass. The best fishing spots are usually around the mouths of feeder streams and the outlet where a river leaves the lake. Shallow reefs, especially off a string of islands, are sometimes very good too. Normally this is early spring fishing, and the fish are in these locations looking for smelt on their way upstream to spawn. Whether you cast or troll near the mouth of a feeder brook is a matter of personal preference. When the fish are hitting, both methods will work.

In the arctic, lake trout normally bite fairly near the surface all summer, and you can actually cast the shoreline for them in some lakes, much as you would do when bass fishing. You can use lures of the bait casting size too, with a wobbling spoon six inches long about right for ten-pounders and up.

Getting back to civilization, small spinning-size wobblers are very effective weapons against brown, brook, and rainbow trout stocked in small ponds. When water temperature gets up around 50 degrees and higher, unsophisticated trout will hit these wobblers much faster than they'll take worms. Casting from a dam or around the mouths of inlet streams can often get you a limit within a half hour or so. The best idea is to reel fairly fast so that the trout has to hit instinctively at the shiny thing that might be food (just like a baby reaches for a gold watch).

In a pond a couple of hundred acres or more, assuming that it's man-made, you can troll a small wobbling spoon approximately where the old stream bed ran, or you can drift and cast over this same area. Around the opening of the trout season, fish will rarely, if ever, show on the surface. Therefore, let your wobbler sink to the bottom before retrieving.

Jigging, either with a small lead-head jig or a wobbling spoon worked gently with an up-and-down rod motion, will catch trout in fairly deep water. It's better to keep the lure moving slowly up and down than to try exaggerated pumping motions. Since you're drifting in a boat, this method lets you cover a lot of pond in a relatively short time.

Deep Trolling

The basic midsummer method of fishing for trout and landlocked salmon, deep trolling requires a good working knowledge of the water fished, for the trout and salmon in a lake will be concentrated along reefs that can't be seen from the surface. This is where modern depth-finding machinery comes in handy by showing not only water depth, but type of bottom, and occasionally even individual fish.

Most of this trolling is in sixty to one hundred feet of water or more. Bait casting or light salt water bay tackle replaces spinning tackle here, as a spinning reel does not take kindly to heavy stiff line, and wire or lead-core line is the best way to get your lure down where it belongs. Even then, most anglers use a keel arrangement plus a sinker to make certain they're down bumping bottom.

Once you hit the correct depth of line, either by hit or miss, or through a guide's advice, knot a bit of colored thread around your line at that point. This tells you immediately when your line is at the right depth. For different depths over different reefs, use different colors. A spot of nail polish or even a bit of colored plastic tape is good too. You'll even find that some trolling lines are made in sections of different colors to indicate depth, which is a big help. Monel wire line, the best for deep trolling because of its small diameter, is unmarked, however, and nail polish is ideal. You need a marker at one hundred feet, at two hundred feet, and at fifty-foot intervals thereafter.

The wobbling spoons and plugs are especially good for lake trout, and the various spinner rigs are used for rainbows, brookies, and landlocked salmon, although there is no hard-and-fast rule, and salmon will hit a wobbling spoon also. The spinner rigs are often used with either a bait fish or a big gob of nightcrawlers following along behind, the theory being that the spinners get attention so that the worms or bait can make the sale. A live bait fish is hardly ever used here as it has to be specially rigged on the hook anyway. A Maine bait fish specialty is a skinned yellow perch about five inches long.

Almost any lure that can be sunk deep enough can be used for deep trolling.

The following are basic:

1. A large wobbling spoon (usually rigged at the end of a long leader attached to a weighted keel).

2. A spinner or spinners (the Dave Davis spinner rig is six feet long) followed by a leader and lure or bait.

3. A plug, rigged like the wobbling spoon. (Sometimes a sinking plug is used without the keel, with the sinker on wire or lead-core line.)

IX.

Fly Casting for Cold water Game Fish

In the Western world at least, fly casting is the oldest form of fishing with an artificial lure. Fly fishing for trout is mentioned by Herodotus and other Greek authors and was practiced by the Romans too. Of course, no casting was involved here as the fly was simply dipped in the water with a short line and a long pole, a type of fishing practiced today in the lakes of Ireland (and elsewhere by smart anglers). By Izaak Walton's time, fly casting was a recognized sport, and artificial flies were fairly well known in the 1600's; but it was not until the nineteenth century that improvements in lines and leaders made possible fly fishing as we know it today.

You can't cast without a weight of some kind to pull your line out. Fly fishing differs from all other forms of angling in that the weight is in the line itself. The lure, for all practical purposes, can be weightless. Another basic difference is that because the line is heavy, it is not cast from the reel. Instead, it is stripped off the reel by hand before casting. Thus, fly casting was possible with very primitive reels and even with no reel at all but a small basket in which to coil excess line.

Possibly because it was the first highly developed branch of sport fishing, or possibly because of its connection with those aristocratic fish, trout and salmon, fly fishing has for generations been established as a recreation for gentlemen as opposed to the common plebeian herd. Of course, today there is no reason why anyone shouldn't enjoy fly fishing , but in some circles a certain note of snobbery lingers on—a refuge for those who dare not compete with the rest of the world on equal terms.

Speaking practically, fly fishing is easy, enjoyable, and a cinch to learn. For the purpose for which it was designed—presenting tiny lures realistically in comparatively clear, shallow water—it can't be beat. This is a very efficient fishing method, and the lower and clearer the water, the more the method's superiority stands out. In late summer, when streams are gin-clear and very low, fly casting will catch fish when bait and hardware won't even get a look. The conventional portrait of the barefoot boy with worms beating the pants off the rich old gent with the expensive fly rod is true enough the first couple of weeks of the season. After that, once the May flies hatch, bet on the geezer with waders, landing net, fly book, and the rest of the regalia. If he knows his stuff, the barefoot boy will be popeyed with envy. Funny, you don't see too many barefoot boys anymore. Barefoot girls are a dime a dozen, but boys now find boots more comfortable, especially on sharp rocks. Besides, once the insects really start to hatch and fly fishing starts in earnest, you don't want anything bare, even your face, around a trout stream. Unless you're well smeared with insect lotion, the black flies, mosquitoes, and gnats will chase you home in a hurry.

Fly fishing is primarily a stream sport. Lake fishing with a fly rod for trout and landlocks is about the same as bass fishing except if you hit it right you can cast to rising and cruising fish instead of just fishing blind. We'll concentrate on stream fishing for trout, with the understanding that the species doesn't make much difference.

Caesar divided Gaul into three parts, and we can beat him by dividing fly fishing into four: using dry flies, wet flies, nymphs, and streamers.

Dry Fly Fishing

This had its start on the chalk streams of England, which are loaded with insect life and with weeds. Because a floating fly would float over the weeds and catch the fish, dry fly fishing was invented. What's the difference between a dry fly and a wet fly? A dry fly has stiffer hackles, which are the leggy portion of the fly. Being stiffer they are less absorbent and won't soak up water and sink. Additionally, they are tied so they stand out straight from the fly body instead of being angled back along the body as on a wet fly. It's considered perfectly all right to dunk your dry fly in oil, or spray it with some, to keep it floating.

Today, fishing lines for dry fly work are built to float. Formerly they were dressed with various secret formulas that mostly resembled paraffin or messy Vaseline. A real dry fly artist wants his line floating, his fly floating, and his leader—now get this!—just under the surface. Why shouldn't the leader float? Because it's too visible to the fish when it floats.

Originally, a dry fly rod was supposed to be stiffer than a wet fly rod in order to pick up a greater length of line from the water. Today's modern rods are more or less a happy medium, and the well-equipped fly caster has need for only one rod (he may have twenty but he only needs one), plus two reels—one with floating line and one with sinking line. He'll also have, depending on his finances, his manual dexterity at a fly vise, or his pure cussedness, an assortment of flies that can range from a half dozen to several hundred.

There are several hundred dry fly patterns of trout flies alone, plus maybe fifty or so dry salmon flies. Does anybody need this many? No! If you want to fly fish for trout near home, the sensible way to buy flies is to write your state or province Fisheries Commission (see Chapter XXXIII for address), tell them where and when you expect to fish, and ask them what patterns and sizes to suggest. Then follow their advice. If you're

The following is a list of suggested basic patterns found to work in every part of North America:

Dry Flies (Tied on No. 12 Hooks)

Adams	Gray Hackle	Red Variant
Black Gnat	Hendrickson	Royal Coachman
Blue Quill	Mallard Quill	Royal Wulff
Cahill Light	Mosquito	
Ginger Quill	Quill Gordon	

For a really complete assortment of dry flies, I suggest that you add the following:

Blue Dun Bivisible	Brown Spider
Brown Bivisible	Fur Ant
Fan Wing Royal Coachman	Light Ginger Spider (No. 16 hooks)
Gray Wulff	Blue Dun Midge
Hair Wing Royal Coachman	Brown Midge
Irresistible	Cream Midge
Light Ginger Bivisible (all use No. 12 hooks)	Jassid*
	Royal Wulff
Blue Dun Spider	Cricket Hopper (No. 10 hooks)

* Jassids imitate insects that live on land and crawl, jump, or fall into the water rather than hatch in the water like nymphs. (No. 20 hooks)

going to distant waters, ask your guide or outfitter for suggestions.

In addition to flies, rod, reel, and line, the dry fly angler needs leaders. The leader is the more or less invisible connection between the fly, which you want the trout to see, and the line, which you hope he won't notice. Before this era of blessed synthetics, fly leaders were made of silkworm gut. This miserable material had weak spots and needed soaking before use, as otherwise it resembled a coil of wire. Thanks to nylon, we now have wonderfully tapered leaders in an infinite variety of sizes. The dry fly addict needs about a half dozen in assorted tip sizes from 1X to 5X. As the X numbers get higher, the leader gets finer, and 4X is about the diameter of a human hair. The leaders are tapered from a heavy butt to a fine tip, because if they were of

Dry flies

Black Gnat

Light Cahill

Irresistible

Royal Coachman

Joe's Hopper

Renegade

Quill Gordon

Adams

equal diameter throughout they wouldn't turn over properly when cast.

Since a 4X leader tests about four pounds before you knot it on the fly and weaken it, it stands to reason that part of the fly fishing game consists of trying to use the heaviest leader possible under the circumstances. Generally, 1X and 2X are quite good, especially at dawn and dusk and on dull days, when no frightening shadows are cast by the leader. Brilliant sun, low water, and so forth can call for leaders as fine as 5X, if your nerves can stand the strain. Gauging your strike to hook the fish but not bust the leader is one of the more difficult tasks in dry fly fishing .

Fishing with dry flies can be easy or difficult depending on circumstances. Arriving at a stream in early evening, you may find some insects already starting to hatch and you may have a perfect match, say a Whirling Blue Dun in size 16, right at hand. Here it's simply a matter of working quietly into position and casting so that you float the fly over feeding fish without alarming them and without drag. This drag, which is the pull of line and leader on the fly, is the worst enemy of the dry fly addict. To avoid drag, you should aim slightly over the surface of the water and cast almost directly upstream. The line and leader will then fall loosely, and by cautious stripping you can work as much as four to six feet of stream, sometimes more and often less, before you have to pick up the line with your rod and cast again. Oddly enough, despite what we've said about drag, you'll sometimes find a day when trout will only hit a dry fly when it starts to drag and gets pulled slightly under the surface. This is an exception to the general rule that upstream casting with as little drag as possible pays off.

Where do you look for fish, and what pattern do you use when they aren't rising and there is no hatch? Besides being at the heads and tails of pools, feeding trout will be in pockets in the riffles both behind and in front of rocks, logs, and other obstructions. The secret of fishing here is to hit the tiny glides of smooth water and pick up your fly before it drowns in the white water.

When nothing is showing, a good many anglers will try a Royal Coachman, a Brown Bivisible, or whatever their favorite might be, and hope for the best. Others will figure that a Quill Gordon or a Hendrickson should be hatching and will stick to an imitative fly rather than the Royal Coachman, which imitates nothing. And it has happened that repeated casting of a fly has appeared to start trout rising by the angler producing a sort of artificial hatch of his very own.

A real horror to the dry fly man is to arrive at his favorite pool and discover trout dimpling the water everywhere, feeding on midges alongside which his tiniest flies look like an aircraft carrier. Some of the better mail-order houses and tackle shops carry midge flies tied on hooks as tiny as No. 24. Especially in June and later, it could pay to carry a few. The only other remedy is to toss caution to the winds and bend on a No. 14 Fan Wing Royal Coachman. This will look like a giant among pygmies, but there's always a chance that some trout is finished with the hors d'oeuvres and ready to dine.

After you get equipped with rod, line, leaders, and flies suitable to your fishing area, the rest of your education must come from experience. Much of the fascination of the dry fly is that you see and hear everything, including the rise of the trout to the fly itself. This works both ways, because you'll see all your mistakes too. The biggest things to remember are

Wet Flies

(Tied on No. 10 Hooks)

Black Gnat

Blue Dun

Cahill Light

Coachman

Cowdung

Ginger Quill

Gray Hackle

Hare's Ear

March Brown

Mosquito

Professor

Quill Gordon

avoiding being seen by the fish, and learning the water so that you know which way currents are going to move your fly. Slickly surfaced pools, especially those full of eddies, often have reverse currents, so that some trout are facing and feeding downstream while others are facing and feeding upstream.

Fly fishing for trout isn't something you can learn overnight, but one easy shortcut is to take time out from your own fishing and observe what experienced hands are doing. You can learn more from watching an expert and asking a few questions, such as "why" and "how," than you would believe possible.

Sometimes lakes and ponds offer opportunity to the dry fly angler. This is usually in late spring, when the water remains cold, but insect life is starting to appear. Large trout will often cruise around the shoreline at this time looking for emerging nymphs and occasionally gulping a morsel at the surface. Far enough north, they may cruise like this in the evenings during much of the summer. You can't just cast your fly and let it sit indefinitely, however. Occasional motion that more or less resembles an insect struggling on the surface will do business, especially as you are generally casting to rising fish.

Dry fly fishing occasionally is used on Atlantic salmon in late summer, when the water is warm, low, and clear. Since these fish really aren't feeding, but hit out of pure annoyance, it generally pays to keep casting over a fish until he either hits or convinces you that he has no interest whatever in your offering. Sometimes in a case like this, a wait of an hour or so and a stealthy fresh approach with a different pattern of fly bring a strike.

Wet Fly Fishing

In this, the oldest branch of fly fishing , the wet fly is fished at depths ranging from just under the surface to near the bottom, depending on water conditions and time of year. There are probably a thousand wet fly patterns, some of which resemble specific insect life, but many—including some of the most successful—look like nothing in particular on this planet.

Just as with dry flies, it's a good idea to contact state or provincial authorities and get their recommendations on patterns and sizes for the area you're going to fish. This will generally result in a varied assortment of colors ranging from very bright, such as Parmachenee Belle, down to the very dark Black Gnat. Brook trout usually go for large bright patterns, and the farther north you fish, the brighter fly you can use. Brown trout, on the other hand, prefer small dark flies for the most part, and rainbows like something between the two extremes.

Here are some classic wet patterns in use throughout Europe and eastern North America. Hook sizes No. 6 and No. 8 are generally preferred in Canada.

Amherst	Jock Scott
Black Dose	Silver Doctor
Durham Ranger	Silver Gray
Highlander	Thunder and Lightning

You can fish wet flies upstream like a dry fly, which gets them deep and gives them no action except that imparted by the current. This is very difficult fishing since you often can't tell when you have a strike. Therefore, the most common wet fly fishing method consists of casting across or downstream, letting the fly swing around and retrieving with a series of short jerks. Fishing downstream in this manner presents a problem: The wet fly angler is walking right into the current-facing trout instead of sneaking up behind them as in dry fly fishing. For this reason, a wet fly fisherman has to watch his feet, his rod, and his shadow very carefully.

In dry fly fishing only a single fly is used at a time. Many wet fly anglers use two, three, or even four flies in a combination called a cast. A small dark fly or nymph can be used at the tip end of the leader, a slightly brighter fly tied to a dropper farther up, and a large bright fly used nearest the butt end of the leader. This bright fly indicates a strike on the other invisible flies. At any suspicious pause or wobble of the indicator fly, you set the hook—sometimes in nothing, sometimes in a fish.

There is really no significant difference between dry fly and wet fly water except that wet flies give you a better chance to fish riffles and rough stretches where you couldn't float a dry fly. Additionally, since part of wet fly fishing is imparting action to the fly, drag is often of minor consequence.

Wet fly fishing in streams gets result all season long, except in very low, clear water. Trout obviously do most of their feeding underwater, on tiny minnows and crustaceans as well as insects and their larval forms, and the wet fly evidently gives a good approximation of these minute forms of life. Fishing with wet flies in a lake or pond is much the same as casting hardware except that fly and fly rod are used. Generally, you row or drift along in a boat off a shoreline or shallow reef, cast in, and retrieve by stripping line in short or long jerks. While a spring sport in most areas, wet fly fishing can be carried on in high mountain lakes all summer. And whether you fish from shore or boat, remember to keep the fly moving like a swimming creature.

Fly casting for Atlantic salmon is essentially wet fly fishing , mostly with special salmon

Any complete selection of nymphs should include the following patterns:

Black Creeper	Dark Hendrickson	Leadwing Coachman
Black Midge	Dragon Nymph	Light Cahill Nymph
Breadcrust	Gay's Grub	March Brown
Brown Bomber	Golden Quill	Montana
Caddis Larvae	Grande Stone	Mosquito Larvae
Cream Nymph	Green Caddis	Zug Bug
Damsel	Hellgrammite	

Stone fly nymphs

Glass head pheasant tail nymphs

A good collection of streamer flies would include the following patterns, on No. 4, No. 6, and No. 8 hooks for stream fishing, No. 2 and No. 4 for lakes, and No. 1 and No. $^1/_0$ for trolling:

Black Ghost	Little Brown Trout	Parmachenee Belle
Green Cosseboom	Magog Smelt	Red and White Bucktail
Green Ghost	Muddler Minnow	Silver Garland
Grey Ghost	Nine-Three	White Maribou

patterns. Most experts state that salmon cannot be caught on trout fly patterns, which makes some sense because trout patterns imitate food, and salmon aren't feeding. The success of Moose Flies and other local patterns that could pass for a black bivisible or even a black gnat makes me wonder, however, whether this inability to take salmon on trout flies is basically a question of everybody believing what nobody has tried. Certainly trout will hit salmon flies with relish. Anyway, in fishing it pays to follow the successful crowd, so if you're going after salmon, get yourself some salmon flies as recommended by your outfitter. Most lodges and fishing camps catering to salmon anglers have flies available on the premises or will bring them in from a local pier or the nearest town.

Nymph Fishing

A nymph is simply a wet fly tied without wings to represent the larval form of some species of caddis fly or May fly. It is fished with a sinking line as close to the bottom as you can get. Originally, nymphs were used mainly in high muddy water in early spring by fellows who would rather go fishless than use a worm. It took a while for nymphs to catch on, but today they are very popular indeed, partly because they do hook some mighty big trout at times when fish simply can't be found at the surface.

Nymph-fishing is bottom fishing, and some nymphs are tied with a bit of lead foil in the body to help sink them. The most difficult part of this fishing method is telling when you have a strike, so an indicator fly tied well up the leader will be a big help. To get your nymph down on the bottom, you should cast upstream in a forty-five degree angle and gingerly bounce it along in deep water. Experimentation has found that nymphs are effective in all waters that hold trout, and they are as popular in Patagonia as they are in the Beaverkill.

One interesting fact about nymphs is that they often work well when fish seem to be feeding on the surface. If you can't hook feeding, surfacing trout with dry flies, look very carefully to see if the fish are bulging or tailing. If you see a dorsal fin or a tail, switch to nymphs because the fish are wheeling around to feed on bottom.

Nymphs are very effective trout lures in lakes too. Simply cast, let sink to bottom, and retrieve—very slowly—with just enough wiggle to indicate some life.

Streamers and Bucktails

These are minnow imitations; when tied with long feather wings they are streamers, and when tied with hair wings they are bucktails. In shallow water you cast them on a floating line, and in deep water you use a sinking line. Generally, the bucktails work best in streams and the streamers in ponds and lakes, but even this isn't always true. One sure thing is that these are among the most effective lures for very large trout. In stream fishing they are usually worked like a wet fly but retrieved with more dashes and darts to simulate a darting minnow. Lake fishing with streamers is the same as with wet flies or nymphs.

The biggest streamers of all are used in landlocked salmon trolling, mostly in New England. Designed to imitate a good-sized smelt, these big trolling flies usually have tandem hooks to catch short strikers and are generally worked from a rowboat or canoe paddled near the mouths of streams where landlocks lurk.

As previously mentioned, streamers are very effective in bass and pickerel fishing. Additionally, they're the only type of fly that brings results in salt water. Streamer patterns vary greatly, depending on what kind of bait fish they are trying to imitate. In stream fishing, the most effective are fairly dark, both to imitate stream fish (a recent success is called the Little Brown Trout), and because in clear water minnows generally appear dark. As with other wet flies, it pays to have an assortment ranging from dull to bright and use the white, red, and yellow patterns on dull days and the more natural Grey Ghost and similar dark flies on bright days. Although this may seem contradictory to what has been said about fish vision (fish see best in dull light, and not so well in bright light), in actual practice bright colors work best under dull conditions because they create a contrast and the fish do see them. In the bright sun bright colors seem to become lost in the general glare and sparkle.

Most trout streamers are tied on No. 6 and No. 8 hooks, while those for landlocked salmon are on No. 1 and No. 2 hooks. There are no streamer patterns for Atlantic salmon, as they supposedly won't work on this fish. Since British salmon are often caught baiting with prawns (a type of shrimp), a shrimp imitation might make some sense. If you want to pioneer, take a few Pink Shrimp designed for bonefish on your salmon safari.

Fly-Tying

This is a great hobby, and there are several books available dealing with it.* You basically need a jeweler's vise, tiny pliers and scissors, a stiletto to pick with, and, of course, the thread, feathers, hooks, and tinsel. All of this can be bought in kit form with instructions

---

* Especially good are *Fly-Tying*, Helen Shaw, Ronald Press; and *Flies*, J. E. Leonard, Barnes.

from both sporting-goods shops and mail-order houses. Certainly few satisfactions beat that of catching a fish on a fly you tied, and maybe even designed, yourself. If you're good with your hands, get a small kit and give it a try. Even if you live in an area without trout, you can catch bass, pickerel, northern pike, and panfish on homemade streamers, nymphs, and wet flies.

X.

Bait Fishing for Cold Water Game Fish

Lawmakers have to run for election, and to satisfy the public, trout fishing annually opens in most areas about a month earlier than it really should. Snow on the stream banks and ice along the shoreline isn't very conductive to fly fishing . It really isn't very good for bait fishing either, but you're left with a choice between nymphs or bait—or nothing.

Worms

Everybody knows that trout are interested in worms, but not everybody realizes that worm-fishing, especially for trout, can be something of an art. Folklore about the deadliness of the worm and bent pin to the contrary, during most of the fishing season the successful angler is the fellow with a book of artificial flies. Worms are, nevertheless, good in their place: for early season high-water use, on rising water after a rain, and in certain small brooks too tiny to be fished any other way.

In Australia, there are earthworms a yard long. Something like this would scare a trout half to death. Big worms don't always catch big fish, and the worms you come up with in spading a vegetable patch are just about the right size for most bait fishing. Hook them lightly through the head and serve, sometimes with a split shot or two, depending on water conditions. Sometimes big nightcrawlers get better results than small worms. These should be hooked lightly through the collar.

A worm that floats along or bumps bottom in a more or less natural position with the body wiggling indicates mealtime to a trout. One that is all bunched up on a hook may smell all right, but its appearance is all wrong, and fish definitely notice the difference.

Early season worm-fishing in a stream is simply a matter of adding enough split shot so that you can bottom-bounce your bait downstream without anchoring it in any one place. When the water is less than 45 degrees, trout don't bite much anyway, but you'll pick up a few in the middle of deep pools and similar places. Casting a worm with a fly rod is what Franklin D. Roosevelt once called an "iffy" business. It can be done, but spinning gear will do it better.

In artificial ponds the best opening-day worming method is to add enough split shot for casting weight and get out near a dam or inlet if possible. Then, very slowly, retrieve your worm inch by inch along the bottom. In weedy areas, you can't do this, so add a cork float and figure the depth so that your worm will just clear the weeds. Because trout generally gulp their food without a lot of preliminaries, they are easier to hook than bass. A couple of tugs and then they'll rush off with the worm and generally your hook.

As spring turns into summer and the water gets lower and clearer, trout lose interest in worms. A shower or rain that dirties the water a bit and causes it to rise will still bring good worming results. In midsummer, worms are most successful when used at night for big brown trout; the size of fish caught at night on bait can be quite surprising. In low water at night, you can bounce worms along the bottom of long pools without any sinker at all.

Most trout streams have tiny little feeder brooks running through alder thickets or assorted brush. Some of these have deep pools and good trout. The only way to successfully fish such a place is with a small worm on a small hook. If the ground is soft you really have to sneak in, as the slightest tremor will scare the fish back under the bank or into some other hiding place. By simply dipping your worm on a short line you can generally get a trout to flash up and grab it as soon as it starts to sink wiggling. (Be sure not to try fishing a place like this without insect lotion in ample supply.)

As with warm water game fish, a worm-and-spinner combination will get results even when other lures fail to produce. A tiny spinner, about the size of a fingernail, is a good attractor for trout. The worm-and-spinner combination in a stream is fished just like a wet fly, cast across or down and retrieved back up against the current so that the spinner blade will spin. A small Colorado spinner is good with a small worm hooked on each of the treble hooks.

Worms, and grubs of all kinds, are good bait for grayling and whitefish. You can find grubs in rotten stumps and under rocks, and they can be fished just like worms.

Minnows

The term minnow can include any small fish from a sucker to a smelt, and small fish are especially good bait for large trout. Normally they are hooked through both lips on a No. 4 hook and drifted like a worm. Minnows and other bait can be cast with a fly rod by strip-casting. This involves stripping line from the reel, coiling it so it can go out without tangles, and bringing the rod back slowly and moving it forward so that the loose line, pulled by the weight of the bait, shoots out through the guides.

Various small chubs and shiners are especially effective in big streams. The best places to use them are the deep pools at the base of a waterfall, or where a feeder brook meets the main river. Minnows, usually cast with spinning tackle, are used in ponds and lakes for trout and salmon. They are cast with a single split shot for weight, allowed to sink, and retrieved slowly.

In midsummer, when the fish are in deep water, New England lakes in particular see a form of fishing known as plugging. The name is deceptive because you don't use a plug at all, but bait. You anchor over an underwater reef and let out sixty to eighty feet of line to reach bottom. (Although this is mostly done with clincher sinkers, a three-way salt water swivel should offer an advantage.) Then you bring up a foot or so to get your bait off the bottom and wait. You may wait fifteen minutes or all day. Modern depth-finding equipment could be a real help here as it is in most deep-water fishing. In addition to minnows or smelt, plugging can be done with worms and other bait. For relaxation it can't be beat, as most of the time nothing is happening at all.

Grasshoppers and Beetles

Just like people, trout like variety in their diet. There are times in August when nothing will catch fish like a live grasshopper. You can buy special grasshopper hooks with light wire for attaching the critter unharmed, or you can use a regular Carlisle hook, about size 6, and strap him on with a light rubber band. The objective is to cast the hopper so he falls into the water as if he tumbled off a grassy bank. It should be noted that some artificial grasshoppers and crickets work as well as the real thing.

At times trout are interested in beetles of various kinds, and these can be used for bait without much trouble. Since beetles don't move much in water, the best idea is just to drift them down with as little drag as possible.

Frogs

Most frogs are too big for trout bait. If you can get tiny ones you run the risk of catching an enormous trout, especially if you fish a stream that courses through a meadow or has waterlilies in shallow stretches. You have a choice of either fishing the frog on the surface and letting him kick himself along, or sinking him to the bottom and giving him some motion with your fishing rod. Frogs are much more suitable for bass bait, since 90 per cent of trout aren't big enough to be interested.

Salmon Eggs

Salmon eggs, fresh or preserved, are great trout bait, particularly in early spring. In steelhead waters, salmon eggs are the accepted lure and are drifted right on the bottom in deep

Hatching mayflies mean food for fish and success for anglers.

pools. Steelhead going upstream to spawn follow about the same course each year and stop to rest in deep holes and runs somewhat similar to those used by Atlantic salmon; however, they don't really stop feeding and will snap up a bunch of salmon eggs with relish.

In the eastern United States where steelhead and big migratory rainbows are caught in the early spring in streams running into the Finger Lakes of New York State, salmon eggs were such a great bait that they were banned. The natives thereupon dyed tapioca pink, which works quite well, as do phony salmon eggs of Vaseline. (If I get up there to fish some day, I'll bring some Maraschino cherries along. A small Maraschino cherry could double for a giant salmon egg, couldn't it?)

May Flies and Other Winged Insects

If you can see size 22 hooks, which are about the smallest size made, you can sometimes use live May flies as bait by simply impaling a couple of them. You can't cast them, so you sort of tickle them along the water. This is quite a specialty in Ireland, where May-fly dapping is an art, and long poles of fourteen feet are used with what amounts to light silk sewing thread as line. You can't do much of this in any kind of current, so it is basically a lake and pond operation. Bees also make good trout bait, if you can get them without their getting you!

Miscellaneous Baits

Trout, grayling, and other cold water game fish will bite on all kinds of things from time to time. Little cubes of cheese are very popular with bait bouncers in some waters. Certain hatchery-truck followers (unsportsmanlike anglers who follow state hatchery trucks filled with trout, and fish where the trucks dump the trout in a stream) swear by bits of raw or cooked beef liver. Doughballs, which can be made by mixing flour and water and heating the mixture until a thick paste is formed or by soaking and then squeezing out pieces of bread, can also be used. A very good brook-trout bait is the pink-and-white ventral fin of another trout. (This is supposed to be the origin of the Parmachenee Belle fly.)

XI.

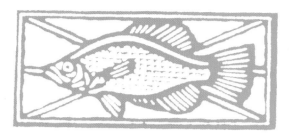

Ice Fishing

Something amazing has happened in this century: people have learned to enjoy winter. Until nearly the 1930s, winters were considered horrible except by children. Adults who considered themselves too old, too dignified, or too brittle for coasting and skating could either tinkle along on a sleigh ride or huddle by the fireplace. Winter was nothing but a time for grouching and looking forward to spring.

Nowadays, devout skiers follow the snow from Colorado to Chile and enjoy breaking their bones slaloming through the Andean winters during July and August. Ice fishermen haven't quite reached that stage of dedication to the sport, nor do they break many bones, but they do get enjoyment from being out-of-doors in the bright-blue, blinding, winter weather.

Unless you sit and watch a bobber, most fishing calls for quite a bit of concentration and undivided effort. Ice fishing usually doesn't. Therefore, it's probably the easiest, most sociable form of fishing there is. You need a lake with fish in it and sufficient ice on it. Notice I said lake. Some ponds are safe enough too, but you should never go ice fishing on a body of water with perceptible current unless you have a couple of feet of ice. Where there is current there are eddies, and where there are eddies there is weak ice. Every year automobiles and trucks go through weak ice, and sometimes people get drowned. If you refuse to take chances you may catch less fish that day, but since you'll live longer you'll make up for it. A professional fisherman or an Eskimo has to get fish or go hungry. He must sometimes take chances. When you're sports fishing, it doesn't pay to risk your neck for recreation. Of the people who do, a sizable proportion end up wishing they hadn't.

Inside a shanty, ice fishing is mostly a matter of using a handline. Outside, most anglers use tip-ups, which incorporate a small reel and a device that springs a red flag in the air when fish bites. After a hole is bored in the ice, the tip-up is installed so that the reel is underwater. (This is to prevent freezing.) The number of tip-ups an angler can use varies

Ice fishing for cisco on Bear Lake, Utah/Idaho

Yellow Perch

widely according to law. The theory is that you set out a batch of widely spaced holes and then, as action occurs, you move the isolated tip-ups into the "hot" area.

Fish Species and Techniques in Ice Fishing

Yellow Perch, Pike, Pickerel, and Bluegills

Probably the biggest species in quantity for the ice fishing addict is the yellow perch. It's a school fish, so that when you locate one you can catch a bunch. It's excellent eating, and winter perch are apt to run in size a bit larger than summer perch. Eastern pickerel and northern pike are big ice fishing species. This is primarily minnow-fishing, especially in the East. West of the Alleghenies, shanty fishermen use a live sucker or sometimes even a wooden decoy to lure pike and even muskellunge up high enough to spear in states where spearing is permitted. Especially in the upper middle western states, bluegill sunfish are sought by ice anglers. They are caught on about the same equipment as yellow perch, but usually over shallower water.

Except that you use minnows for pike and pickerel (sometimes for perch) and worms and grubs for perch and bluegills, fishing for these species is basically much the same. The best idea is to start your holes in areas where fish are caught in the summer in from five to fifteen feet of water—generally, an area off a shallow point or in the middle of a bay. The length of your line in relation to water depth can be very important, as the fish range from right on the bottom to within a foot or so of the surface. Your rigged lines should carry enough lead to get them down fast, and fairly heavy monofilament line, about fifteen-pound test, is ideal. Monofilament won't freeze, and the rather limited light under the ice makes a heavy line less visible than in the summer months. A No. 6 hook is about right for perch and bluegills. A No. $1/_0$ Carlisle will do for pickerel, and about a $3/_0$ Carlisle for pike. Minnows used in ice fishing should be hooked through the back just behind the dorsal fin so they swim level in the water. (At one time dime-store goldfish were extremely popular for ice fishing bait. They are very tough, and their color attracts fish. They are now illegal to use in many parts of the United States and Canada, however, because anglers who put their surplus bait into the lake started populations of wild goldfish, which sounds nice except that goldfish are carp, and carp are undesirable in game-fish lakes.)

Trout and Salmon

In parts of New England it's legal to fish through the ice for landlocked salmon and trout. This is bait fishing, with the first objective usually being to find grubs to catch smelt, which are later used as bait for the trout and salmon. Nothing is very different from ice fishing for pike or perch except that you are fishing in probably thirty feet of water or more. You start over the same reefs you would fish in the summer and work in towards shallower water if possible.

Smelt

These little fish are very popular wherever they are found, which includes the Great Lakes eastward into Maine and west into Michigan, Wisconsin, and Minnesota. Because they are so small and bite so delicately, smelt fishing is mostly done in heated shanties. Usually these have no windows, but enough light filters in through the ice for daylight visibility. Areas with smelt have cold enough winters (smelt fishing through the ice is a big sport on Lake Champlain and in part of New England) so that the shanties, mounted on runners, can be towed out to the fishing grounds by car or truck and left on the ice until spring threatens to arrive. Usually the runners are removed when the shanty is put in position over a long-favored location. In smelt fishing three to seven hooks (where legal) are used on a handline and double headers are frequent. Bait is tiny bits of earthworm or small grubs fished on a No. 12 hook.

Other Species

Bass, various sunfishes, white perch, walleyes, and many other species are occasionally (in the case of walleyes, often) caught ice fishing. These are not normally considered as ice fishing species, however.

Lures and Bait for Ice Fishing

Artificial Lures

Jigging an artificial lure is sometimes a very effective ice fishing method. In recent years ice flies, which are very sparsely tied wet flies without wings, have become very popular with bluegill and perch anglers. These are used just like bait except that they are moved up and down slowly. Nymph patterns or nearly any wet fly with the wings cut off will produce results. A real grub is often hooked on an ice fly for extra results.

Small wobbling spoons can also jigged with good results in perch and pickerel habitat. You don't have to worry about too much reflection under the ice, so that nickel and chrome get best results.

Natural Baits

How to get bait and keep it from freezing are perennial ice fishing problems. Earthworms are good, but unless gathered in the autumn and kept in a wooden crate in the basement, you won't have them when you need them. Grubs and maggots of all kinds get action too. With a pocket knife, you can find grubs in the thickened galls found on many plants. Wood borers or sawdust worms can be easily acquired nearly anyplace by splitting rotten logs, and they will live for months in sawdust.

The nymph or larval stage of nearly any insect makes good bait if you can find them. Put a seine or even an old window screen in a nearby brook and overturn some upstream stones. Dislodged larvae will almost always wash down and cling to the screen.

The best way to get minnows in the winter, aside from buying them, is to use a glass minnow trap. This is rather like a bottle with a funnel pointing inward at the bottom. The fish swim in the funnel after bread crumb bait and can't get back out again. Because minnows will freeze in a minnow bucket on the ice, many fellows dig a surface ditch in the ice and let water in through a tiny hole in the bottom of the bucket. The minnows won't swim down through the hole unless you make it too large. A similar larger trench will keep your catch alive and unfrozen until you're ready to quit and go home.

Ice Fishing Equipment

Ice fishing equipment can range from a tip-up or two, plus a crowbar and a tin can full of bait, to elaborate shanties complete with stoves, lights, and chimneys. Since this is all fresh water fishing, equipment should always include a fishing license. Additionally, check your state's or province's fishing regulations to make certain ice fishing is legal on the lake you expect to fish. In some localities resort operators have been able to stop ice fishing with the argument that so many fish are caught their summer business is suffering.

Clothing should include insulated underwear over which you wear a wool shirt and pants, and over that you should wear an insulated zipper suit for good measure. In skiing and other active winter sports, you can get by with layers of thin clothing because you are exercising and generating body heat. Ice fishing isn't that active, and you have to bundle up like an Eskimo to stay warm while standing still. Rubber boots worn with two pairs of socks are very good for the feet, but insulated leather boots aren't too bad. The best head-gear is the kind that pulls down right over your face. Don't care if small children scream with fright when they see you—warmth, not beauty, is the objective.

In tackle for outside fishing you'll need the legal number of tip-up rigs bought at a sporting-goods store. (You can make these, but it's hardly worth the bother unless you love to tinker.) You'll need hooks in sizes appropriate to your quarry, with No. 4 a good pickerel-perch combination. Clincher sinkers are easier to handle than split shot, and you'll need weights up to about a half ounce. A few ice flies and wobbling spoons will complete your gear.

The best thing for making holes in the ice is a special auger device sold for this purpose. The next best thing is a big crowbar or wrecking bar with a chisel end. If you use this or a smaller chisel, be sure to tie a line to it securely and the other end to your wrist or sled. Otherwise you'll break through, let go of the crowbar, and it will vanish into the deeps forever. You can also chop a hole through the ice with an axe or hatchet. This isn't recommended, as one mistake on slippery ice could cost you a foot, or your life.

Practically indispensable to the avid ice angler is a child's sled. You load this up with your equipment and drag it along on a rope behind you. Another great thing if you expect to spend much time in one place is a tarp and couple of light poles you can rig as a wind-break. A sterno or gasoline or kerosene cooker is very good for warming hands and making coffee or a hot lunch. (Don't use these in a closed shanty unless you have a stovepipe properly installed.) On very thick ice or on a snow-covered beach, you can gather drift-wood and start a good blaze to thaw out by, but on any kind of thin ice your fire is apt to suddenly vanish into the lake. (This is fine unless your cooking equipment and lunch goes with it!)

Early in the season, before the ice is full of snow, skates are a lot of fun and get you around to check distant tip-ups at good speed. A skate sail can do this even faster. Standing around in skates makes for frozen feet, so bring boots to switch to when you're weary of speeding.

A vital piece of equipment is a good knife. The sheath style is best because folding blades are difficult to open in the cold. An inexpensive fishing knife with a wooden handle is as good as anything.

While you may not feel your automobile or truck is part of your ice fishing equipment, you do need it to reach the lake. Be sure you have chains or studded tires before trying to drive on slick ice. Also, be sure you have adequate antifreeze to face a biting wind at near zero degrees. Never, never drive on ice unless you are absolutely positive it is safe. If there is the least shadow of doubt, bore a test hole. Snow-covered ice can be extremely treacherous. Danger-loving ice addicts who want to drive on a lake usually have buggies with the doors removed. This gives them a chance to avoid being trapped inside. Dangerous ice isn't always noisy either; soft ice doesn't creak or groan, it just gives way.

An added piece of equipment to bring ice fishing is a Coleman cooler or insulated fiber-glass bag for your lunch—not to keep it cold, but to keep it from freezing. Also, if you aren't building a fire or bringing a stove, a thermos of hot soup or coffee certainly hits the spot. While there are always people who want something stronger than coffee, you're smart to wait until after fishing hours.

Unlike summer anglers, who mostly want to get off alone, ice fishermen are generally a convivial gang, and ice fishing contests are big affairs west of the Great Lakes. Towns and Chambers of Commerce offer all kinds of prizes, and a local lake may have so many cars on its surface it looks like a regular parking lot.

Are there any best hours or times for ice fishing? Oddly enough, late afternoon seems to be generally the best time of day, and a high barometer indicates best fishing. In some places, night ice fishing in shanties is popular. Be sure the way is well marked before you get out on the ice to join a group for this. Getting lost on a big lake at night is not only possible but absolutely no joy whatsoever.

If you live in a climate where you can try ice fishing, give it a try. The initial cost is very small, and who knows, you might be hooked!

XII.

A Survey of Fresh Water Fishing Equipment

Before you invest money in a fishing outfit, you should have some idea what you are buying—and why. The following outline analyzes the faults and virtues of every type of equipment, starting with the cane pole and working on up—financially and maybe aesthetically—to fly casting.

What's best for you? This depends on where you expect to fish and what you expect to catch. Check with any anglers you may know and with your local conservation people for their ideas. Meanwhile, it may help to know a little more about the different kinds of tackle and fishing methods.

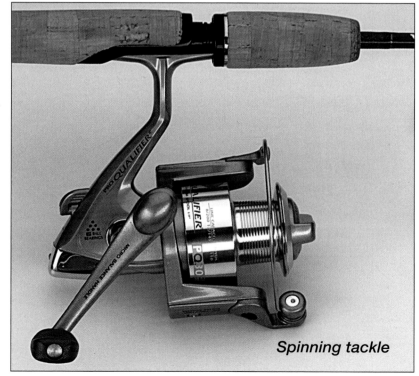

Spinning tackle

Cane-Pole Fishing

Obviously this is the oldest and the least complicated form of angling. In addition to your pole, which should be about twelve to fourteen feet long when assembled, you need about twenty-five feet of braided line of twelve to twenty-pound test. Don't use monofilament line, as constant exposure of a short length of this type of line to sunlight will make it wiry and weak.

CANE OR FIBERGLASS POLE (NO REEL REQUIRED)

Advantages:

a. Price. This is extremely reasonable; even modern sectional poles are very inexpensive.

b. Ease of use. It takes only minutes to learn how to handle a pole and flip your rig under hand out into the water.

c. No mechanical problems. There's nothing to corrode or get out of order.

d. Easy to store. Put it in a corner or up on your garage rafters and forget it.

Disadvantages:

a. You can fish only a limited area of water about one and a half times the length of your pole.

b. Landing big fish is a difficult problem. (With the old cane poles, you simply tossed the entire pole into the lake or stream and let the fish drag it about until he tired. Then you sneaked up and grabbed the butt end of the pole and yanked him in. Before you try this with a fiberglass pole, be sure it floats.)

c. Fishing methods limited mostly to bait fishing with a bobber. You can try skittering for pickerel or dapping flies for trout with a pole, but it's about comparable to hunting with a muzzle loader: it works, but modern equipment works better.

d. You are apt to be classified by other anglers as being in a low socio-economic category or as a "meat" fisherman rather than a sportsman. (Of course, this is nonsense. Sportsmanship is an attitude that has nothing to do with equipment, and some millionaires enjoy fishing with a cane pole.)

Equipment for Bamboo or Fiberglass Pole

1. **Pole.** Should be seven to fourteen feet long and jointed for easy carrying. Many poles have telescoping sections that fit inside each other. A pole should have a ring guide at the tip and possibly another guide nearer the butt. Tie your line to the guide nearest the butt end of the pole and run it out through the guide at the tip.

2. **Line.** For best results, your line should not be more than one and a half times the length of your pole. Best line for pole fishing is braided nylon in ten- to fourteen-pound test. Color isn't too important except that solid white and solid black are considered too visible. Pepper and salt, sand, and various shades of light green are best.

3. **Bobber or float.** Cork bobbers are best by far. Tapered bobbers will give best results because they are most sensitive to nibbles and offer least resistance to biting fish. A small bobber is much better than a large one. Bobbers are often painted in bright colors to make them easier to see against the water. If you paint your own bobber, a coat of yellow enamel gives top visibility.

4. **Sinkers.** Cheapest and best is split shot. BB shot is about the right size. Clamp a single shot about six inches above your hook to make sure your bait gets down to where it belongs. In water with no current, you may do better with no sinker at all.

5. **Hooks and leaders.** If you buy snelled hooks (they have a looped length of nylon wrapped to the hook with thread) you won't need a leader. Ringed hooks, which come in little boxes (you can buy a big assortment for twenty-five cents), are much cheaper. If you use these, buy a ten-yard coil of ten-pound test monofilament leader material. Tie about two feet of this between your hook and your line with a fisherman's knot. A No. 6 hook is correct for most fresh water pole fishing.

6. **Bait box or minnow bucket.** To start with, you can use a small plastic pail or the cheap metal buckets sold to painters. If you find yourself using minnows for bait, you'll need a minnow bucket; this is usually a double bucket with a liner. You can place the liner in the water while fishing to keep your bait alive.

7. **Stringer.** The metal ones with safety-pin snaps are best. Hook fish through both lips and keep in water. You can release a live fish you don't want to take home.

8. **Landing net.** You don't really need one; swing your catch ashore.

9. **Pliers, knife, scaler, measure or ruler.** You'll need all of these.

10. **Tackle box.** The small plastic boxes are long-lasting, inexpensive, and can't rust.

Basic cane-pole equipment consists of a cork or plastic bobber, a box of assorted hooks in sizes 2 to 8, and a few small split shot used to keep your bait from drifting up to the surface. Because your bobber is vital to your fishing success, you should choose it carefully. For most fishing, the smaller, longer, and thinner you bobber, the better. The round globe shapes are all right in small sizes, but the big ones offer a lot of suspicious resistance to a biting fish. Even worse, they fail to tell you exactly when to set the hook.

You can easily learn to tell what's biting at your bait simply by watching your bobber. With small fish you get tiny erratic jiggles. Game fish generally offer a few warning taps, and then your bobber will either dive suddenly and take off underwater or stand on end and move along the surface. If your bobber starts to move away very slowly either on or just under the surface, you've got a really big fish biting.

As indicated, the best way to cast with a cane pole is underhand. Simply raise it and swing the line out and away from you. This will let it settle easily into the water. If you toss your bobber overhand with the pole, it will make a fish-frightening smack as it's banged down into the water.

Spinning Tackle

REGULAR SPINNING TACKLE (OPEN-FACED SPINNING REEL)

Advantages:
  a. Minimum skill required. Anyone can learn to cast with a spinning reel and become quite expert in an hour or so.
  b. Can be used for nearly every kind of fishing. (By adding a clear plastic weighted bobber, you can even fly-cast with a spinning outfit. This is prohibited in most fly fishing -only areas, however.)
  c. Easy maintenance. A little reel oil is essential on occasion.

Disadvantages:
  a. Poor for deep-water fishing and for very heavy fish, and not well suited to any sort of trolling.

An open-faced spinning reel is the easiest equipment with which to learn casting. You can teach yourself without trouble. Since the reel spool is stationary instead of revolving and is parallel to the fishing rod itself, a cast simply pulls line off the end of the spool, making backlashes impossible. Open-faced spinning reels are designed to go under the rod because they were developed in Europe, where the place of a reel is always considered to be underneath the rod. The original patent on this type of reel was held by an Englishman named Bache-Brown, who developed it to solve the problem of casting tiny lures and baits on nearly invisible line to sophisticated fish.

With a spinning reel you should use monofilament line, which is a single strand of nylon rather than several smaller strands braided or twisted together. Eight-pound test is about right for most fresh water fishing. In areas of heavy weeds you need ten-pound test line.

Recently, so-called ultralight spinning gear has become popular. This is identical with regular spinning tackle except that it is much smaller and lighter. It calls for lines testing from two pounds to four pounds. Ultralight equipment obviously puts much more sport into catching very small fish and is a good way to get hits from very sophisticated fish. You can use it to catch much bigger fish than you'd think possible, and four-pound test line has landed many fish over twenty pounds for careful anglers under ideal conditions. A necessity in landing large fish is a heavy shock leader of ten- to twenty-pound monofilament carefully fastened to the end of the regular line. This foot of leader protects against chafing, rocks, and so forth. Unless you're fishing only for panfish, I'd suggest starting with conventional spinning tackle and getting into ultralight gear after you've had some experience.

Spinning rods come in all weights and sizes, but a six-and-a-half-to seven-foot model with a fairly whippy action is about the best. The most important thing to look for on a spinning rod is good guides. Examine than carefully for nicks or scratches that could chafe your line and lose your fish—and lures too. Nearly all spinning rods today are made basically of graphite with a long cork butt. A rod with a screw-on type reel seat is best, especially for occasional anglers. Other reel seats that simply hold the reel on the rod by a couple of rings pushed into position tend to let the reel fall off at some crucial moment.

After placing your spinning reel on the rod (the handle will be on the left side) run your line down the guides and over the reel bail before tying it on the spool. Put a pencil through the spool of line and let somebody hold it while you wind the line on the reel. Now you're ready to practice casting.

First of all, never practice with a lure. Use an inexpensive casting weight that you can buy at nearly any store handling fishing tackle. These are made of rubber or plastic in the official spinning weight of 3/8 ounce. Besides the obvious danger of hooking a dog, cat, friend, or yourself, lures with hooks tend to get stuck even in a lawn. Although some people spend so much time and effort on casting tournaments that they hardly, if ever, see a fish, you should get out and practice casting on a ball field, golf course rough, industrial plant lawn, or even a rural road, before going fishing. Then when you're doing the real thing, you can concentrate on catching fish instead of the mechanical details of using your equipment.

To cast, leave about a foot of line between the tip of your rod and the casting weight. Then (assuming you're right handed) use your right forefinger to hold the line firmly against the rod, and flip back the bail with your left hand. Bring the rod tip smartly back over your shoulder, and release your finger from the line as you whip it forward. (You bring the rod tip back to increase momentum when you start forward in your cast.)

The basic secret in all casting is to relax and not try to use brute strength. Timing is the thing to learn. If your weight sails up straight at the sky, you released your finger too soon. If you bang into the ground at your feet, you held tight too long. It may take you a few trials to really catch on. Then it becomes easy, and you can start aiming at old inner tubes, rubber rings, and other suitable targets. The ability to put a lure exactly in the right place is the most important skill in fishing. This is what separates the skilled from the unskilled and is one reason why less than 10 per cent of all fishermen annually catch more than 90 percent of the fish.

Spin Casting

SPIN CASTING TACKLE (CLOSE-FACED SPINNING REEL)

Advantages:
a. Minimum skill required. To cast, you push a button.
b. Excellent for most fresh water lure-fishing.
c. Especially good for night fishing because there is no bail with which to get tangled.

Disadvantages:
a. Maintenance can be a problem, especially when the line gets tangled inside the reel cover.
b. You can't switch from heavier to lighter lures without trouble. The heavier lures put the line under tension, and when this is lessened with a lighter lure, the line releases into a mess inside the cover.
c. Very poor for bait fishing, trolling, and deep water.

The spin casting reel is an American adaptation of spinning that utilizes the American bait casting rod and bait casting lures. It was developed to combine the effortless casting of spinning with the short rod and the reel-on-top fishing to which North Americans are accustomed. A good spin casting reel of a top manufacturer, used only with lures suited to it, will give good service. Don't try to use it with light lures or for bait fishing or trolling. (You can bait fish with a large heavy bobber equivalent to the weight of a lure—about $5/8$ ounce.)

The biggest problem with spin casting reels is that if the line is wound too tightly on the spool it springs loose when released for a cast and gets caught and tangled inside the casing. My personal feeling, although many experts will vigorously deny this, is that spin casting, like many hybrids, offers some of the virtues and all of the vices of both parents.

Spin casting calls for a short rod, about five feet or five and a half feet long, and stiffer than a spinning rod. Most of these rods have offset reel seats, and this is neither a plus nor a minus. The reel comes with line already on the spool, so assembly of the outfit is easy. Run the line up through the guides and tie on your casting weight.

To cast, bring the rod back smartly over your shoulder, as in spinning, and push the release button as you bring it forward. It's easy! The important thing is not to try for too much distance at first. And when you reel in make sure you're not winding the line too tightly. One way to avoid trouble is to pump by raising the rod and then reel slack as you lower the rod.

Equipment for Spinning and Spin Casting

1. **Fishing rod:** Should be graphite and six to seven feet in length. (If you expect to do most of your fishing in salt water, get the eight-and-a-half-foot rod called a "steelhead rod." Developed for fishing in west coast rivers, this slightly heavier rod is excellent for light surf-casting and bay and ocean fishing.)

2. **Spinning reel:** A medium-priced reel of a well-known fishing tackle company will give good service and should come with a guarantee. Many spinning reels are imported from Europe and should also have a guarantee together with convenient repair stations in this country. Spin casting reel. If you want to try this close-faced spinning reel, get the best you can. They are nearly all made in the United States and should have a service guarantee. Many spin casting reels come with line already on the spool. Eight- to twelve-pound test is best for most fishing. (Don't get a spin casting reel for salt water fishing. They aren't made for it.)

3. **Line:** Mono is a Greek word meaning "one," so monofilament line is a single strand of nylon, usually colored mist or blue and nearly invisible under water. Before nylon monofilament became available, all lines were braided or twisted from many individual fibers, much like a tiny rope. You can still buy some braided lines for spinning; however, the monofilament is today generally accepted as the best. Get the limpest monofilament line you can, even if it is more expensive. Hard, wiry line will cause you kinks and trouble.

4. **Bobber or float:** A cork or plastic bobber is used in many types of fresh water and some salt water fishing. An important thing to consider is weight. A bobber should weigh at least $\frac{3}{8}$ ounce for easy casting. (Very heavy is worse than too light.) If you can find a solid cork bobber that is tapered rather than round, you'll have the best.

5. **Sinkers:** Split shot in BB size is about right unless you are fishing in very deep water or strong currents. If

Equipment for Spinning and Spin Casting *(continued)*

you are going surf-casting or ocean fishing, you'll need some 1 $\frac{1}{2}$ - and 2-ounce sinkers.

6. **Hooks:** You'll save a lot of money with eyed hooks (also called ringed hooks) instead of snelled hooks that come with a short leader wrapped on. Tie an eyed hook directly to the end of a monofilament line. Remember: hook sizes start at 1 and go down to size 22, and they also go up from size 1 to about size $^{12}/_0$. There are many styles of hook made. My personal preference for most fresh water fish is sizes 6 and 8 Carlisle. This has a long shank that makes unhooking the fish easier. For fish larger than perch and sunfish, especially when using live bait, shift to sizes 1 and 2. You'll find little boxes of assorted hooks in most places that sell fishing tackle. These are inexpensive, give you a wide range of sizes in economical quantities, and have a chart of sizes to help you.

7. **Leaders:** These are unnecessary with monofilament line, as the entire line is the leader. However, when you're fishing for pike, pickerel, or other fish that have a mouth filled with sharp teeth, a short wire leader is a good investment, especially when you use lures. You can buy these about six inches long, with nylon covering the wire, a snap on one end for your lure, and a swivel on the other.

8. **Lures:** A book could be written on spinning-tackle lures. If you expect to fish for largemouth and smallmouth bass, pike, and pickerel, you'll want a small selection of plugs, spinners, spoons, and poppers. Buying useless lures is a habit that many anglers fall into; never buy a lure unless you are absolutely certain that you are going to try it.

9. **Miscellaneous:** There are a great many little extras that can come in handy.

   oil: a small can of light oil is essential for reel lubrication.

   screwdriver: for reel repairs and tightening.

   pliers: for putting on split shot, unhooking problem fish, etc.

   fishing knife: indispensable.

   scaler: very good thing to have.

   stringer: helps keep your catch alive.

   landing net: useful, but not essential.

   tape measure: a good idea, as many states have legal minimum lengths on all game fish.

   tackle box: a small plastic one should be the best.

   insect repellent: always carry it!

   After you start fishing, you'll add other items as you need them.

Bait Casting

BAIT CASTING TACKLE (MULTIPLYING REEL)
Advantages:

a. Gives a better "feel" and a feeling of control than you get with spinning and spin casting equipment.
b. Best for trolling and every kind of deep-water fishing.
c. Best for solitary fishing, as you can handle with one hand and work boat with other hand.
d. Easy maintenance.
e. Takes most sizes of lures and live bait, providing you have enough weight for casting.

Disadvantages:

a. Most difficult casting method to learn.
b. Best suited to heavier lures and baits.

The bait casting reel is an American invention that was developed in Kentucky after the Civil War by watchmakers who loved fishing for bass. Their early reels were all handmade, and the gears were cut by hand. The best-known early bait casting reels were made by Sam Meek, a watchmaker who introduced such refinements as jeweled spool bearings. I have been told that his reels were so well made that some are still in use a century after their manufacture.

Bait casting is a distinct departure from the European fishing tradition that calls for the reel mounted underneath the rod. (This started with fly casting because the reel balanced better underneath and, even more important, was out of the way.) A bait casting reel, which is a small winch geared so that the spool revolves about three and one-half to four times while the handle revolves once, sits atop the rod with the handle on the right side. Besides the revolving spool, most models have a level-wind device geared to the handle, which insures that the line will be evenly distributed on the spool as you wind. Most top quality bait casting reels today also feature a free-spool lever that disconnects the spool from the handle for casting. This accomplishes two purposes: First, it prevents the whirling handle from dusting your knuckles as you cast; secondly, by removing the drag on the spool caused by the revolving handle, it clears the way for maximum casting distance.

Bait casting was designed for relatively heavy plugs and spoons and only recently has tackle been developed that puts bait casting in nearly the same category as ultralight spinning. The standard bait casting tournament weight remains $5/8$ ounce, however, nearly double the spinning weight.

A good deal of skill is required to use a bait casting outfit successfully. It is more difficult to learn to handle than either spinning or spin casting gear. Generally, a specific outfit will handle only a limited range of bait and lure sizes. Why, then, is it popular? First of all, bait casting tackle lets you really feel what is happening, since you control the line directly with your thumb. Then too, it is without doubt the best equipment ever devised for deep-water fishing, trolling of any kind, and using heavy lures and sinkers.

In bait casting as in spinning, the reel is the most important piece of equipment. Get a good one, something made by a well-known company with pride in its product.

Bait casting rods are traditionally four and a half of six feet in length and stiffer than spinning or spin casting rods. As with other rods, the basic differences between top and lower quality are found not so much in the basic fiberglass material as in the guides, reel seat, and windings. A good rod gives you a better "feel" than an inexpensive one because it is carefully balanced.

Until about the early 1950's, bait casting reels were used with braided silk or nylon line. Today, most reels are built to handle nylon monofilament, in the same weights used with spinning tackle. Braided synthetics remain easier to cast with, especially when learning. The basic advantage of monofilament is that you avoid any need for a leader in 90 per cent of all fishing. The disadvantage of monofilament is that it can become less supple and more brittle with extended exposure to the sun. A ten-pound test monofilament or braided line equivalent is ideal for most fresh water bait casting. It's light enough to handle easily and strong enough to take care of any fish you might have to cope with in fresh water except the giant garfish of the lower Mississippi basin, for which you need tuna tackle.

Monofilament line is sold at different prices, but it pays to get the best. The better line costs more because it has been stretched and treated and dyed so that it is limp, will not kink, and is nearly invisible underwater. Cheap line is wiry, springy, and tangles easily and often. The small difference in price between the best and second best can mean a huge difference in fishing fun. If you want to save money on line, fill your reel spool about half full with any kind of cord and finish off with fifty yards of good line. Another thing to remember about monofilament line is that it deteriorates in sunlight and should be replaced after a season or two.

To put your bait casting tackle together, put the reel on the rod. You wind clockwise. Run the line down through the guides, through the level-wind device, and tie it to the spindle in the hold or groove you'll find for this purpose. It helps to have an assistant hold the spool while you wind. When you're working with more than one spool, your buddy should hold one edge in his fingers and let the line slip off the edge nearest you.

After tying on the casting weight, hold your rod with the thumb of your casting hand firmly on the reel spool. Then bring the rod tip back smartly and come forward releasing thumb pressure. Take it easy! Too much oomph at this stage can cause a monumental

Bait Casting Equipment

1. **Fishing rod:** Today, most bait casting rods are graphite. They usually are from four and a half to five and a half feet in length. Get one marked "light action" unless you are going to fish in salt water, or for very large fresh water fish.

2. **Bait casting reel:** The reel is the heart of any outfit. Get one with a guarantee from a reliable manufacturer. A level-wind device should be built into the reel. Light-weight spools of aluminum or plastic make casting easier. A star-drag on the handle costs money and isn't necessary for most fishing. You don't need a free-spool reel to start with.

3. **Line:** Monofilament line (as described in Table II) in ten-pound test is a good choice for most bait casting outfits. Many people prefer the older braided lines because they are easier casting than monofilament.

4. **Sinkers:** Clamp-on sinkers in $1/8$- ounce to $1/2$- ounce size are usually used with bait casting gear. You could also use a few sinkers up to 1 ounce in the standard bank shape.

5. **Hooks:** Ringed or eyed hooks are fine. Get an assortment of sizes from No. 1 down through No. 8.

6. **Leaders:** You'll probably want a couple of six-inch wire traces to keep sharp-toothed fish from cutting your line. These are much better when used with lures than with bait. When bait fishing for pike use a long-shanked hook such as the Carlisle. If you use braided line, buy a ten-yard coil of ten-pound test monofilament leader material and tie a few yards to the end of your line.

7. **Lures:** You'll need a small assortment of plugs, spoons, spinnerbaits and spinners in standard bait casting sizes. Ask the advice of a local fishing expert but don't overload yourself.

8. **Miscellaneous:** Reel oil, screwdriver and small wrench, fishing knife, scaler, snap swivels, pliers, and a tackle box to hold everything round out the complete bait caster. A tape measure comes in handy for fish that you're not certain meet legal length. Insect repellent is a necessity. If you get a float, get a big one: it should weigh nearly $5/8$ ounce.

backlash, with the spool revolving faster than the line is peeling off. Bait casting was developed by jewelers with a delicate sense of touch, so it may take you a while to get the feel of it.

When you get a backlash—and you will—stay calm. Sit down and work it out gently. You can probably count on several practice sessions before you feel really competent with your bait casting gear. But it's fun to use. You'll enjoy it.

Fly Fishing

Fly fishing was originally developed in Europe to catch trout and was later extended to salmon; however, it is a great method of fishing for largemouth and smallmouth bass, panfish,

---

FLY FISHING TACKLE (SINGLE ACTION OR AUTOMATIC FLY REEL)

Advantages:
 a. Only fishing method that lets you cast weightless lures and flies.
 b. Easy to learn (although it looks difficult).
 c. Best method for stream fishing. (Other methods are prohibited in some trout and all North American Atlantic-salmon waters.)
 d. Maintenance is negligible. (As in cane-pole fishing, there is nothing to get out of order. Heavy line makes tangles easy to solve.)
 e. You have a psychological advantage in that a fly fisherman is looked upon rightly or wrongly as a gentleman.

Disadvantages:

 a. Very limited in that it is only useful in comparatively shallow water and with flies or other weightless lures.
 b. Becomes almost impossible to use in windy weather.
 c. Limited usefulness with bait.

---

pike, and pickerel in shallow water. Despite the fact that it looks difficult, fly casting is very easy. Best of all, it's fun; and this is why fly fishing is undergoing a big surge of popularity. (Spinning brought a huge army of new fishing novices into the sport. Fly casting gives them a challenge when casting spinning lures becomes too easy.) Despite any remarks you may hear to the contrary, fly fishing in shallow water will often out-fish all other methods by a large margin. The tremendous advantage of a weightless lure small enough to be an insect and light enough to float and dart like a shiner can't be duplicated by any other angling method.

Fly casting operates on an entirely different principle than other types of fishing. The lure, a tiny bit of fluff, weighs nothing; the weight needed for casting is entirely on the line. The reel, so essential in spinning, bait casting, and spin casting, is simply something to store on and balance the rod. Early fly casters didn't even use a reel.

Since the weight of the line itself pulls out your cast, it must be balanced with a long, flexible rod. A heavy, strong rod requires a heavy line; a lighter, more delicate rod, uses a lighter, more delicate line. Within the past two years, the American Fishing Tackle Manufacturers Association has established numerical standards for matching rods and lines, so that each rod when bought has marked on it the numbers of suitably weighted lines. Any line by any maker with the correct number will work well with a fly rod made to handle this specific number.

A new fly rod will be marked with at least three of these numbers, indicating a level line, a tapered line, and a weight-forward line. Originally, all fly lines were level lines, and size was indicated by a letter, with A being the heaviest line made and H the lightest. (A D level line was about standard for most fishing.)

About thirty years ago, some bright genius decided that plunking a D level line into the water interfered with his casting pleasure. It also necessitated extremely long leaders because unless the leader on a D level line tapers down gradually from butt to tip it will not shoot forward properly on a cast but tend to fall backward on the line. And so the tapered line was invented.

The tapered line retains the D body for casting weight, but the final five yards are tapered down to H at the tip. Starting a leader at the end of an H line is much easier. The leader butt can be considerably thinner, and a shorter leader can be tapered down. Within nine feet you can taper a leader from .018 monofilament down to .007 monofilament. (This is .007 inch!) With the D line, you had to start with .021 monofilament or even heavier and add three additional feet to your leader.

Both level and tapered lines are still made and sold, with the majority of tapered lines being tapered at both ends—the so-called double-tapered line. The double-taper had a good selling point in that you could cut the line in half in the center, splice each half to backing line that would fill the reel, and have two casting lines, each on a separate reel, for the price of only one double-tapered line.

The final fly-line development is the so-called torpedo-shaped, or weight-forward, line. The theory behind this is that since the weight of the line does the casting, you want this weight in the forward part of the line. If you have this weight forward, the remaining line can be very light so that you can readily shoot it through the guides with as little friction as possible. After a great deal of effort, various makers constructed lines that rapidly tapered from H to C in a couple of yards, kept the C weight for about five yards, and then went rapidly back to H for the rest of the line length. This gives you the tapered-line advantage of short, fine leaders and fine connection, the level-line advantage of casting weight, and the special advantage of light line that follows the heavy casting head without falling in an arc under its own weight.

For no-leader, low visibility fly fishing, weight-forward lines are now, to the delight of anglers everywhere, readily available.

You can buy floating fly lines, sinking fly lines, and sinking tip (3-5 feet sinking and the balance floating—very easy to use) thus eliminating the need for greasing a line to fish dry and removing the grease to fish wet. And while fly lines in bygone years were made of enameled or waxed silk, today they are entirely synthetic, with nylon used for most lines, including the floating lines, and dacron utilized for sinking lines. A serious fly fisherman needs both floating and sinking line, which means he requires one rod and two reels. A fly reel is flat and can be easily carried in a pocket and changed in a minute.

Unless you expect to fish for salmon or steelhead trout or saltwater species, a regular fly reel big enough to hold your casting line is all you require. It should balance properly with your rod, so try rod and reel for balance in the store before you buy them. For big fish, you need a larger capacity reel. This won't weigh any more than a smaller reel but will let you add one hundred yards of light braided nylon as backing behind your casting line. When a salmon or steelhead takes off on a run, you have to give him his head, and this is where the backing is essential.

In fly casting, as previously mentioned, the reel goes below the rod. If it were mounted atop the rod, it would tend to keep turning the rod over in your hand. Also, it would constantly get in the way. Because fly fishing originated in Europe, and the fly reel was the first reel, it's the European custom to mount all reels underneath the rod. Here in the United States, the bait casting reel was invented by men who knew nothing of fly fishing . They put the reel on top of the rod for easier thumb control of the spool.

Fly rods range in length from pygmies of six and one-half and seven feet to monsters of fourteen feet. The former are very good on tiny brooks and for panfish. The monsters are used in Europe for Atlantic salmon—not so much to handle the fish as to cast very large flies. Especially in Scandinavia, the water is icy cold and the fish lie deep under a torrent. To reach them, flies tied on $6/0$ hooks are sometimes used, and it takes powerful two-handed fly rods to handle a fly tied on a tuna hook.

For about 90 per cent of all fly fishing , you need a rod that measures from eight and one-half to nine and one-half feet and has what is called medium action. A rod with dry fly action is very stiff and necessitates much extra work in casting; it is advantageous only when fishing large lakes or in areas with few trees and high winds. A mushy, or soft, fly rod, usually a bargain-basement rod, is no bargain at all. It is so lacking in stiffness or spine that casting with it is like casting with a piece of spaghetti or a wet noodle. First-grade carbon filament rods by good makers are reasonable enough, so you can start with the best. A few manufacturers, notably the Orvis Company in Manchester, Vermont, turn out split-bamboo fly rods for anglers who want the very finest equipment. These cost double or more the price of a top-quality fiberglass, composite or graphite rod. Are they worth it? Quite a few anglers think so, but most fishermen are content to stick with fiberglass, especially since it requires practically no maintenance.

Leaders were originally knotted together from sections of silkworm gut imported from Spain. (Prior to silkworm gut, they were made of horsehair.) Silkworm-gut leaders had a lot of faults. They were brittle when dry and had to be soaked an hour or more before use.

Fly reel

They were subject to weak spots, since quality and diameter weren't uniform. Tippets drawn down to 4X (.007 inch) were sometimes unreliable. Today's lines are always uniform and are available in all diameters; there are even tapered one-piece leaders that eliminate the knotted sections of the silkworm-gut era completely. For trout and panfish, use leaders tapered down to 2X and 4X, or six-pound and four-pound test respectively. Bass fishing requires a slightly heavier leader to handle heavier lures, and most bass leaders taper down to 10-pound test (.011 inch). For northern pike and other sharp-toothed fish, add about a foot of twenty-pound test at the tip of the leader to guard against being cut off.

In order to cast with the fly rod, first assemble the rod and fit the reel onto the reel seat. When you are setting up your equipment, make sure that your reel and line are loaded to

Fly Casting Equipment

1. Fly rod: For trout and panfish, a light (3 to 5 weight) seven-and-a-half-foot rod offers easy casting. For bass and other larger fish, you need a more powerful (upwards of 7 weight) eight-and-a-half-foot rod to handle the larger lures and flies that will be cast.

2. Fly reel: Fly reels come in a variety of types and levels of complexity. Higher end reels, complete with internal bearings and gear systems to regulate drag, can really make fly fishing much easier and more smooth. But, it is essential only to have a place to store the line you aren't using, keep your line untangled and balance out your rod. It is really up to you how much you want to spend.

3. Fly line: Available in synthetics constructed to float and others constructed to sink rapidly. Also in tapered and torpedo-head construction, which cost more than level line. Make sure your line matches your rod (both rod and line are marked). The torpedo head is easiest for casting, and the floating line best for most fresh water fly fishing .

4. Leaders: For fly casting, tapered leaders are a must. Buy a few with tips of 1X, 2X, and 3X.

5. Lures. Flies, of course! : With over 1,500 patterns in twenty sizes, the choice is nearly limitless. Consult a local expert, such as the conservation officer or local fly shop employee, for his advice on patterns and sizes. If your fishing will be in lakes, you'll want a few feather minnows, popping bugs, and hair frogs. Mice made of deer hair are excellent fly-rod lures. Spoons, plugs, and spinners do not generally make good fly-rod lures. Small spinners, mostly in the Colorado style, are often used in conjunction with a worm. (This is really bait fishing, however.)

6. Miscellaneous: Boots or waders, a landing net, fishing knife, tape measure, fly box, oil for reel, fly dope (to float dry files), and insect repellent are all essential. You also need a nail clipper (handier than knife or scissors for trimming knots, cutting loose ends, and so forth).

suit whether you are right or left handed. If you are right handed, you should cast with your right hand and strip (control your line) with your left, so you should have the winding side of your reel facing to the left, and that your line feeds smoothly off the reel while facing the proper direction.

   After assembling the rod and reel, run the line down through the snake guides and tie it to the spindle of the reel. Then crank it up by turning the handle. Putting line on a fly reel is a very easy operation.

You don't need leader or fly to practice fly casting. Simply strip out about twenty-five feet of line from the reel with your left hand so that it falls in loose coils by your feet. Then, letting out about fifteen feet of line in the process, snap the rod back to a vertical position so that the line is pulled up and behind you. When you see that the line has straightened out, bring the rod forward quickly to about a forty-five-degree angle with the ground. As you bring it forward let the rest of the line shoot out through the guides. The back cast is really the most difficult step in the process. If you start forward too soon, you snap the line like a whip, and snap your fly off when fishing. If you start too late, everything falls in a heap.

False casting consists of working out a good length of line by moving the rod back and forth. With practice, you'll be able to keep about thirty feet of line in the air and shoot an additional thirty feet with your final forward cast.

Don't believe anything that you might hear about fly casting being a wrist motion. Many of the best casters use their entire arm and shoulder, much more so than with spinning or bait casting gear, and don't use the wrist at all. The important thing is not to wave the fly rod back and forth over too great an arc. Don't bring it back much past a vertical position on your back cast, and don't bring it forward parallel with the water. A good model is the face of a clock: if you are the center of the clock, and your rod, when vertical, is at 12 o'clock, then when casting, you should never bring your rod beyond 11 o'clock (behind you) and 1 o'clock (in front of you). Too much forward follow-through simply pulls your cast down short of the mark. A short casting arc lets the rod do the work.

XIII.

How to Cast like a Pro

Supposedly, practice makes perfect. In actual fact, the wrong kind of practice simply confirms you in your mistakes. This is why golf and tennis pros can stay solvent and in business. You can live a long lifetime without rubbing elbows with a professional caster, however, which simply means you have to teach yourself. This isn't as difficult as it might sound. Your casting errors become obvious to you because you have a line attached to your lure.

If it makes you feel like an idiot to practice casting in public, drive out to some empty countryside for casting practice, or go to a lakeshore with plenty of room and no trees. Any kind of beachfront out of season is ideal and generally as devoid of humanity as a place can be. During the 1930's I had an ideal practice area, a polo field near home. Nobody could afford polo, but the field was kept mowed. (Today it lies under a housing development.)

After you've become more or less used to the feel of things, start trying to cast for accuracy. Whether you use spinning, spin casting, bait casting, or fly gear, you want to be able to drop your lure in a precise target area. If you don't want to aim at old peach baskets or inner tubes, copies of old magazines, especially the big pictorial magazines, make fine targets that you can use over and over again.

When you're trying to hit a target with a lure, the most important thing is the position of your feet. (Any golf, tennis, or baseball pro will tell you this too. So will every skeet shooter.) Stand comfortably, and if you're right-handed, figure that your point of aim will be along the line of your left foot.

Start with your targets about twenty-five feet away, and when you can hit them consistently, move them out farther. If you reach the point where you can drop a casting weight or a fly on target at seventy-five feet, you can outcast probably 90 per cent or more of all anglers today and could even win accuracy casting events.

A strong wrist and fluid movement make all the difference in a successful cast

If you're casting into a head wind, try to keep your cast as low and flat as possible. With a tail wind, you can let your lure soar a bit. Regardless of your fishing method, never cast side-arm but always overhead. Side-arm casting is all right under certain conditions but is very dangerous to your fishing buddies.

The biggest problem with spinning gear is to avoid winding loops onto the reel spool. If your line continually twists into loops, throw it away and buy a new one. With both spinning and spin casting gear, avoid the temptation to fling the casting weight a mile. Keep yourself under tight control and work up to maximum distance slowly. Also be careful not to wind the line too tightly on the spool when you retrieve. Set a very light drag as a warning, and walk up to your casting weight instead of dragging it back to you.

With a bait casting reel, adjust the tension on the reel spool so that the casting weight will just about pull line off the spool when you hold the rod parallel to the ground. There are ways to avoid most backlashes:

1. Don't try too hard for distance.

2. Stop the spool with your thumb the instant the casting weight is about the hit the ground or the water.

3. Keep a fairly tight thumb on the spool when casting into the wind.

In fly casting there are a couple of tricky things you'll want to learn. In the roll cast, you pick your line up from the water or the ground and roll it around, up and out in a single motion. This is a short cast that avoids the room needed for back casting in situations where you're fishing in front of heavy brush or trees. The double-haul cast is easier to learn by watching than from a description. Good for extra distance, it involves using the left hand to pull the line back as you start the rod forward. This increases tension on the rod and line and enables a longer line to be cast. You don't need this for most fresh water fishing, but it does come in handy on big salmon and steelhead rivers, where every added foot of distance can make the difference between fish and failure.

With a correctly balanced fishing outfit of medium to good quality, you will have no problem in becoming at least an adequate caster. Do yourself a favor and practice before you go fishing. You wouldn't start any other sport without lessons, and casting—where you can't really get lessons—needs practice as a substitute. Furthermore, the ability to toss a lure where you want it is a huge fishing asset. Poor casters spend much time climbing trees and uprooting lily pads when they should be fishing. Poor casting is frustrating too, especially when fish are hitting and you're losing time because of tangles and backlashes. And what's the use of finding feeding fish, when you can't present a lure to them without scaring them away? At the risk of sounding like an old-time hellfire and brimstone preacher, I repeat that good casting is the key to fishing salvation, and the only way to become a good caster is to practice until you have the knack. Like bicycle riding or ice-skating, once you can cast, whether with spinning, spin casting, bait casting, or fly rods, you'll never forget how.

XIV.

Artificial Lures—
How and When to Use Them

We've already discussed the different types of lures, but a number of questions remain. For example, "When should you use lures, and when should you use bait?" Generally speaking, lures work best from dusk through sunrise, and bait is preferable at midday or in bright sunlight. Like every rule of thumb, however, this has plenty of exceptions. Another generality is that bait works best in early season before the water warms up, and from then on lures become more and more effective. In streams flies are more effective than bait as the water becomes lower and clearer.

Much depends on the exact fishing situation and what you're trying to catch. Here are a few things to keep in mind whether you're using hardware or flies.

Popping and Surface-Agitating Plugs

Cast these into shallow-water target areas at dawn and dusk, especially when there is little or no wind. Sometimes surface lures work well on overcast days. Generally, they will out-fish other lures at night. A special time to use surface lures is when schools of fish are chasing bait on the surface. Also use them when large swirls indicate that fish are rising and feeding near the top of the water.

Wobbling Plugs

Usually, these are more effective in the smaller sizes unless you are fishing for large pike and muskellunge. Cast them inshore to target areas and retrieve fast enough to get proper action; or troll them parallel to the shore line, especially around specific target areas. You can use wobbling plugs all day, but you'll find they foul up badly in weedy areas and in lily pads. They work best outside the weeds, around rocks, and in streams.

Diving and Sinking Plugs

These are for deep-water fishing, usually in midsummer. They can be either cast or trolled but generally are cast over reefs in deep lakes. Bottom-scraping plugs can be used all day. These are especially effective in the South, including the TVA lakes and similar reservoirs with smallmouth and spotted bass plus bottom-seeking largemouths.

Spinnerbaits

Spinnerbaits are a highly effective and versatile lure. In larger sizes it appeals to muskellunge, pickerel, pike and especially bass, while in larger sizes can be used to hook perch, rockbass and bluegills. Keep these in mind for lakes that have a lot of weeds, grasses and other various obstructions.

Spoons and Spinners

Weedless spoons are the best lure at any season or time of day when you're fishing weedbeds and lily-pad areas. Casting spoons and wobbling plugs can be substituted for one another. Generally, pike fishermen prefer spoons, and bass fishermen plugs. Spoons have an advantage on dull days; plugs are often better on bright days because they don't flash enough to frighten the fish. Different lakes and streams call for plugs or spoons depending on what the fish are feeding. Spoons are easier to cast into the wind than plugs and offer a big advantage on windy days, especially with an overcast sky.

Spinners are usually well-suited to fishing on top of a weedbed. They are also an excellent deep-water lure. Either a heavy spoon or a spinner will do everything any plug will do. Spoons and spinners also offer a definite advantage in muddy water and are preferred over plugs for trout and landlocked salmon. Both spoons and spinners are traditional standby lures for trolling.

Jigs and Rubber Worms

Like diving plugs, these are mostly midsummer lures and are worked right on the bottom, very slowly. They are especially popular for bass and panfish and will take fish in both deep and shallow water. Rocky lakes are especially well suited to these lures. You can use them at any time of day.

Fly-Rod Lures

When fishing lakes for bass, the same rules hold as for spinning and bait casting lures. Surface lures will work best at dawn and dusk on windless days, and also at other times when fish are showing at the surface. Fly-rod hair frogs are usually weedless and can be used in regular frog habitat, around lily pads, and so forth without much trouble. Popping lures work especially well in May and June, when bass are very easily annoyed into striking.

Streamer flies are probably the most effective all-around lure for fly fishing in a lake or pond. You should get local recommendations as to patterns and sizes. As mentioned in connection with landlocked salmon, some special streamer flies are made for trolling and are used a great deal in New England, especially in Maine.

Trout fishing is sometimes more selective. After May 1, you usually have to try and imitate a hatch with a dry fly pattern. At other times, if you can catch a trout, clean him and discover what the fish are feeding on. Then try to get a nymph or wet fly that imitates the natural food. Small streamer flies work very well when trout, especially large trout, are feeding on minnows.

Salmon fishing calls for special patterns depending on locality, with wet fly fishing generally most productive. Steelhead fishing is another special pattern sport, with salmon-egg imitations the goal of most fly-tiers in the Northwest.

There are three basic reasons for using lures:

1. It's more fun.
2. You catch more fish.
3. You can't get bait.

XV.

What Every Angler Should Know About Live Bait

Some of the time for all fish, and all of the time for some fish, bait of one kind or another is the only thing that makes sense. Of course, you'll always find a few people who sneer at the thought of using worms or minnows for catching bass or trout; but fishing is for fun, and part of the fun is catching fish. Sportsmanship depends on the individual angler and has nothing to do with his equipment. To paraphrase an old expression: It's not what you do, but how you do it. Before we leave fresh water fishing for the briny deep, then, here are some details on baits and how to use them.

Earthworms

Worms are to fishing as popcorn is to the movies: you can get along without them, but they're nice to have handy. Earthworms are practically a universal bait for every kind of fresh water fish except possibly northern pike and muskellunge.

Although today there are worm farms that raise bait for market and sell their output through sporting-goods stores, you can save money and dig your own in moist, rich soil with a spading fork. In addition, you can find nightcrawlers after dark with a flashlight. They come out in large numbers after a rain, and a well-watered lawn will have them every evening. Why do worms emerge from their burrows at night? The answer is to mate. Even though they have no eyes, earthworms are sensitive to light, and instinct tells them that after dark they are safe from birds and can gambol on the green without fear.

Regardless of their reproductive urgings, worms are very sensitive to certain vibrations. When you go out after nightcrawlers, walk softly, and when you spot a worm or worms in your flashlight beam, sneak up and grab him like an Indian. A red filter on your flashlight will frighten worms less, but it makes seeing them more difficult. My best results come with a regular flashlight, but once a worm is spotted, I avoid shining the bright beam on him.

If you want to save your lawn from spading and get worms scientifically, you can buy an electric vibrator that you plunge into the ground. Rather than frightening worms, its vibrations bring them up to the surface even during daylight. A homemade variation of this is to stick your spading fork deep into the dirt and whack it gently with a baseball bat or broom handle. These vibrations work well in fairly damp soil.

In wooded areas look for worms under logs; in rocky soil you'll find them under rocks, especially after a rain. You'll also find centipedes and other insects that make good bait. Manure heaps or compost piles usually always have worms living under them. During drought periods look under manure piles where the ground hasn't dried out. Plowing, roto-tilling, and hoeing of vegetable and flower gardens become a prime source of worms because of the rich soil. A little raking later will find you even more.

Worms are easy to keep on hand. Unlike higher animals, they never make noise, need toilet training, or demand exercise. You can buy commercial worm bedding, but a wooden crate filled with rich soil is a good substitute. Leftover milk, beet greens, and other vegetable discards should be added as food from time to time. If you want really wiggly fishing worms, keep another box of damp moss and transfer worms to it from the soil box a couple of days before your fishing trip.

The way to hook a worm depends on your quarry. For panfish, hook a small- or medium-sized worm through the head and again farther down the body, leaving about an inch to trail. For larger game fish, hook a big worm lightly through the collar or two or three smaller worms through the head so that they trail out behind the hook.

Minnows

There are dozens of species of chubs and minnows that make good live bait. Other small fish such as young suckers, catfish, carp, and yellow perch are also excellent. If you're going to catch your own bait, you'll have to be able to distinguish between legal bait species and game fish. Otherwise, you could get an expensive fine.

Most species of minnows are silvery or brassy. Some are translucent with a silver flash down each side. None of them have any spines, and none have more than a single dorsal fin. You'll find minnows living primarily in shallow water over sandy or muddy bottom with weeds in which they can hide. They often congregate around boat docks and pilings near shore, and are usually found along with small perch and sunfish.

If you have the time, catching your own live bait is very enjoyable. It's especially exciting to catch them on a hook, and you'll need size 12 or 14 or even 16 hooks for this and a monofilament line or leader of two- to four-pound test. Tossing bread, oatmeal, or even

Selling bait has always been a mainstay for young entrepeneurs—even in 1935

small white pebbles and bits of shell into the water will attract schools of minnows. If you're camping, a few potato peelings or leftover cereal will draw minnows, but this type of garbage dumping is undesirable and even forbidden in most civilized areas. Bait with a tiny speck of worm or a little doughball made by dunking white bread in water and squeezing it dry. Drop your baited hook and let it sink. When it vanishes, strike! You need a keen eye and a quick hand for this, but it gives you something to do in the heat of the day when the fish aren't biting.

An effective way to obtain minnows is with an umbrella net that you can buy at most sporting-goods stores. You lower it to the bottom like an upside-down umbrella and toss in bread crumbs to attract them. When you see minnows darting around over the net, bring it up. It can be trickier than you'd think from this description.

Check your state fishing laws before you use a seine, which is a long net with floats to hold up the top and little weights to sink the bottom. Most states specify the maximum length allowed and also forbid their use in certain waters, especially those stocked with trout. In some areas only a resident may legally use a seine. For best results you need two people, one at each end. It also helps to use a pole at each end (a section of broom-handle is ideal) to which you tie the leaders from the top and bottom of the net. The poles will help keep the net spread vertically in the water.

The best places to seine are over sandy bottom without rocks or sunken logs and other obstructions. Don't plunge into mud-bottomed areas unless you're sure the ooze ends somewhere, even though clinging mud and quicksand won't suck you down. Move slowly and you can swim right out of it. It pays to seine over dependable bottom only, however, as seining in muck is not only dangerous but usually unrewarding in terms of results.

Especially in streams too small for seining and over broken and treacherous bottom, a minnow trap is a handy gadget. These come in wire and glass, with glass preferred. They have a funnel into which minnows swim to get at the bait, bread crumbs or oatmeal, and out of which they haven't the brains to extract themselves. In areas with a large number of minnows, a couple of traps will keep you supplied as long as you keep them baited.

The care of minnows is more difficult than that of worms. You need a minnow bucket of some kind. These mostly are double buckets; the inner pail is perforated and has an air-chamber so that it can be floated beside your boat or dock. This will keep a lot of minnows happy as long as it is overboard. Transporting minnows is a problem. In hot weather a cake of ice dripping into the bucket is a big help. You can also buy aerating pills that give off oxygen and even devices with tiny pumps. Another type of bucket, especially good for carrying minnows, is made of papier-mâché. Since this is porous and absorbent, it cools by evaporation and lets the water inside "breathe" through the bucket wall.

Generally speaking, the larger the minnow used, the larger the fish that will be caught. When cast and retrieved slowly, dead minnows will serve as well as live, but for still-fishing with a bobber, you should change minnows regularly to be sure you have an active one to attract fish.

Why use minnows when worms are easier to obtain and keep? First, many fish prefer minnows, especially after early spring. Worms are not already a natural fish food. They don't live in water and are only found in lakes and streams because of flooding. Secondly, worms are so attractive to panfish that it is often almost impossible to catch a decent bass when using a worm for bait. The panfish steal it first!

Grasshoppers and Crickets

These make wonderful bait, especially from August through October, when hoppers of various species are plentiful along the banks of creeks and lakes.

The best way to catch grasshoppers is to get out early in the cool of the morning with a butterfly net. When the temperature is below 60 degrees, you'll find them numb and slow. Grasshoppers are found in nearly every hayfield and weed patch, and all species are good bait.

Crickets are found under stones, beneath logs, and in other places a cricket can hide, including houses with damp basements. Crickets are great ventriloquists but are slow and easy to catch when compared with grasshoppers.

The best idea for using both these very soft insects is a little harness that can be bought in many stores handling fishing tackle, or you can make your own with a No. 8 hook and some tiny rubber bands. With either a fly rod or spinning gear, you can cast near enough a bank so that the hopper appears to have made a strategic error and leaped into the water. You can also hook these insects on about a No. 10 hook and fish them dead, underwater, with a bobber.

Frogs

These amphibians are wonderful bait, with the smaller green, leopard, and pickerel frogs especially good. You may feel a bit silly waving a butterfly net, but it's a good tool for catching frogs, especially after a rain when they come ashore on wet lawns and other grassy areas. If you have no butterfly net, try a hat (an old one). Catching frogs by bare hand is a difficult proposition—for both human and frog—at any time.

An excellent way to keep frogs alive for short periods is to put them in an old nylon stocking and tie a knot so they can't wiggle out. To keep them for a longer period, you need a little pen made of hardware cloth or mosquito netting. This should be wired on top and bottom as well as the sides and must be kept in the shade. You can keep frogs dormant in an icebox too. Simply put them in a cardboard box, and they'll go into hibernation for a week or maybe much longer. Don't put them in the freezer compartment, as they can't take anything under about 40 degrees.

Frog harnesses are available, but most people simply hook them through both lips or sometimes through a leg and let them swim around. For smallmouth bass, you can use very tiny frogs with enough sinker to get them down near the bottom, where you use them the same as you would a minnow.

Lampreys

These are found in most streams of major watersheds. Before leading a parasitic life young lampreys live in muddy and sandy stream bottoms and feed on vegetable matter. Rooting up the bottom with a spading fork will uncover them; they're quite easy to catch in shallow water. They make very good walleye bait and can also be used for bass in deep water. Few anglers try these for bait, but they'll take almost any game fish, including many salt water varieties too.

Hellgrammites

Larvae of dragonflies and other big insects are found in streams and ponds. You catch them by putting an old mosquito screen, frame and all, downstream from where you are turning over rocks. The hellgrammites you loosen will drift down and hook onto the screen. They aren't pretty but when hooked through the collar are excellent bait for smallmouth bass.

Crawfish

Actually a miniature fresh water lobster, this little crustacean is tiny but good eating, just as good as ocean lobsters, and a mainstay of Cajun restaurants everywhere. For bait, the best crawfish are those which are still soft from having shed their shells. Turn over rocks and you'll find their hiding places. Occasionally, you'll get a soft one. Hook them through the tail when using them for bait; crawfish, like shrimps and lobsters, move backward rather than head first. These are good bait for smallmouths in deep, rocky lakes and in large streams. Catfish like crawfish tails, particularly when soft.

Catalpa Worms

These are parasitic on catalpa trees, so all you need is a backyard catalpa to get plenty of bait. Nothing is better when fishing for bream and other sunfish south of the Mason-Dixon Line and in the Midwest.

Salmon Eggs

Mostly available preserved in jars, salmon eggs are good trout bait and are particularly popular on the West Coast with the steelhead crowd. Either single eggs or a little bunch is bounced along the bottom just like you'd fish any other bottom bait.

Pork Rind

This is some inner pigskin that is preserved in jars and usually cut to size. Most pork rind is white and incredibly tough. There is some question as to whether it is a lure or a bait, but it adds life and action to spoons and spinners, especially the weedless types. Additionally, a tiny fly-rod strip of pork rind weighted with a split shot just above the hook is very effective on very big sunfish.

Perch Belly and Strip Bait

A strip, including the two orange ventral fins, cut from the belly of a small yellow perch is a terrific pike and pickerel bait when worked on a weedless hook around lily pads and weedbeds. The old-time cane-pole market fishermen used this with telling effect. Strips of fish are good bait for catfish, and can be used to substitute for pork rind.

Other Miscellaneous Baits

In addition to those already listed, there are many other excellent baits. If you live near salt water, you can use grass shrimp, which are just as effective on fresh water fish as they are in a bay or sound.

Cheese, hot dogs, bacon, bread, oatmeal, cornmeal, chicken gizzards, and beef blood have been used for bait. Fresh water mussels are sometimes worth a try. Fish eyes are good panfish bait. And if you're really hard up for bait, use a small piece of white soap. You'll get catfish on it, and maybe sunnies and perch too.

Rather than cook up a special recipe for doughballs, it's much easier to buy a can of niblets and use the kernels for catfish, carp, buffalo, and other bottom-grazing species. In some areas it's a standard practice to empty a can of creamed corn in your fishing area as chum to attract the fish.

As you may gather from all this, I definitely think that using bait is part of fishing. Lures are usually more fun to use, but there comes a time when you either go bait fishing or come home empty-handed. Besides which, anyone who looks down their nose at bait fishing doesn't know what they're missing. Depending on circumstances, it can be just as challenging as fly casting.

XVI.

Offshore Game Fish and Charter Boat Fishing

Standard advice to the lovelorn always used to include the phrase, "There are plenty of other fish in the sea." Despite overfishing and pollution, salt water fishing remains excellent in most locations, and you can literally fill sacks with fish within sight of such cities as New York and San Francisco. While most salt water sports species can be termed game fish, the offshore species include swordfish, marlins, sailfishes, tuna, and several sharks. These, along with their little cousin—the bonito, mackerels, and bluefish—are pelagic fishes. They are mostly deep-sea migrants who wander the waters of the world.

Although some scientists strongly believe that the bluefin tuna in the Atlantic migrates in a circular pattern from the Bahamas to Newfoundland, across to Norway and the Mediterranean, down the west coast of Africa and back again across the South Atlantic to the Bahamas, most deep-water species are comparative stay-at-homes. Fairly localized populations of marlin, yellowtail, and so forth present a great deal of fishing opportunity. Various species may be widely distributed as self-contained individual colonies between which there is very little communication. Bluefish, for example, are found in all the oceans except the eastern Pacific, but nobody has advanced the theory that bluefish from New Jersey migrate to the Black Sea. They do migrate, but only over hundreds rather than thousands of miles.

The fast-swimming, ocean-traveling fishes do not seem much affected as yet by man-made pollution. Many species spawn, live, and die far out at sea. Atlantic mackerel, for example, are becoming more abundant; however, the development of long-lining and tremendous deep-water netting equipment is cutting into the supply of bluefin tuna and the various marlins. These big fish simply do not seem to reproduce at a rate that can cope with both nature and man. This has become a topic of international concern, and conferences have been held with representatives from most of the large commercial fishing nations of the world, including Japan and Russia. Incidentally, unknown to most Americans, the United States has revised its continental limits from three miles to twelve miles offshore to cope with invasions of foreign trawlers. Since the three-mile limit was originated as the farthest point to which eighteenth century shore-based cannon could fire, it was a bit outmoded in any case.

Most fishing for offshore game species, both large and small, is conducted by fleets of chartered or private craft, and this is basically an expensive proposition. A fully found luxury cabin cruiser with oversize power plant and costly loran and navigational equipment can represent an investment of $200,000 or even more. Add upkeep and depreciation and divide by the number of times you could use it a season, and you'll see why ownership of such a craft is financially unfeasible for many people.

Charter boats—usually owned and operated by their captain—give you what amounts to your own luxury fishing yacht on a daily charter or rental basis. In addition, you get the service of a professional captain and mate to find the fish and prevent you from becoming lost at sea. A charter boat sailing for tuna, marlin, sailfish, or other glamour species of off-shore game fish usually rents for about $200-$300 a day. When you consider the skipper's financial investment, the wages of a mate, the gasoline bill, dockage, and other costs, you can see why a charter boat captain is lucky to make ends meet and keep his family eating.

Outside the United States, charter craft are often small commercial fishing vessels; the wage scale is lower, and rates are less. If you ever intend to fish in the far corners of the world, however, it's sensible to make all arrangements, including financial, before you leave home. Misunderstandings are no fun for anyone.

Charter boat fishing has much in its favor. You get a good craft, professional guidance, and in American waters, tackle and bait supplied. All you really need are your clothes, including rain gear, and seasick pills.

Seasickness is a real curse. The old saying about it, "First you're afraid you are going to die, then you're afraid that you won't!" is true. Nothing except some fatal disease can make a human being so miserable. I've actually seen a skiff running down the Jersey shore under power with nobody at the wheel. All hands were so overcome with mal-de-mer they didn't care what happened to them!

My observation about seasickness is that if martinis don't bother you, seasickness won't either. If a couple of libations are inclined to make you dizzy, you're subject to mal-de-mer and had better take the pills. Modern seasick pills are small and tasteless and definitely work. Follow instructions, which usually call for taking the first tablet a half hour before sailing. There are a variety of other remedies that have also proven to be highly effective— most importantly some clever behind-the-ear patches that seem to be infallible in preventing nausea.

Eating or not eating seems to have little effect on seasickness. Drinking carbonated beverages, including beer, is helpful in moderate amounts. If you're going out in the oceanic sun, you're courting trouble with hard liquor, though. Having only beer and soft drinks afloat is a good policy and will help you enjoy fishing more.

The best way to select a charter boat is through the recommendation of a personal friend who has actually spent some time aboard it. There are many other good ways, including that of going down to the dock some afternoon and seeing who comes in with the biggest pile of fish. This can be deceptive for many reasons: A better captain may have had a load of whoopee-making conventioneers aboard, or a bunch of light-tackle fanatics happy to take all day to subdue a couple of kingfish. Check with local Chambers of Commerce and look in the telephone-book yellow pages for listings; most captains registered with either expect to be in business for a good time to come. Reading the output of the local newspaper's hunting and fishing scribe is a good idea. If you can reach him by phone and ask his advice, so much the better.

Try not to make a charter just by telephone. If at all possible, go down to the dock, look at the boat, and meet the skipper. If you want to bring and use your own tackle tell him about it. Charter captains have to be businessmen, and if they feel their business is directly related to the size of the pile of fish they unload on the dock they won't want you using light gear. The best captains are secure enough in their bookings so they couldn't care less; in fact many of them enjoy fishing for something else than sheer poundage. A good many boats do carry light gear for use by anglers as contrasted with tourists. Most skippers today, especially in southern ports, expect you to bring lunch for them and their mate as well as your own party. This could be a good point to clear up in advance.

It's not sporting to return to the dock with more fish than you can possibly use or even give away. In charter fishing, however, this is part of the game. In may cases the captain even expects you to leave surplus fish at the dock. Whenever possible, he'll either give them to charity or sell them; however, all fish caught aboard your chartered boat do belong to you and you have no obligation to give any to the skipper. There are disreputable fellows in every trade, and some charter captains will insist all fish are theirs, especially when it's a species with a good market value. Don't believe them!

In the last twenty years, big-game fishing has begun (rightfully so) to be included in the umbrella of conservation and species preservation. Instead of pulling in as many big fish as they can and hauling them all to shore just to have a picture taken, some charter companies are encouraging catch and release policies in the offshore market. The oceans aren't as plentiful as we like to think sometimes, and there isn't as much demand for the meat as there is for trophy photos and the result is a lot of unnecessarily wasteful fishing. When checking out a charter boat, ask about catch and release programs.

The time to decide whether you want a sailfish mounted for over your fireplace is before you leave home, not in the excitement of returning to the dock with a whopper. If you do want a mounted fish, you want the best job possible for your money. This can take a little research. If you have a local museum or aquarium, get the opinion of experts. Top taxidermists don't grow on trees. They are skilled artists, and most artists don't advertise themselves much. If you find a taxidermist whose work you like before you take your trip, make arrangements to ship your prize to him if, as, and when.

Of course, in the glow of victory you may be receptive to your captain's suggestion that "This marlin will make a beautiful mount." He'll get you a job from a wholesale taxidermy studio that pays him for referrals. The only trouble with a mounted fish from one of these places is that they operate a mass production plant, and your specimen will lose its individuality. Also, it may not be very lifelike. Quite frankly, your charter boat captain is perfectly entitled to take a commission for arranging work for a taxidermist. Even some doctors, despite their screams of ethics, are remunerated in some measure for referring patients to specific colleagues, and a commission, whether in scotch or cash or cocktail parties and social introductions, is payment for services rendered.

On a charter boat, the captain and mate do practically everything for you. They rig the lines, select lures or bait, and choose the area to be fished. This is all specialized knowledge for which you're paying them; you'll need to know all of this only on a private boat of your own.

XVII.

Some Facts about Offshore Big-Game Fish

Most people think that any fish with a beak is a swordfish. Actually, they are divided into several groups of species with many differences among them. Because they are all game fishes of the highest order, they offer a good place to begin a discussion of offshore big-game fish.

Swordfish

The true swordfish, as distinguished from his relatives, the marlins, has a broad flat sword, or beak, and relatively short fins. With tremendous weight and strength and muscular coordination, swordfish have sunk small craft. Although they have been known to ram their sword through twelve inches of oak planking, they use their weapon mostly to whack away at mackerel and other small fish that they can stun and then swallow at their leisure. Swordfish are not at all gregarious and are found singly in all the oceans of the world, but appear most commonly in the North Atlantic, the South Pacific, and parts of the Indian Ocean.

Together with some of the bigger sharks and ocean sunfish, swordfish have a habit of coming up from the depths where they usually live and basking at the surface. This is when commercial fishermen quietly slip up and harpoon them. It's also when they're at the surface that sports fishermen try to tempt them into striking by towing a bait, usually a squid or mackerel, very slowly past the quarry's nose. If the fish hits, the angler throws his reel into free spool so that the bait flutters dead in the water. He also lets out about one hundred feet of line that has already been taken off the reel and coiled in the cockpit. Then the swordfish may grab it or ignore it. After the fish has taken all loose line and is running freely, the angler throws the reel into gear, rapidly takes up all slack, and strikes with vigor two or three times. Speeding up the boat helps set the hook. At this point the fight is usually

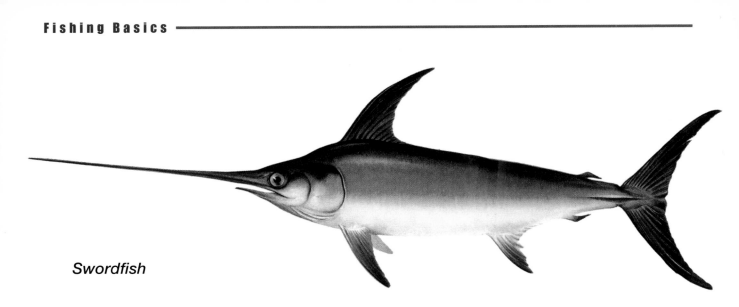

Swordfish

on, and it can last for hours. Even with heavy tackle, fighting chair, and shoulder harness, swordfishing is a game for robust athletes in top condition. Most broadbills weigh between 175 and 300 pounds, but 500-pounders and over are common. A fish weighing a half ton is possible.

Among the requirements for taking swordfish is a big, fast boat with enough speed to get out of the way if the fish charges. In the days of wooden ships and iron men a few commercial harpooners were killed because their boat was rammed and sunk or because the fish actually jumped into the boat; an angry swordfish in a small boat can easily beat a man to death with either sword or tail.

Marlin

White and blue marlin in the Atlantic and striped, blue, and black marlin in the Pacific and Indian Oceans are the recognized species. Marlin differ from swordfish in many ways. They have a fairly short, round bill with a rough feel almost like sandpaper; the swordfish's flat bill is smooth. More colorful than swordfish, marlin have vertical stripes, or bands, that may vary from white to deep blue. Their fins, especially the pectoral fins, are longer and more graceful than those of a swordfish. Most species have brilliant blue fins and various markings. Also, they are more tropical in habitat. For example, the best marlin fishing on the east coast of North America during the summer is centered off Maryland, Virginia, and North Carolina, while most swordfish action at the same time is up in New England and Maritimes waters.

White marlin, the smallest species, is found in the Atlantic within a range that extends from Cape Cod to southern Brazil and east to Africa. Averaging about forty to sixty pounds, these colorful, shimmering fish provide a jumping, rushing battle that must be seen to be believed. In addition to being caught on bait, white marlin are regularly taken on trolled lures, especially the Japanese feather. If they rush up and grab the lure without swatting it first with their bill, you have a fight on your hands. If they hit the lure first with their bill, they'll recognize it as a phony, and that marlin is a lost cause. The Bahamas in April and May, and Ocean City, Maryland, in August usually provide plenty of action.

Blue marlin are much larger and more heavily built fish than the white marlin. They are also more tropical and rarely taken north of the Carolinas in the Atlantic and Mexico in the Pacific. Fishing for blue marlin is essentially the same as swordfishing, and with fish weighing from three hundred to eight hundred pounds the angler can do a great deal of work. It was a blue marlin that Hemingway wrote about in The Old Man and the Sea, with his locale the coast of Cuba. The coast of Venezuela probably provides the most consistent fishing for both Atlantic marlin species.

Striped marlin usually weigh about two hundred pounds, and there is quite a sports fishery for them off the coasts of both New Zealand and Peru, with Hawaii being another hotspot area. They are also the staple fish of the Japanese long-line fisheries industry. These long lines consist of a main cable that may be a mile or more in length and is buoyed at intervals. To this are attached baited shorter lines at intervals of about a hundred feet. This gear takes large numbers of marlin, swordfish, sharks, and tuna with such efficiency that sports fishing is being threatened. (Fortunately, the Japanese recognize the existence of this problem and have been quite cooperative in voluntarily staying away from some prime game-fish waters.)

Black marlin, the giants of the clan, are scattered about the Pacific and Indian oceans, with the best fishing off the Peruvian coast and much action in the Hawaiian Islands and New Zealand. Fishing methods, as with striped and blue marlin, are just about identical with those used for swordfish, and probably 95 per cent of all fish taken are caught on bait. The only difference between marlin fishing and swordfishing is that with marlin you often go out and drift or troll a bait without much hope of seeing fish on the surface.

Spearfish

Intermediate between the marlin and sailfish families, spearfish of two species, the longbill in the Atlantic and the short-bill in the Pacific, are occasionally taken by sports fishing. With the flat body of the sailfish rather than the rounder body of a marlin, these spearfish look exactly like a sailfish without his giant sail. They have a smaller sail-like dorsal fin than the sailfish, but it is much bigger than that of a marlin. Spearfish are really an accidental catch for the most part, largely because they live too far at sea to be accessible to sports anglers, probably 99 percent of whom confine their fishing to a single eight-hour day.

Sailfish

Sailfish

Thanks to the various Florida Chambers of Commerce, everybody knows what a sailfish looks like. Usually the January newspapers of northern climes are filled with pictures containing two objects: a sailfish and a pretty girl, both looking the worse for wear.

It's now recognized that Atlantic and Pacific sailfish are separate species, with the Pacific fish being much larger. Together they range over most of the world's tropical oceans and seem to congregate annually in certain choice areas. Luckily for Americans, one of these is off Palm Beach, Florida, during December and January. Unluckily for the same Americans, this fishing is best off Florida when the ocean is roughest. The west coast of Mexico is noted for Pacific sailfishing; a big fleet of charter boats at Acapulco specializes in this type of angling for the tourist trade. Fishing continues excellent at least right down to Panama, where the Club de Pesca de Panama offers guests the opportunity to hook as many as fourteen or sixteen sails a day.

Good light-tackle fish, sails are noteworthy in that they are one of the few salt water species protected by some conservation practice. Tons of sailfish, which are not noted for their eating quality, were gaffed, killed, and left to rot until the law of diminishing returns started to set in and sportsmen and boat captains were forced to either take action or lose fishing. This has resulted in a sailfish release program on both coasts, and today most skippers insist that only one fish be kept for mounting or pictures and all others should be unhooked and set free.

Sailfishing is very much like fishing for white marlin, with a bit more emphasis on looking for individual fish on the surface. Because sails, like marlin, generally hit their prey with their beak to stun it, a small bait fish of some kind works much better than an artificial lure. Incidentally, while it is true that sailfish have been caught on two-pound test line, this is completely a stunt—as soon as the fish is hooked near the boat, the captain backs right up to the leader, and the mate seizes the wire leader and hauls in the fish. That's how some of these pseudo-records are set!

Sharks

It was Zane Grey fishing New Zealand's Bay of Islands in the 1920's who recognized the gameness of the mako, or mackerel shark. World-wide in distribution, the mako is noted for its terrific leaps when hooked. Also, it's one shark that can be eaten with pleasure; the flavor is almost impossible to distinguish from that of swordfish. Today the International Game Fish Association keeps records on a few shark species, and there are a number of anglers who spend a great deal of time and money at shark fishing.

Captain Frank Mundus on Long Island has showed you don't have to fish the tropics for some respectable shark catches. He annually got many makos and white, blue, and tiger sharks close to New York City. The finest shark grounds in the world are off the coast of Australia however, where husky specimens of down-under manhood have landed white pointer sharks and white sharks weighing well over a half ton.

Although most sharks are not beauty-contest winners, the mako, porbeagle, and blue sharks are very handsome fish, with metallic blue backs and sides shading into a white belly. A colorful appearance does not make them any less vicious, and all sharks should be regarded with great caution until 100 percent dead. Being low on the evolutionary scale, sharks seem to have absolutely no sense of pain. They have been boated, gutted, and

Mako shark

Great blue shark

returned alive to the water, where they actively started feeding. And there have been numerous cases where a "dead" shark has returned to life and given some careless person a nasty bite.

Sharks, though, aren't man-eaters in the sense that a lion or tiger is who starts hunting people. A shark is simply an everything-eater; he'll try to make a snack of everything that won't eat him. Since fish and birds lie on the surface and flop when in trouble, a shark dimly figures that anything splashing on the surface is ringing the dinner gong for him. All of this indicates that great prudence should be exercised in shark-infested waters.

Shark fishing in a serious manner differs from billfishing for swordfish, marlin, and sailfish because it usually involves chumming with ground fish or blood from a slaughterhouse rather than trolling. Except when fishing for real monsters, tackle in the 80- to 130-pound test class is generally sufficient. Bait is usually a chunk of fish. Probably because they rely heavily on their sense of smell when feeding, sharks are rarely caught on lures.

Tuna

Of the several tuna species, only three are of any importance as big-game fish. The others, including the blackfin tuna, which rarely weighs over ten pounds, are too small and in a class with the bonito.

The Allison, or yellowfin, tuna and the bigeye tuna often better the hundred-pound mark. Except that they are caught in the tropics, with the Allison tuna a popular sports fish as far north as Bermuda, there is no distinction between fishing for them and for bluefin tuna, the major species, which is found nearly everywhere in the world like the swordfish.

At one time, in fact until after World War I, the Atlantic bluefin tuna on the North American coast were usually called horse mackerel and considered a trash fish even while the same species supported a big fishery in the Pacific. Today, with the Pacific tuna supply depleted by over-fishing, giant tuna clippers from the west coast are appearing in North Atlantic waters, where they have been greeted by shrieks of rage, dismay, and horror; however, as long as people buy canned tunafish, you can be sure some enterprising fellow will supply it for them.

As a game fish the tuna is big, strong, and will give anyone a real workout, but they are not easy to find. Not nearly as spectacular a fighter as a swordfish or marlin, he usually runs and sounds (dives down deeply), so that you spend a long time trying to get him back up top again to have him repeat the performance. In shallow water a tuna will take off like an express train, and individual fish have towed good-sized boats for many miles. Fishing for big, economy-size tuna is hard work, for which you should be in top physical condition.

XVIII.

How to Catch Salt Water Big-Game Fish

I f you have the time and money to go out after giant tuna, swordfish, sharks, and marlin on your own privately owned boat, you should hire a professional guide or charter captain to come along at first and help show you the ropes. Even after that, you need a friend or hired hands as your mate and assistant to look for birds and signs of fish, handle the boat while you're hooking and fighting a fish, and come up with the gaff at the right moment. At least once, an experienced angler has baited, hooked, gaffed, and boated a good-sized swordfish unaided, but this is so difficult as to be almost unheard of.

Boat

Big-game fishing requires a seaworthy craft with an oversized cockpit, outriggers, a fighting chair, and a hoist of some kind. Depth-sounding equipment, ship-to-shore telephone, and even navigational radar are very useful, with the ship-to-shore almost a must for checking with other skippers and getting help in an emergency. A live well for keeping small fish healthy before use as bait is another asset. The way to buy your own boat is to get as much expert advice as you can, check over as many possibilities as feasible, and then make up your own mind. You can save a great deal of money with a second-hand craft providing you are reasonably certain of its condition, especially in regard to the power plant. Marine engines, except the heavier diesel models, generally need replacement every few years because of heavy use.

The most expensive item in a boat is speed. Fuel consumption goes way up geometrically as speed increases arithmetically. If you're in no great hurry, or fishing grounds are near port, a slow, seaworthy craft will be much more economical to operate. On the other hand, speed is a safety factor, especially when you see signs of a storm brewing. The important thing to remember in buying a boat is that the initial cost, which can run one thousand dollars a foot, is just the start. You'll have at least one hundred dollars a foot in annual costs, including upkeep, insurance, dockage, fuel, motor overhaul, and a host of other extras. If you can moor your craft behind your house and are an expert mechanic, you can save a good deal of this, but big game fishing is expensive no matter which way you look at it.

Tackle and Equipment

Generally speaking most private boats carry one 130-pounds test outfit for heavy fish, a couple of 80-pound test outfits, and maybe five lights rods with 30-pound test line that can be used all at the same time for albacore, king mackerel, small school tuna, and similar fish. Heavy tackle is very expensive and you can spend several hundred dollars for a $^9/_0$ reel without even trying.[*][*]Salt water reel sizes should not be confused with those hook sizes that are larger than a No. 1 and therefore use the /0 configuration also. The number in the reel sizes indicates how many yards of old-time linen nine-thread line testing twenty-seven pounds will fit on the reel in question. Thus, a 9/0 reel will hold nine hundred yards. Light gear is, of course, much cheaper, and on your 30-pound outfits you can use regular $^2/_0$ surf reels that will hold a couple of hundred yards of this 30-pound test line.

You need an assortment of spools of cable wire of various weights for use as leaders, and swivels to serve as a connection between leader and line. The basic reason for the leader isn't to conceal the line, but to keep the fish from breaking off by striking the line with its bill or tail. Along with the cable you need a crimping tool and soft copper sleeves to fasten on the hooks and swivels. (In the old days everybody used piano wire for leaders, but cable, especially the nylon-covered kind, is much less apt to kink and snap and lasts much longer in use.) Depending on what you're fishing for, cable can test anywhere from 20 pounds up to 240 pounds. For fish weighing over one hundred pounds, a twenty-five- or thirty-foot leader is fairly standard.

Hooks for big-game fish usually run from $^5/_0$ up to $^{12}/_0$ in size. In addition, you'll want smaller sizes down to about $^1/_0$ for catching bait fish. Specially forged shark hooks, usually with a short length of chain welded on, are available, but these are generally used on the end of a stout rope.

Most big-game fishing is bait fishing, pure and simple. In southern waters balao and half-beak (closely related species usually never over a foot in length that are characterized by having a greatly extended lower jaw) are often used along with flying fish, small Spanish or Sierra mackerel, and even bonito. Sewing these properly on the hook is a fine art. Strip baits—either a fillet from a fish, a strip of squid, or even an oversized piece of pork rind—are much easier for the amateur to handle. You simple pass the hook through the head of the strip a couple of times, and away you go.

Lures are often effective on tuna and will sometimes hook white marlin and sailfish. The Japanese feather—in various color combinations of red and white, green and yellow, white and black, and blue and white—is probably best of all to this day. Trolled at a good rate of speed, ten to fifteen miles an hour, it will provoke plenty of action, especially from the smaller game species. Spoons of various styles also get results on occasion, but plugs are rarely employed except as teasers, which are big hookless plugs put overboard on a hand-line to lure billfish. Usually they are used in pairs. The teaser is yanked in when a fish makes a pass at it, and a bait fish or strip bait tossed into the wake in its place.

A gaff is a big barbless hook on a pole and is plunged into a big fish alongside the boat to both kill it and serves as a means of dragging it abroad. You can see, therefore, why you can't generally gaff a fish and then release it. Gaffs for every big fish, including giant tuna and sharks, come with detachable heads on a line. The pole comes loose on this so-called flying gaff. With small sailfish and white marlin, the mate grabs the bill in gloved hands, unhooks the fish, and tosses it back.

Fishing for the big offshore species consists largely of cruising and looking. Most charter and private craft have a tuna tower of aluminum pipe. The mate usually goes aloft and keeps an eye cocked for birds, fins, and anything else of interest. Once you get into an area where fish are likely to be, a baited line is put over and trolled; in sailfish and marlin waters several baits are put overside, with the outriggers used to skip a couple of them right along the surface. Especially when the ocean is rough, a single fin is very difficult to see, and in most big-game fishing areas you can sometimes spend hours or even days without sighting much of anything. This doesn't always mean you go fishless, as barracuda, king mackerel, mahi-mahi (a.k.a. dolphin), skipjack, and other species enjoy wrecking nice marlin baits, and get themselves caught in the process.

Generally speaking, swordfish are the most difficult quarry, and sailfish and white marlin the easiest. Tuna, depending on the season of the year, are some place in the middle. Fishing for giant tuna is usually done by chumming rather than trolling. Chum, in the form of mossbunker, is run through a meat grinder and flung overboard in an area where tuna, like drugstore cowboys of the sea, are congregating. Mossbunker, or menhaden as they are also called, are small, oily fish that stink with an effluvium from their entire body.

If all goes well, tuna will gather around a chumming boat like crowds around a free lunch counter in an old-time bar. You can look overboard sometimes and actually see them lying like trout in the pool of a brook, except that these trout can be six feet long. Getting them to take a chunk of fish containing your hook is sometimes very easy, but it is often a nightmare. Imaginative minds have even devised lady's hairnets surrounding a gob of chum to give the fish the illusion that there's no sticker to the antipasto. Small live bait, including fresh-caught ling and whiting, are probably best of all. Often these, slices of herring, and other bait are used with a cork float, the same as for sunfish in a pond, except bigger. When a tuna strikes, your cork really takes a dive!

Hooking any big-game fish is just the beginning. Landing him, even with a helping hand at the boat's wheel, is another story entirely. The best idea is to make sure your drag is properly adjusted slightly below the breaking strength of your line before you start fishing. Then, when you hook a fish, leave the drag alone. More big fish are lost by popped lines and pulled hooks caused by worried anglers tightening drags too much than by any other cause.

Most big fish of any species will start off with a flashing burst of speed, often followed by a leap into the air. Then they usually wheel and dive or take off at another angle. A good helmsman will keep your chair always pointed directly at the fish.

It's much easier to whip a big fish in shallow water, where he can run himself into exhaustion but can't dive, than it is far out in deep water, where he can sound and defy you to pull him back up. Big marlin, swordfish, and tuna have been known to reach depths where the pressure has killed them and from which it is almost impossible to raise them. In a case like this you should get the boat well away from the fish and try to pull him up an imaginary inclined plane under water rather than straight up from the bottom.

With proper tackle and a good skipper, many anglers have whipped very big fish in fifteen minutes. Sometimes it can take much longer. Tuna in particular have been known to tow a dory for fourteen hours and more. Again, commercial netters have, for a long time, taken more than is necessary out of the oceans. It's time to go the way of fly fishing, and implement active catch and release programs for big-game fish.

XIX.

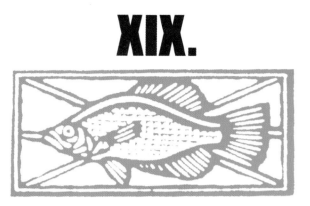

Smaller Blue-Water Game Fish

T he fun fish of the open sea aren't the giants. It's work to tangle with a monster. Smaller species are easier to find and generally good to eat. Here are a few typical examples.

School Tuna

Young specimens of the bluefin tuna weighing from twenty to ninety pounds are fun to catch and great eating. Generally, they are caught trolling. If you've done fresh water fishing, you think of trolling as slowly moving along as quietly as possible. Trolling for school tuna and their relatives, the false albacore and bonito, will come then as quite a shock. The boat does not scare these fish, as in fresh water fishing; instead, the wake attracts them, and they swim fast enough to flash by a slow-moving lure and know it's a fake. Therefore, when you troll for school tuna, you move along at from twelve to fifteen miles an hour—about half as fast as a water skier. You fish your lures from ten to twenty feet behind the transom, right in the churned-up wake. When you have a hit you really know it!

The best tackle for this fishing is a light salt water trolling rod, a regular multiplying reel, and about two hundred yards of twenty-five- or thirty-pound test line. You also need a leader that can be either a short length of thirty-pound test cable-wire or sixty-pound test monofilament. Because the fish come up from behind the lure, the visibility of the leader isn't critical in trolling the way it is in most fishing. The connection between leader and line should be a small barrel or toggle swivel, and the leader should end at a snap so that lures can be readily changed.

You can get into a big fight when you start arguing about trolling lures; everybody has a favorite. Lures for school tuna and their buddies in the sea range from the old lead-head cedar squid through various types of spoons, jigs, and feather lures. My personal feeling is that the Japanese feather lures and nylon lead-headed jigs are as good as anything and have the great advantage of not revolving and kinking your line at high speeds. Another choice is the umbrella rig. It carries four or more arms tipped with small hookless lures and a larger lure (with hook) slightly trailing dead center. Although this lure is not castable, it is the marine equivalent of the spinnerbait.

In July and August school tuna are a favorite of the private and charter fleets from New England south to North Carolina. Overfishing has created a problem on the Pacific coast.

Bonito

This beautiful fish is one of the best eating of the entire tuna-mackerel clan. No oilier than a mackerel, it can be baked or broiled without special treatment. Usually caught along with school tuna and skipjack in late summer around New York, it is basically one of several closely related species of Atlantic bonito that migrate down to the Bahamas and Florida in the winter months. The average size is from two to ten pounds. Pacific bonito are caught along with yellowtail especially around the Coronado Islands.

Skipjack

Also known as oceanic bonito, this world traveler is found over a wide range of ocean. A study in blue, purple, and silver, heights even prettier than he looks. In fact, he'll make a tuna double his size appear tame. The basic fishing method is fast trolling.

Albacore

In the Atlantic this fish is really the little tunny, a different species from the long-finned Pacific albacore of commercial fishing. Atlantic, or false, albacore weighup to forty pounds, and all of it is fighting weight. Sometimes they'll come right up to the beach, hit the lure of

Little Tunny

a striped-bass fisherman,and usually get away trailing yards of broken line. the long-finned Pacific, or true, albacore is the white-meat tuna of the supermarkets. Usually, he's caught on live bait rather than by trolling.

Mackerel

The Boston mackerel of the North Atlantic, the Spanish mackerel of the southeast and Gulf coasts, and the Pacific Sierra mackerel are closely related. These small, streamlined speedsters average a couple of pounds in weight and will hit a lure with a terrific wallop.

Boston mackerel are usually caught by drifting and jigging. Chum is used to bring the fish around the boat. Spanish mackerel, the mainstay of a big Southern industry, are usually caught trolling. Many Florida anglers cast lures for them in the big sounds and bays, with small spoons and plugs the most effective attractors. On the California coast Sierra mackerel are often caught while live-bait fishing for yellowtail.

All mackerel species are found in huge schools, sometimes nearly two hundred miles in length. Thus mackerel fishing is mostly feast or famine. There are days when you could sink the boat with your catch, and others when you either can't find fish, or if you find them, can't get them to show interest in anything.

Mahi Mahi (a.k.a. Dolphin)

So as not to be confused with the small porpoise of the same name, which is a mammal, this beautifully colored fish has undergone a name-change in the past decade or so. They

Mahi Mahi (Dolphin)

are found in all the warm waters of the world, and also many of the best restaurants. Most are caught by trolling at a good speed, especially around floating debris of any kind. (They seem to like to hide in the shadow of an old plank, a barrel, or even a few sheets of newspaper.) Mahi Mahi are very fond of flying fish and will come completely out of the water when chasing them. Their average weight is from ten to twenty-five pounds, but some, especially around the Hawaiian Islands, come quite close to the hundred-pound mark. The only people who don't like them are marlin fishermen; a mahi-mahi likes nothing better than to sink his teeth into a marlin bait.

Wahoo

Among the fastest swimmers in the ocean, this giant mackerel is shaped like a javelin and found, never in large numbers, in all the warm seas of the world. Quite a few are caught around Bermuda, and occasional specimens have been taken as far north as New Jersey, generally by boats fishing well offshore for marlin and tuna. A large number of wahoo are also caught in the West Indies and west into the Gulf of Mexico. Trolling is the only fishing method used, although most wahoo are caught accidentally.

King Mackerel

Also called kingfish, this hard-hitting, hard-fighting fish can weigh up to fifty pounds and more. He's especially popular in Florida and west to Texas, but he ranges south to Brazil, and north to the Chesapeake Bay. King mackerel are caught by trolling, but a great many anglers prefer to cast lures and live bait around offshore oil rigs and reefs. This is the Gulf of Mexico's most plentiful offshore game fish; tarpon are the most plentiful inshore game fish.

Bluefish

A world roamer, bluefish are found almost everywhere except the eastern Pacific. Usually weighing from two to ten pounds, this may be the most important North Atlantic game fish from Massachusetts south to Georgia. Many bluefish are caught trolling, but the best trolling method is quite different from tuna and albacore fishing. Bluefish are often found on bottom, and slow trolling with wire lines, just like fresh water summer fishing for lake trout, is often effective. Wobbling spoons and nylon "eels" are top trolling lures.

The most popular east-coast bluefishing method is chumming. Tremendous tonnages of mossbunker are used every summer as bluefish chum. A small amount of ground mossbunker is mixed with seawater in a bucket, and the mixture is scooped overboard. Slices of butterfish are the usual bait. Either a very long shank hook or a short wire leader must be

Bluefish

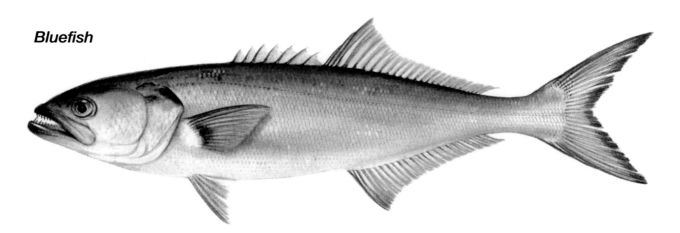

used, or else the bluefish will cut the line or monofilament leader. These fellows have a sharp-toothed mouth that serves as a very efficient pair of shears.

If you go bluefishing, be careful when unhooking your catch. Blues, like some people, bite; and they'll snap at anything, yourself included. There's a famous, although possibly exaggerated, story about a character who won a hundred-dollar pool for the biggest fish aboard a party boat with a good-sized bluefish. Feeling no pain, he picked the fish up, said, "I love you, honey," and bestowed a kiss. His prize-winning bluefish promptly bared its fangs and bit off a good chunk of his captor's nose. The business end of a bluefish is as dangerous as that of the famed piranha of the Amazon, so take care!

Yellowtail

This member of the jack family is southern California's answer to the Atlantic's bluefish. A trim, beautiful fish, yellowtail are mostly caught from giant party boats and private craft that have live-bait wells aboard. When the fishing grounds are reached or a school of fish is sighted, bait is tossed overboard to attract them. Then the anglers, using long, flexible rods, bait up and cast into the feeding fish. (You need a flexible rod so as not to cast off your live bait.) Along with yellowtail, you may get white sea bass, albacore, bonito, Pacific barracuda, and literally dozens of others species, but the yellowtail are the prime attraction. This is seasonal fishing, with best results in midsummer from Catalina Island south.

Many additional species of far-offshore game fish could be listed. As a practical matter, however, the only time most anglers get to see these fish, with the exception of bluefish and mackerel species, is on a very occasional charter boat trip, where the skipper provides the tackle and instructs in its use. Even with the boating boom and prosperity, the economic facts of life are such that very few anglers have big, fast boats for far-offshore work, and most salt water fishing is still done within a mile of the beach.

XX.

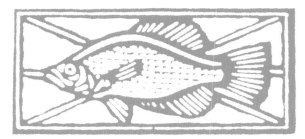

Party-Boat Fishing— The Urbanite's Delight

I f the term "party boat" conjures up the vision of orgiastic revels, I'm afraid you'll be sadly disappointed. A party boat is nothing more than an open boat, which means that it is "open" to all customers until a capacity load of passengers is reached, and has nothing to do with a cabin or lack of same. Thanks to the U.S. Coast Guard, which determines the capacity and licenses both boat and captain, there hasn't been a serious accident on a party boat for a long time, despite the fact that they carry all kinds of people out to sea in all kinds of weather except a gale.

Ever since the ill-fated Pelican sank off Montauk in heavy seas because the weight of excess passengers made her top-heavy, there has been strict observance by party-boat skippers of the Coast Guard regulations. You are probably safer on a party boat than aboard any other type of craft, and much safer than in your own home. Aside from hooking yourself, cutting yourself, or becoming wretched from seasickness, practically nothing can happen to you except a good time and, very likely, a good catch.

Since most party boats sail every day, their captains are very well informed on where the fish are and on what they are biting. There's nothing like being constantly out fishing to get the feel of the game, and a competent boat skipper develops this feel and hones it to a fine edge. Because his boat's reputation and his livelihood depend on results, you can be quite positive that a party-boat captain will do anything in his power to help you catch fish. Follow his advice on rigs and baiting and you'll load up. Be obstinate, and he won't be able to help you.

In addition to the skipper, who is usually also the owner, most party boats carry one or more mates who double as deckhands and instructors. They cut bait, grind chum, gaff or net big fish, untangle snarled lines—all in addition to their chores of casting off lines at dockside, lowering and raising the anchor, and generally acting as the skipper's eyes, ears, and arms. The mate generally operates the boat's pool, which is a sort of lottery in which each interested passenger can contribute a dollar (sometimes more), and the biggest fish wins it all. Party-boat pools on a big craft can run into amounts of well over $100. Some of the larger craft operate several simultaneous pools. Depending on the area, either the entire pool goes to the lucky winner, or the mate gets a small slice off the top as handling charges.

Before entering a party-boat pool be sure you understand what species of fish are eligible. On a well-run craft this is pulled out in detail so that you know that ling, dogfish, skates, lobsters, and so forth aren't included. Sometimes, especially on mackerel trips, the pool is simply drawn from a hat. In a school of mackerel the fish may run exactly the same size and weight down to a fraction of an ounce.

The best way to win a pool, besides being lucky, is so take good care of your catch. Bring a garbage can or an old washtub aboard and buy a cake of ice to toss in it. The difference in weight between an ice-cold wet fish and one that's been lying in the hot sun all day can make the difference between putting a load of folding lettuce in your wallet and being an also-ran. If the boat won't allow washtubs, a potato sack with some ice in it will do a good job for you too.

Another job of the party-boat mate is usually to collect the fares and give you a receipt. If the day is a complete failure, this receipt may become a free pass for a make-up trip at your convenience. (Sometimes, it will give you a discount on your next trip instead.)

Where can you find a boat? In major metropolitan areas this is no problem. Boats and captains' associations advertise in the sports pages of newspapers, especially those with a fishing and hunting editor. Additionally, you'll often find them in the yellow pages of the telephone book under "Fishing Boats." Practically every United States and Canadian seaport in a population and vacation center supports a fleet of party boats. The New York City area has one of the biggest party-boat fleets in the world, with craft leaving from Sheepshead Bay (near Coney Island); Westchester Avenue, the Bronx; Great Kills, Staten Island; Hoboken, New Jersey; Highlands and Atlantic Highlands, New Jersey; and Babylon, Long Island. From Brielle, New Jersey, on the Manasquan River, north and east to Montauk, Long Island, and New London, Connecticut, every inlet and docking space has one or more party boats, and this is only one metropolitan area. Miami, Los Angeles, San Francisco, Portland, Seattle, Mobile—all have party boats. You can find them overseas too, with at least one craft sailing daily for codfish and mackerel from Oslo, Norway, during the summer months.

Asking how long a party-boat trip is, is like asking the famous rhetorical question about how long a man's legs should be. (Lincoln answered, "Long enough to reach the ground.") Areas where fishing is close to home often offer half-day trips in the morning and afternoon. Where it's a long boat ride to the fishing grounds, a full day, generally from 8 a.m. to 4 p.m., is customary. In the Los Angeles-Long Beach-Santa Barbara area you board your boat the evening before sailing, rent a bunk, and go to bed. The boat sails late at night to put you out in yellowtail territory at sunrise.

Party-boat fares range widely too. You'll pay a moderate amount for a half-day trip and double that for a full day, the price depending in part on the type of fishing and the bait supplied. What about tipping? If the mate gives you special service, a few dollars is only fair. There's no need to tip a party-boat captain, just as you wouldn't necessarily tip any other business owner.

What kind of fish can you catch from a party boat? In many areas party-boat fishing is basically bottom fishing. Starting in the Maritimes and New England, codfish, haddock, and flounder are the staples in the summer, with mackerel providing action for the light-tackle fan. From Connecticut south to the Carolinas summertime is bluefish time for party boats too; this is mostly chumming. A large number of boats also sail for sea bass, porgies,

Great Barracuda

blackfish (also called tautog in some parts, flounder, and fluke (summer flounder). In the Chesapeake Bay area croaker, sea trout, and Norfolk spot make up most of the party-boat catch, with some small boats specializing in rockfish (striped bass) for small groups. (The biggest concentration of party boats specializing in stripers has been at San Francisco.)

From the Carolinas south you get into sheepshead, flounder (a southern species), and a horde of varieties of tropical and semi-tropical reef fish. Florida party-boat fishing is mostly reef fishing for a wide range of snappers, grunts, and other colorful southern fish. Along the Gulf coast red snapper is the major party-boat fish, and king mackerel the major charter boat quarry; however, some Louisiana, Alabama, Mississippi, and Texas boats sail for sea trout, croaker, and redfish (channel bass to northerners).

Along the southern California coast yellowtail are the most important party-boat quarry, along with albacore, barracuda, and bonito. There's also excellent bottom fishing for a wide range of perch and rock bass. Farther north, salmon and striped bass become the staple quarry, and in Washington State party boats take their passengers trolling for Coho and king salmon with the aid of giant cannonball sinkers that keep individual rigs well down and away from others. Washington and Oregon also have sensational bottom fishing for a wide range of fish, from cultus cod to halibut. On west coast boats from San Francisco north you may have to provide your own bait. Check this before sailing.

Although party boats on the east coast seldom if ever engage in trolling, trolling for salmon is standard party-boat fishing in the Northwest. The boats are fairly small, and cannonball sinkers, which can weigh as much as ten pounds and are released when a fish strikes, keep your line away from that of a half dozen fellow passengers. The sinker is generally fastened on a wire line to which a device similar to a clothespin clips your fishing line near the sinker. When a salmon hits, he pulls your fishing line out of the pin, and you then play him without the sinker.

South of Boston on the Atlantic coast, party boats often sail year round, with maybe a slack month in February. As the water cools in the fall, winter species replace those caught during the summer, but fishing continues, and January off New Jersey can produce more action than June. It's about the same on the west coast too, although with the end of the tourist season and the salmon runs a good many boats, especially in the Northwest, lay up rather than fish bottom.

For most party-boat fishing you'll be adequately equipped with what is sensibly called a boat rod. This is short and stiff, with a medium-long butt. You can't cast with it, so don't even try. You can never have a rod that's too stiff for most bottom fishing because you need this backbone to handle a heavy sinker, possibly a pound or more in deep water, and set the hook firmly in a fish's mouth. With a limber rod, you strike, the rod bends prettily, but no power goes down the line to set the hook. Most party-boat anglers prefer a multiplying reel; spinning reels are not good for heavy sinkers and deep-water angling. The reel should be loaded with nylon monofilament or braided line of at least twenty-pound test. For codfish, red snapper, and other heavy bottom fish, you can go to forty-pound or even fifty-pound test line. This type of fishing consists of hoisting up a heavy fish from possibly sixty to over a hundred feet of water, so light tackle is strictly out of order, will ruin your day, and annoy your fellow passengers.

One time that light tackle is sufficient aboard a party boat is when you're fishing for California yellowtail. You have to cast a light bait well out from the boat, so you need a steelhead or flipping rod with a fast tip, combined with a good multiplying or spinning reel with a couple of hundred yards of fifteen- or twenty-pound test line. You can't bulldog a yellowtail. You just let him run against the drag. Fairly light tackle is also useful when bluefishing on the Atlantic coast. When you chum for bluefish, it's a good idea to try and play your fish out beyond most of the spider's web of lines about the boat and then bring him in very fast.

In many areas you can buy all the tackle you need aboard the boat, and you can also rent rods, reels, and handlines. Away from major population centers this isn't always so, and in such places the smart party-boat angler brings along, in addition to a stiff rod for bottom fishing and a lighter rod for top-water fish (if he expects any), an assortment of sinkers from four to sixteen ounces, diamond jigs in sizes to eight ounces, snelled hooks ranging in size from 1 through 6/0, and some three-way and barrel swivels. (Diamond jigs, which most bottom species will wallop when worked up and down just off the bottom, are used especially when fishing is fast and furious to save you from spending time with bait.) When party-boat fishing in a new area that you are positive will have all the necessary equipment available, make it your policy to get your rigs, including hooks, sinkers, and lures, at a local tackle store, at the dock, or on board the boat. It party-boat fishing, the skipper finds the fish and provides the bait; yet it's up to you to bring them up and over the rail, and the proper rig can make an amazing difference.

Party boats that bottom fish very often drift rather than anchor. When there's a crowd aboard, drifts are made with alternate sides to windward. When you're fishing the windward side, your line goes out easily from the boat, and it is wise especially for bottom feeders, to let out plenty of line even after you hit bottom. This puts your line at a more acute angle so that all the hooks on your rig are on or just off the bottom. When fishing the leeward side, use a sinker heavy enough so you can fish straight down, as letting your line drift under the bottom of the boat causes various kinds of trouble. You can get tangled with the lines of fishermen on the windward side. You can hook a fish, scrape across the bottom of the boat, and cut your line. (This is easy, as all boats have sharp barnacles in salt water.) Worst of all, you can hook a fish that will wrap your line around the lines of anglers on the opposite rail of the boat.

Always remember that there's an art to using bait. When you get clams, conches, or other mollusks, don't just roll them into a hunk and stick your hook in the middle. Drape them artistically, so that the point of your hook is in position to go to work on a biting fish. When using slices of fish or squid, remember that they are supposed to resemble a bait fish, and a long, thin piece hooked through the head end with a long, trailing tail looks more like fish food than a square chunk hooked so as to move through the water sideways. The best idea with sand eels, spearing (a small, silvery bait fish), and other small dead bait is to use a rig with a small bait-holder hook at the head end and a bigger hook ready for business at the tail end. Live bait can be hooked lightly through the back, through a gill cover, or through both lips. Through the back and behind the dorsal fin is generally preferred, especially when at anchor. When drifting with live bait, hook them through both lips or use the bait-holder hook.

What do you need aboard a party boat? First, as already mentioned, you need a washtub and a cake of ice for your catch, or at least a potato sack or feed bag. Check, preferably a day ahead, about bait. If you need it, ask the skipper for ideas. Along with rod, reel, and tackle box complete with rigs, hooks, and jigs, you should have a spare spool of line and an oil can for your reel. In freezing weather use powdered graphite instead of oil; in fact, you want no oil in your reel then, as oil gums in the cold. A knife and fish scaler are handy to clean your catch with on the ride back to the dock. Most boats will provide a hose with running salt water to help you. Don't forget your lunch and a thermos of coffee in cold weather or some cold drink in hot weather. Many party boats sell soft drinks and beer aboard, and some have a regular galley. If you're certain of this, you might want to buy everything on the boat.

Warm clothing is a must in cold weather, and it's much colder standing still aboard a boat than moving about ashore. In the summer, take a sweater to be safe. If you sunburn, take enough suntan lotion. There's very little shade aboard most party boats except down below, and if you're at all queasy you won't like the smell of bilge and diesel oil that is present in every cabin. Rain gear of some kind is necessary in some areas, and a good idea everywhere. You can use it to wrap up your camera, if for nothing else.

The best footgear is anything with a non-skid sole. In cold weather low rubber boots are essential to protect your feet from freezing spray. A very handy extra is a carpenter's apron with many pockets. You put this on over everything else and place such items as spare rigs and hooks in the pockets. Gloves and mittens aren't much help unless they are waterproof, but insulated rubber gloves for icy water are now available at very little cost. If you have the least doubt about seasickness, take appropriate measures before leaving the dock. Charter and private boats can sometimes put an ill passenger ashore, but party-boat skippers aren't about to spoil the day for the rest of their fares. If you get sick on a party boat, you'll just have to suffer for the next several hours.

Sometimes, if you're party-boat fishing far from home, you may be faced with a big catch of fish you don't know what to do with. When this happens, call a local hospital, orphanage, or old-folks home. If you can't find any charity, ask the local newspaper for suggestions. The captain will often take care of your catch for you, but giving it where it will be appreciated is better.

Party boats offer good fishing opportunities near big cities and in vacation spots. Using them can save you a big investment of your own in equipment, and save you much time in finding a good fishing spot. You get professional help in finding fish, in rigging up, in baiting, and even in landing and cleaning them. If you're a beginning fisherman interested in salt water, this is a good way to start. If you're an expert, you'll still have fun on a party boat.

XXI.

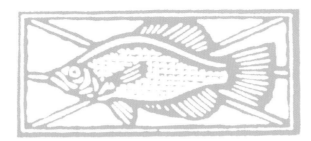

Surf, Pier, and Jetty Fishing

For the angler who likes to stand on his own two feet and find, fool and land his own fish, few sports can top surf-casting. This is one type of salt water fishing in which no boat captain tells you what to do or where and when to do it. You've nothing to go on but the look of the water as waves that have traveled thousands of mile across the seas spill out the dregs of their energy upon the sand. The colors of dawn and sunset on the ocean,

the screams of gulls and terns, the shifting bars and beaches, the amazing ebb and flow of the tides—all give surf-casting a certain allure that no boat-based angler can really know.

Comparatively few people think of surf-casting as an effective way to catch fish. Most of them believe that ocean fish hesitate to come into shallow water. Maybe they've seen a few characters spend all day on a corner of a bathing beach in midsummer trying futilely to land even a flounder. Surf-fishing is a seasonal activity; and depending on the latitude and the calendar, it can be either excellent or terrible.

Why would any sensible fish come into the surf when he has the entire ocean in which to roam? The basic answer is to eat. Waves and eddies in the surf uncover luscious soft crabs, break up clams and other mollusks, and wash worms out of their burrows. In the spring and fall, schools of spearing, sand eels, rainfish, mullet, and other bait fish migrate north and south in the surf comparatively safe from their deep-water enemies, but at the mercy of predators equipped to chase them into the shallows. Therefore, providing your timing is right, surf-casting can unlock an entirely new world of angling for you. This is true in Maine, Oregon, New York, California, Texas, and every other state with a seacoast. Nor is surf-casting restricted to the United States. Great Britain, New Zealand, Australia, Hawaii, Argentina—nearly every country bordering the ocean offers some form of surf-casting to the interested angler. You may stand on a boulder instead of a beach, or cast from a cliff instead of a sandy strand; but if you can catch fish from the surf in one area, a slight adjustment in lures, rigs, and methods will bring you success elsewhere. Whether the quarry is kingfish (not king mackerel) in Delaware, spotfin croaker in California, striped bass in Rhode Island, or channel bass at Oregon Inlet, the experienced surf caster will make a strong showing and sometimes introduce a new idea that will beat the natives.

Because fishing methods are probably more important than anything else in surf-casting, we'll take a quick swing around North America and discuss each region separately.

Maritimes and Northern New England

Except for occasional beaches, this is an area where granite cliffs come right down to the water, so surf-casting here is almost an unknown sport. The natives either fish for trout and salmon or go out by boat for cod and pollock, and most tourists aren't equipped to fish from slippery, rocky shores. Mackerel, striped bass, and pollock do come inshore; and a good caster can reach them with a stainless-steel squid. Because of a plague of bergalls (a species of small fish with sharp teeth and a frantic appetite for bait) bottom fishing is generally not worthwhile, although you can pick up some very nice tautog and flounder in places.

Southern New England

The area from the tip of Cape Cod west into Rhode Island is a surf caster's paradise in the summer. Striped-bass action starts at the end of May and continues into October, and bluefish are on tap beginning in June. Both species are mostly caught at night with big, heavy plugs and jigs. Because long casts are imperative, big, heavy rods are favored; and surf sticks from eleven to fourteen feet in length are used with both multiplying and big spinning reels.

Cape Cod, with its miles of sand beaches, offers good camping; and many of the regulars spend a large amount of money on beach buggies with oversized tires and four-wheel drive. With these, they cruise the beaches looking for breaking schools of bass and blues. A recent addition to surfing equipment here is a small aluminum boat with a big motor, usually at least eighteen horsepower. When the surf is too flat to fish, these can be used to run out to offshore bars and look for action. Some monster stripers have been caught on live mackerel bait from these little cartop boats. You need a light jigging outfit for the macks and a fairly heavy outfit with about thirty-pound test line for the bass. A cut-down surf rod about six feet long is best for this fishing.

You can fish with bait in the surf, of course, and catch bass, blues, and summer flounder, plus tautog near the rocks. The basic surf rig is a three-way swivel, with the line on one terminal, a sinker (usually a four-ounce pyramid) on another, and a hook, ranging from No. 2 up to $^6/_0$ in size, on the third at the end of an eighteen-inch leader. Bloodworms and sandworms are good bait for almost everything, but shedder crabs, strips of squid, killies (called mummies in New England), and cut fish are also used. Along a sand beach you look for holes in the bar, which you can spot by their darker color a patch of green water in the midst of a long line of white foam. This effect is caused by the waves riding over the deeper water in the hole and breaking farther inshore, whereas alongside the bar itself they're pounding themselves to pieces.

West of Cape Cod you get into rocks again. Because a bait sitting on a rocky bottom often results in the fishhook getting caught on an obstruction, plugs and squids and eel rigs of various kind are very popular west of the Cape Cod Canal and on into Rhode Island. Striped bass and bluefish love to eat eel, especially at night, and casting a rigged eel, eel tail on a jig, eelskin, or even imitation rubber-and-plastic eel lures is a successful method after dark. Nantucket, Martha's Vineyard, and Cuttyhunk offer excellent fishing from the surf and even better fishing from boats.

Once you get west into Connecticut and Long Island Sound proper, surf-casting dies off quickly. There's no surf, for one thing. You can fish from shore with light spinning or bait casting gear for flounders, tautog, and scup (porgies), but this has nothing to do with braving the pounding breakers.

Long Island, New Jersey, and Delaware

From Montauk to Maryland there's extraordinary surf action on almost a year-round basis. Rocky Montauk, at the tip of Long Island, offer Rhode Island-type fishing and conditions, with lure slinging toward offshore rocks and rips for striped bass and bluefish very popular with those who are capable. The rocks vanish as you go west toward the Hamptons, and from there to Maryland the only rocks along the shore are in the form of man-made jetties.

The sandy beaches from Easthampton south and east to Manasquan Inlet offer good summer surfing for everything from striped bass down to blowfish (a pest species that is such good eating it's becoming popular). Summer flounder (fluke) are the traditional summer specialty here. The basic surf rig for them is the three-way swivel already described, with a long-shank Carlisle hook in size 3/0. The best bait is either a strip of squid or a spearing. Fluking is a daytime game, and the object from June until early August is to cover as much bottom as possible. After a long cast you work your rig in rapidly along the bottom. A fluke will either give your bait a sharp rap or simply hand on to the bait. If you feel a mysterious lightness to your rig, hesitate a couple of seconds, and then sink the hook.

A May and June species is the northern kingfish, related to the southern-surf whiting and not to the big, mackerel-like kingfish, or king mackerel, of the Gulf coast. This little fish goes for small bits of worm, shrimp, and crab. When fishing for kings you need about a No. 4 hook on a short leader (just long enough to clear your sinker). A bite seems to create the effect of a trap drummer playing a short roll: one swift, continuous peck. Tremendously strong for their size, a one-pound kingfish that is hooked sometimes gives the illusion of a giant striped bass, at least for a few moments. Look for kingfish in the same places you would look for striped bass: in the holes along the south or west sides of jetties and in holes on a sand bar. Often they'll come in within a few feet of shore, so long casts aren't really needed.

The New Jersey shore north of Manasquan Inlet has long been famous for good striper fishing. The building of literally dozens of stone jetties to combat beach erosion has improved conditions by creating additional areas of rips and swirling currents where bait fish hide and bass play.

Since much of his fishing is done from and near jetties, the New Jersey surfer is adequately equipped with a lighter, shorter rod than that used by the New Englander or North Carolinian. Regular "steelhead" or freshwater flipping rods are ideal for light plugs, small eels, and lightweight bait fishing in this area.

The basic striper technique here is to fish from the beach about dusk with plugs or rigged eels, and cover jetty after jetty until you find fish. Generally, if bass are around a jetty, you'll know it after a few casts. If they're not, you might as well move on.

Many old-timers still prefer bait fishing for striped bass. They rake soft and shedder calico crabs from the sand around jetties at low water and use them for bait on the rising tide. Sandworms are another favored bait, especially in spring, but have the disadvantage of being extremely soft and difficult to keep in one piece when cast, especially if they are hooked only through the head as they should be. Clams are good bass bait, particularly after a storm, when you can pick them up right from the beach. (These big surf clams are also wonderful eating; the small ones are especially good steamed, and the bigger ones are very good either sliced and eaten raw or in chowder.) When using crabs or clams for bait in any surf area, you need a spool of light sewing thread (red is a good color) with which to tie your soft bait on the hook to prevent the undertow from washing it away.

Some Helpful Hints on Successful Surf Casting...

1. Find out what tide stages are best in your area and plan to be on the beach then.

2. A good wind and choppy seas usually produce excellent fishing. Big, smooth swells or total dead calm usually aren't very good. Dirty, discolored water needn't stop you from fishing, especially when you can cast beyond it. At the very edge of sandy or silty water you'll find many fish who come in for churned-up bait but prefer to stick at the edge of the silt rather than swim around in it.

3. In most areas night fishing is better than day fishing, especially in hot weather.

4. Always look for holes in sand bars; holes around the ends of jetties; and screaming terns and gulls, which signify something is going on under the surface.

5. Striking up a chat with successful anglers will usually result in new ideas you can use for your own fishing pleasure.

6. Keep away from bathers. They won't help your fishing any, and hitting somebody with a sinker can result in a lawsuit.

7. Bottom conditions are always changing in the surf. Last season's prize hole may be completely filled up this year.

8. Surf-living fish stay on the move. This means you should move about until you find the fish, rather than staying in one spot and waiting endlessly for action. A quarter mile or less can often be the difference between success and failure.

9. Be a sportsman. This means you don't cast across the line of a fellow who has a fish on it. You don't leave garbage on the beach or rocks. You give the other fellow a break. Sometimes the loan of a plug or some bait can lead to a worthwhile friendship.

10. Safety first! In a crowded area be sure to look behind you before casting. Watch your footing around rocks. Give sting rays, Portuguese men-of-war, and other unpleasant creatures a wide berth.

11. To feel a bite, you have to keep your line tight at all times. Don't pull so hard that you move the sinker, but be sure you can feel everything. And just don't cast and let your bait sit until doomsday. Move it a few inches every few minutes. After a quarter hour without a hit reel in and cast again—or move to some place more promising.

12. Don't get discouraged. Surf-casting can be good one day and not so good the next. The one thing that makes for success once you know your area and your business is consistency. Fish enough, and the law of averages is on your side.

Mid-Atlantic striper surfing is generally at its best in June and October, but northern New Jersey and Long Island have some fish all summer long. In the spring and fall daytime fishing is much better than nighttime fishing, whereas probably 90 per cent of all stripers caught in the summer are taken between dusk and dawn.

If you're bait fishing and find that something is chewing up your offerings, you'd better move. Crabs are doing it, and this is a sign that few fish are in the area. If you land a sea robin along the New Jersey shore, cut him open, and you'll very likely find some soft calico crabs in his stomach. Use these for striper and kingfish bait.

Tautog (also called blackfish) are easy to catch around jetties during calm water in spring and fall. (They stay all summer, but quit biting.) The best method is to use old junkyard nuts for sinkers, tie them on with weak line, and buy some Virginia blackfish hooks. You can dig sand bugs for bait on any beach, especially at low tide. Blacks will also hit worms, clams, and especially calico crabs in small sizes. The place to fish for them is at the very edge of the rocks. Keep the point of the hook buried in the bait to lessen the possibility of snagging a boulder. Blackfish run to a good size, with many in the five- to eight-pound class and even larger.

Unlike more northern areas, the mid-Atlantic offers surfing activity at least through New Year's Day. This winter fishing is for whiting, also called silver hake, which come into the surf after dark from November through January and again in May. In sandy areas without jetties you can catch these fish on a cold night by frost fishing, which is running along the shoreline with a flashlight and waiting for a wave to wash them ashore alive and wiggling. Whiting will strand themselves like this in a medium surf while chasing spearing and sand eels, and you have to grab them before the following wave washes them back out to sea. A cousin of the cod, whiting are great eating, and places like the Long Branch Fishing Pier groan under the weight of the mob assembled to catch them. It's a startling sight to see hundreds of people fishing in midwinter—startling to anyone who associates all angling with sun and balmy weather, that is.

Most whiting are caught on bait, usually sliced herring. Spearing and slices of whiting are even more deadly. Since these fish will also hit a small lure, a large number of whiting anglers now fish the New Jersey jetties with plugs and squids at dusk.

Maryland to Florida

Here we get back to the unbroken sand beaches again. (They start south of Atlantic City, New Jersey.) This is a region of very seasonal fishing. The fine white sand is good for bathers, but has little nourishment for fish life; therefore most surfing is for migratory species on their way up and down the coast. This means bluefish in April and October, weakfish and spotted sea trout in late fall, and channel bass and striped bass in April and October, although they are often caught in May, September, and November as well.

Channel bass—also known as red drum to distinguish them from their lazy relative, the black drum—have a couple of big spots, one on each side of the body near the base of the tail. The outer beaches of the Virginia barrier islands and the North Carolina outer banks are famed surfing areas for channel bass.

Fishing is much like Cape Cod striper angling except that cut bait, usually the head end of a mullet, mossbunker, or lafayette sliced diagonally, is used. Shedder crabs are good bait too but subject you to bother from kingfish and other little pecking species. Like New England, this is the land of the big, oversized surf rod; and you'll need plenty of muscle to plunk a half pound of bait and sinker about a hundred yards offshore. Also, like Cape Cod, this is beach-buggy country; and most anglers use one (rented) to cruise along the waterfront looking for suitable sloughs and holes and the flocks of screaming birds that hover over schools of channel bass or bluefish cutting up the bait fish.

Rather than a three-way sinker, many channel bass addicts use a fish-finder rig. The fish finder itself is made of heavy wire and has a snap at one end for attaching the sinker and a ring at the other end through which the line is passed. A rawhide thong connects the line and leader and serves as a stop for the fish finder, so that the sinker can't run out to the hook. When you have a hit, you can pay out line without the weight of the sinker frightening the fish.

Fishing for channel bass is mostly done during the day; and since the fish seen in the surf are rarely under twenty-five pounds, anything you hook will probably give you a battle to remember. You can get all kinds of other things too, including sharks and sting rays, black drum, and occasional oddities up from the tropics.

Surf-casting success south of Cape Hatteras generally diminishes until you reach the Florida peninsula. The problem is that the extremely flat sand bottom doesn't hold enough food to keep a fish population happy. Both good fishing and the slope of a shore are directly proportionate to the size of the shore's rocks and/or sand. If there are rocks and large pebbles, the shoreline drops off abruptly. Also, the rocks serve as a home for mussels and other animals in the ocean food chain. On Long Island and in northern New Jersey the shore is made up of rather coarse sand, and there is a good slope. From the Carolinas to Florida, however, the beach is practically like white talcum powder; and the flats of a very gentle slope extend quite far out. The result is negligible fishing. Another problem is that the farther south you get, the less effect you have from migrations. This doesn't mean that you won't get some sea trout, small channel bass, and blues while surf-casting from the Georgia Sea Islands, but these aren't exceptional surfing spots. Cape Hatteras, on the other hand, is at the edge of currents ridden by migrating hordes of fish and is therefore unusually productive.

Florida—East Coast

Surf-casting is good, if seasonal, down the Atlantic shore of the Florida peninsula. For one thing, there are tropical species here; and for another, many northern species end their migrations in Florida and adjacent waters.

Fall is pompano time for the Florida surf specialist. This is very similar to channel-bass fishing except that the best bait generally consists of beach bugs, the same little gray-and-white crustaceans that work so well with tautog farther north. The preferred rig is like a northern whiting rig, with a sinker at the tip end and a couple of leaders spaced up the line. A No. 1 hook is about right; and with rig, sandbugs, and the ability to cast a country mile, you're in business. Shrimp and pieces of clam are also good bait, and shedder crabs should work very well too. Pompano don't weigh over a couple of pounds, but even on a heavy surf outfit they give a respectable account of themselves. There's no tastier fish in the ocean.

The Florida surfer also carries a bunch of jigs and plugs for casting at schools of bluefish, Spanish mackerel, sea trout, channel bass, and other species that chase bait fish into the surf to feed, especially at dawn and dusk. Beaches near inlets—such as St. Lucie Inlet, Sebastian Inlet, and Jupiter Inlet—are especially good because fish cruise inshore to feed on bait fish swept out to sea from the fertile bays lying behind the beaches. Although best in fall and spring, Florida surf action continues all summer, especially from dusk until dawn; high noon at June on a Florida beach is a blinding experience that even the fish don't enjoy.

Florida to Mexico—The Gulf Coast

Since there's little surf in the Gulf of Mexico, you can hardly call fishing here surf-casting, but the light-tackle fan can have a good time fishing near the various passes (inlets) for sea trout, tarpon, and channel bass (known as redfish on the Gulf). This is mostly plug-casting with the same lures as those used in fresh water fishing for largemouth bass. Surface plugs with propellers fore and aft and poppers are especially favored, and the idea is to make a great commotion with the lure. Matagordo Island, north of Corpus Christi, Texas, is a particular favorite of the Gulf coast wading fisherman. You can also use bait and catch flounder, whiting (related to northern kingfish), and croakers, providing the plentiful salt water catfish and other pests don't spoil your fun. Throughout the Gulf region shrimp, whether alive or dead, is the standard bait for nearly all salt water fishing.

Pacific Coast

For practical purposes Pacific coast surf-casting can be divided into two areas, with San Francisco as the juncture. South from San Francisco there is a variety of surf perch, corbina, spotfin and yellow-fin croaker, opaleye, kelp bass, and rockfish. The rigs are basically the same as those used for bait fishing on the east coast, except that there is a bigger tendency toward a two-hook rig for surf perch and other small species. Mussels, clams, pile worms, and sand crabs are the principal baits used.

Around San Francisco itself, from Rockaway Beach to the Golden Gate, there is some surf-casting in the early summer for striped bass. This again is mostly bait fishing with sardines; however, the fish will sometimes hit stainless-steel jigs and plugs.

North of San Francisco the surf perch begin to dwindle; and there are more rockfish, cabezon, and greenling, plus flounder, ling-cod, and even a chance of halibut. Some years there are striped bass too, especially in the Coos Bay area of Oregon and even up into Washington. Additionally, surf-casters at the river mouths start taking salmon.

The cabezon, a close relative of the sea robin and other sculpins, is a weird-looking fellow who lives in rocky pockets and makes very good eating. Fishing for him is similar to east coast blackfishing. You hop around from rock to rock and lose many sinkers and hooks, but have a good time anyway.

On the Atlantic coast, the beaches south of New England are all sand; and many of them are long sandbars serving as barrier beaches for big salt water bays. The Pacific coast features rivers running directly into the sea. North of San Francisco there are almost no bays until you reach Coos Bay in Oregon, and from there north to Astoria the same situation prevails. Since their fishing environment has many more rocks than sandy beaches, most Pacific surfers are less interested in long cast and more interested in saving tackle. In rocky areas small tobacco sacks loaded with sand are favorite sinkers.

The only sandy areas north of San Francisco are a few Oregon and Washington beaches plus sandbars at river mouths, and these are greatly utilized by salmon-fishing enthusiasts. These men joyfully fling spoons and bait (usually sardines or anchovies) well out from shore into tidal pools. Seasonal timing, of course, is the most important thing here. August is probably the best month, featuring all kinds of contests, with prizes ranging up to automobiles for the biggest fish.

Pier and Jetty Fishing

The big advantage of a pier or long jetty is that it puts the angler out to sea a good deal farther than he could reach by casting from the shore. Aside from this, fishing is basically for the same species that you would get from sand or rocks ashore.

Because shifting sands and heavy storms are a bad combination for piers, there are only a few of them left on the Atlantic coast north of Florida, which still has quite a few. At least one pier near Wilmington, North Carolina, has had a large number of sailfish caught from it by anglers who utilize a unique rig that has a balloon to blow their live bait well out to sea from the end of the pier. Florida pier patrons catch many king mackerel and barracuda along with their Spanish mackerel and bottom species.

Pier fans can enjoy themselves in California, which has many fishing piers along the coast from Oregon to Mexico. Several species of croaker, surf perch, smelt, and corbina are caught, along with a few halibut, kingfish, rockfish, and occasional flounder. In New England, Oregon, and Washington, where rocks come down to the sea, there is little need for piers. A few erected in Massachusetts and Rhode Islands for millionaire striped-bass buffs a century ago are in ruins today. (In those days the prime bait was lobster tails!)

Fishing from a pier has both good and bad features. Some of the good features are that bait and tackle are available, fees are cheaper than those on a party boat, and you can get advice from the pro who runs the place. Also, the presence of a crowd of fishermen with

Surf, Pier, and Jetty Equipment and How to Use It

The basic thing about shore-based fishing is that like big-game hunting, you have to have enough gun to do the job. Translated into angling terms, this means that you must be able to reach the fish, so it's better to have too long a rod and too large a reel than you really need in order to be certain you can cast out to where the fish are. Also, a surf caster, like a turtle, has to carry everything on his back; and this means quite an array of equipment. Basically, this is what you need:

- surf rod (in calm weather, you can use a freshwater flipping rod and any reel that will hold at least 100 yards of 10 to 20 pound test line)
- surf reel
- sinkers
- connecting links
- squids, plugs, and other surf lures
- monofilament leader material
- tackle bag (to hold all this)
- gaff
- knife (with scaler)
- thread—for wrapping soft bait, such as pieces of crab
- waders and/or boots and/or sneakers
- dark glasses

- bait, or tools for acquiring same (such as a clam rake or seine)
- line
- swivels and fish finders
- fishhooks
- monofilament leader material
- cable wire (for leaders)
- first-aid kit
- head light (for night fishing)
- long-nosed pliers with wire cutters
- sharpening stone (for knife and hooks)
- reel oil, screwdriver, and wrenches
- suntan lotion
- hat or cap

It may seem like much, and unless you're going out at night or on slippery rocks and jetties you can do without some of it. There are, however, reasons for a load that you might think would break the proverbial camel's back. Seriously, all of it should weigh under ten pounds total.

bait definitely acts to attract fish. Some piers, including one in New Jersey, install chumming machines to lure fish and sink Christmas trees imbedded in concrete to attract marine life of all kinds; many even operate a restaurant or food stand. A pier is especially valuable in places like the southeastern United States coast, where a flat sand shelf extends well out from the beach, with combers too big for wading and water too shallow for fishing.

On the negative side, pier fishing can be crowded and dangerous. (Getting hit on the head by a quarter pound of lead could be disastrous.) Also, your fellow anglers tend to be noisy amateurs who cast over your line and make general nuisance of themselves. Another minus is that landing anything over ten pounds becomes a major project. Some piers have extra long handled nets or special nets on ropes that can be lowered under a big fish. On others, you must try to "walk" your catch ashore along the pier railing.

Jetty fishing is pier fishing on a lower level, usually just above the waves. On wet rocks you need ice creepers on your footgear or at least hobnails. Old golf shoes will do the job in warm weather. Jetties at inlets and harbor mouths can provide excellent fishing at times. Once again, they can be overcrowded and dangerous, especially at high tide. There are certainly thousands of them from Long Island to Florida and a few on the west coast too. They often get you out to where the fish are, and the fact that they break currents and form eddies will in itself attract fish to them; in fact, they are home for mussels, algae, and an entire chain of sea life including fish.

In some areas such as Florida, with its overseas highway to Key West, a good deal of bridge fishing is done. This is exactly like fishing from a pier except that you have to keep an eye out for traffic, and usually you can take advantage of the tide. By casting down-current, in the direction of the tide, and working your bait or lure back up against the current, you are moving your offering out in front of the fish, who lie with their heads up-current. This method and also its direct opposite, drifting a bait with the current, are the two best ways of achieving success from a bridge. Otherwise, a bridge is simply a pier anchored at both ends instead of one.

XXII.

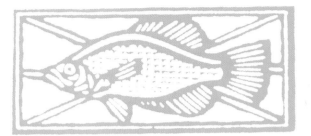

Bay and Inlet Fishing

Starting well out at sea with sharks, swordfish, and tuna, we've come into the surf to fish for striped bass, croakers, and rockfish. Now we're going through the inlets and behind the beaches for a look at the plentiful fish life in the bays.

First, however, one note of warning. Many important species of food and game fish come into bays to spawn and start a new generation. It is unfortunate, therefore, that the pollution of estuarine areas is reaching the point where many bays, especially in the Northeast, will stop supporting marine life. This will certainly have an adverse effect upon fishing. In fact, it already has had such an effect in the New York City area.

Shallow, sand-bottomed, warmed by the sun, and protected from the ocean by sand dunes, the bays of the Atlantic coast are an ideal nursery area for small fish. And where there are little fish, there are also bigger ones too, eagerly in search of dinner. It's odd to realize, but a fish can eat his own children or nephews and nieces without a qualm. All his dull brain knows is that something edible and bite-sized is moving nearby.

Generally speaking, northern bay fishing is mostly bottom fishing, and southern bay fishing is mainly top-water fishing with lures. If you really want to, however, you can use about the same tactics on a Connecticut striped bass that you would employ on a Bahamas bonefish. And, conversely, whether you fish for flounder in Nova Scotia or sheepshead in the Keys, you're bottom fishing with much the same rig. The emphasis does shift from top to bottom as you go north, nevertheless, and this is true on both coasts.

As was done with surf-casting, we'll take a wide swing around North America and look at bay fishing in every area.

New England and the Maritimes

Aside from occasional schools of small mackerel that can be caught on spinning lures, most bay fishing in the Northeast is bottom fishing. Also, because a boat can take you where you ought to go, most bay fishing is boat fishing. Flounders, porgies, blackfish, and a few tom-cod are the major species. The basic rig for all of these is a three-way swivel, a sinker just heavy enough to get you easily on the bottom, and a two-hook rig, with the second hook tied into the leader of the first hook. If you change hook sizes with the seasons, this rig will catch you fish until the proverbial cows come home.

Of course, you've got to locate the right spot. As in fresh water, the fish aren't spread out uniformly across a bay bottom. They concentrate in holes, near rocky shoals, at the edge of tide rips, and so forth. In any new area you should ask directions from a native, especially one who makes a living selling bait and tackle—he wants you to have a good day and return to him.

One big aid that many anglers overlook is chum. This can be anything from a store-bought chum pot filled with crushed clams or mussels to an old onion sack filled with the same, or, where available, even a mossbunker "log." If you can't get anything else, you can lower a well-punched can of sardines or dog food or even canned corn to the bottom and do quite well. When you bottom fish, it makes sense to have your chum on the bottom and a bit forward of your lines so that the fish have to come up-current and hit your rig before they get at the chum.

Another big help to bottom anglers is good eyesight. When you see a fleet of anchored boats busily fishing, don't just come up close and drop the anchor. Look them over carefully and note where fish are coming aboard and where anglers are practically asleep with boredom. If you can, try to anchor about fifty yards or so up-current of those who are having the most success. Of course, if you're fishing for blackfish that live entirely in the rocks, all you can do is look for big, upcropping rocks to fish near.

Other good places to anchor are along the edges of channels. Never in the channel! If you anchor in a marked channel you are subject to arrest by the United States Coast Guard and arraignment before a federal magistrate, who will probably give you a large fine. Don't risk this. Never anchor in a channel or near pilings, bridges, and other obstructions or anywhere two channels meet. And never tie your boat to a channel marker.

The best baits in this area depends on where you fish. One point to remember is that you should use the lightest tackle possible. A fresh water spinning or bait casting outfit will handle any flounder that ever swam, and with ten-pound test line you can get on the bottom with about an ounce of lead. This is a big advantage in feeling nibbles; and since bay fish can swim around your rig, the less conspicuous it is, the better.

Mid-Atlantic

New York, New Jersey, and Delaware bays offer a much broader choice of fish, and one which changes greatly with the seasons. Early spring fishing is for blacks and flounders, as in New England. Then come fluke, kingfish, porgies, bluefish (including tiny snapper blues), and striped bass. In the southern part of this range there are also weakfish. In

177

addition, Delaware Bay offers black drum in June.

When bottom fishing for flounder and blackfish, you should move your rig a bit from time to time (in fact, this is why a light sinker is an advantage). Some of the summer species, especially striped bass and fluke, can be caught better from a drifting boat than while at anchor.

Depending on the latitude and the season, striped bass are found in bays and estuaries between mid-March and mid-May. Around bridges and inlets, and in canals with a heavy tidal flow, probably the best way to catch them is by drifting sandworms just off the bottom. This requires the standard three-way swivel, a three-foot leader, and a light piece of monofilament tied to about an ounce of sinker so that you can lose the sinker if it's snagged without the entire rig going with it. Toss this overboard and let the sinker bounce along the bottom while you putt-putt fairly slowly downcurrent. (If you go upcurrent, you raise your bait too high from the bottom.) Whether you simply drift with the current or get into gear and use the motor is a matter that takes some experimentation to decide. My personal observation is that if your worm is down near the bottom, you can't go fast enough to take it away from a bass that wants to eat it.

Father inland, where the tidal currents slacken, you can still successfully drift with worms for striped bass by using a cork bobber about four feet above a No. 2 Eagleclaw hook. Hook one or two worms through the head and let the wind and tide move you along. If you have a light boat, rowing gently with the tide will move your bait along naturally. This style of fishing is especially effective after dark. Of course, you can anchor too, but the more water you cover, the better; and there are many times when boats anchored in a supposedly good location do nothing while a school of bass is feeding a few hundred yards away. Casting small plugs and lures, even streamer flies, also takes springtime stripers in bays. (This is true in California too.)

After bay striper fishing slackens off, action with bluefish and fluke commences. Most bay bluefish are caught by trolling with a small wobbling spoon and a piece of pork rind. The knack in this is to hit the right speed, which is usually about five to eight miles per hour. In a small boat with an outboard motor the speed you hit with the throttle just below "Start" is about right. Usually, you'll see other boats and can gauge your speed to fit in with theirs. If you see a boat catching fish when you're not, watch two things: (1) Are the fish biting when the boat is going with or against the tide? (2) What speed is the boat traveling at? Unlike fresh water fishing, the lure itself is usually of minor importance as long as it wobbles and is shiny.

Bluefish can also be caught by casting small surface plugs, wobbling spoons, and other lures; this method is more fun than trolling. It's a good idea to troll with light tackle until you locate a school of fish and then drift and cast to them. Fast reeling usually works best, and when working poppers you want them to make quite a bit of noise and to splash on the surface. (This applies to nearly all salt water surface fishing; the reason is that you're not imitating a dying bug or drowning mouse, but a lively top-water minnow scurrying to escape.) Although most bay bluefish weigh only three pounds or less, still be careful when unhooking them. Even the tiniest blue can deliver a nasty bite.

Fluke are probably the most important summer bay fish in the mid-Atlantic region. These big summer flounder are almost always caught by drifting over fairly shallow sandy bottom. With big mouths and sharp teeth, this species and related southern forms feeds on live fish. Therefore, a moving bait is almost a must. Drifting or slow trolling behind an outboard lets you cover a great deal of bottom in minimum time. Again, your best rig is the three-way swivel with a light sinker, a two-foot leader, and either a $^2/_0$ Eagleclaw or Carlisle hook. There's one difference: Early in the season fluke bite very short, and you have to use some kind of tandem hook to catch fish. When the water is cold, fluke will sneak up on your bait, clamp down on its tail, and simply hold on. The so-called sand-eel rig, which has a tiny bait-holder hook in front and a big tail hook, is one solution to this problem. Another is to put the barb of one hook through the eye of a second hook, thus making your own tandem outfit. The best fluke baits are small minnows, called killies in the New York-New Jersey area. Spearing, sand-eels, squid strips, and fish-shaped slices of other fish, including fluke, are strong contenders too.

As with other bay fishing, you should stay out of channels when you're drifting or anchored. Trolling, or even drifting with an idling motor so you can get away from other boats, will enable you to fish the channel edges. Early in the season the outgoing tide is usually the best place for fishing because the water has had a chance to be sun-warmed. Later in the season the tides don't make too much difference except that high water gives you a chance to push into little creeks that can't be fished at other times. With a shallow-draft boat you can often catch fluke in a foot of water faster than in a channel. When the water is muddy, a flasher spinner sometimes makes the difference between fish and no fish. This varies so greatly with the area that there is no hard and fast rule.

As the summer advances, small porgies, white perch, sand perch, croakers, and weakfish are found in the bays. This is mostly bottom fishing that is much the same and in the same locations as flounder fishing except with shedder-crab bait, if it is available. Otherwise, worms are excellent. Use small hooks; No. 4 is about right.

Toward fall, snapper fishing is a big mid-Atlantic bay attraction. These snappers are actually baby bluefish born that spring and grown to approximately six to twelve inches by the first frost. The old cane pole (or fiberglass rod if you're modern), with float, tiny sinker, and long-shank hook, is still good. Be sure you have a long-shank hook though, as the snappers delight in biting monofilament leaders in half. The best bait is spearing hooked through the head and then again through the tail, since snappers usually hit the tail first. Chumming with a few chopped-up mossbunkers dangled overboard in an onion sack and worked up and down occasionally will usually bring snappers right into the boat, especially if you're fishing a channel edge near a grassy shore.

Sophisticates take snappers on tiny trout-sized wobbling spoons cast into the chum and reeled fast. You can use streamer flies too; but you'd better be rich, because the tiny, sharp teeth of these fish will ruin any fly very quickly. (For real action, put a spearing tail on a tiny wobbler and work it deep and slowly.)

Snappers, porgies, and white perch usually leave the bays when the first autumnal storms take place. Striped bass and flounder often move back in, and the flounder (not fluke) will stay and bite until the water temperature goes down into the thirties in December.

No survey of mid-Atlantic bay fishing would be complete without mentioning eels and eeling. Genuine fish despite their snaky appearance, eels have a fascinating life history. After spawning in the Sargasso Sea, they make their way up the coast as tiny elvers. The females run far upstream into fresh water, and the males usually stay in salt water bays and estuaries. When their built-in time clock rings and spawning time approaches, the females descend to salt water and join the males in the long pilgrimage back to the Caribbean, where they spawn and die. Before leaving for the Sargasso Sea, the departing eels lose their usual green-black color and turn silvery. Thus a silver eel is one about to go on its spawning run.

Delicious eating, eels are sought by many people. Most soft-bottomed bays are literally paved with them; they're caught, mostly at night, by hook and line and with an ingenious device called an eel bob. An eel bob consists of a mass of worms, usually a dozen or so big nightcrawlers spiked with a few bloodworms and sandworms. This mess of wrigglers is carefully wrapped in fine sewing thread, and a sinker is used to get it on the bottom. When an eel bites, the angler jerks and catches the eel's fine teeth in the wrapped thread. Swiftly boating his catch, he shakes the bob over a potato sack and the eel falls off—into the bag. This clever method actually works and avoids the very difficult problem of unhooking a writhing, slimy eel whose tail is tying your rig into a tangle. An eel landed by conventional methods is usually hooked deep, and the best idea is to cut your hook off and put him in a bag to be skinned later. If you don't have a handful of sand, an eel is nearly impossible to hold. They're fun to catch, though, and surprisingly strong.

Another method of eeling, which dates from colonial days, is eel spearing. Bay eels go into the mud during the winter months. In fact, they gather in wriggling knots in deep muddy holes on the bay bottom. An eel spear differs from the classical weapon of chivalry in that it's designed to catch the eel on the upstroke rather than on the downstroke. The eel spear has a handle about twenty feet long and is poked into the mud and retrieved by a yank. If an eel is felt wiggling, you pull in the long shaft hand over hand and dump your prize in the boat. If no eel is felt, you keep poking around.

Ice is no barrier to eel spearing. The eelers chop holes in likely spots, poke their long spears through, and move the spears around until they hit a knot of eels. The result is a large number of holes in the ice and much bad feeling between skaters and ice-boaters on the one hand, and the eelers on the other. With prosperity and a waning of the importance of eels in the diet of many families, eel spearing is today a dying art; however, it's quite a lot of fun, and the results, when properly smoked or pickled, are much tastier than any non-eater of eels would imagine. In bygone years huge barges filled with live eels were brought down to eastern seaboard cities from Canada's St. Lawrence River for traditional European cooks to use. An eel is certainly no uglier than a lobster. Give him a try. today, American eels are exported overseas and eeling is regulated.

Besides this common eel there are a couple of other eel species. The moray eel, found only in the tropics, is a vicious inhabitant of holes in coral formations. The conger eel, a milder type, is occasionally caught by bottom-fishing party boats. Both of these are much larger than the common eel, which usually weighs about a pound or two; and neither conger nor moray eels are found in shallow, muddy bays except in rare instances.

Chesapeake Bay and South

Probably no body of water so easily fished by so many anglers is as full of fish as Chesapeake Bay, a hundred-odd miles of wide, shallow, fertile water that runs from north of Baltimore down to the Virginia capes. Because it marks the northern limits of many southern species and the southern limit of northern fishes, the Chesapeake area probably has more varied fishing than you will find anyplace else in North America. In its upper reaches, you can even get fresh water species mixed in.

Following a collapse of the Chesapeake Bay striped bass population, Maryland and Virginia took action. Beginning in the early 1990's, both recreational and commercial seasons were closed for several years while state hatchery resources restocked the entire Chesapeake system. When fishing was again permitted, salt water fishing licenses were required for all anglers, along with special permits for commercial operators. In addition, there are daily bag limits and size limits that are strictly enforced, and the season in which you are allowed to fish is short. Seasons, limits and size requirements may be expected vary a little each year, but the most current information will be found when you purchase your mandatory fishing license. If you fish with a private boat owner or professional captain, there are no license requirements. The vessel operator, however, must have a license that covers all passengers. There are, however, both size and quantity limits based on the number of anglers aboard. Current minimum size for each fish during the open season is eighteen inches in Chesapeake Bay and twenty four inches in the adjacent ocean. There are exceptions, and these will change annually. Be sure to check when you obtain either your individual license or your boat owner or operator license.

Chumming for rockfish with live shrimp is very successful all over the Bay area. This method also brings many weakfish and spotted sea trout aboard. A brand-new fishing method around Love Point near Annapolis consists of chumming with soft clams that are run through a grinder, shells and all. The bait here is a soft clam too. What else?

Other popular Chesapeake species include croaker, white perch, weakfish, spotted sea trout, bluefish, Norfolk spot, and sand perch. Aside from bluefish, weakies, and sea trout, most of these are caught bottom fishing from charter and party boats. Cobia, dolphin, bonito, and other blue-water fish are also found in the Bay, but the amateur boatman isn't apt to run into them.

Farther up the Bay, especially north of Baltimore around the Susquehanna flats, there's excellent fishing for fresh water varieties. It's exactly like shallow-water lake fishing and includes angling for chain pickerel (pike in Maryland), largemouth bass, yellow perch, and sunfish. These fresh water fish are found in brackish waters all around the edge of the Bay, and in many places you can catch white and yellow perch, rockfish, and an occasional largemouth bass all within the same area, a factor which makes for interesting fishing. (A note of interest is that there's very good fishing for largemouth bass in Currituck Sound in North Carolina. This is so far from the sea that the water is mostly fresh, and the bass fishing is like that in any other good largemouth area.)

May is usually shad-fishing time on the Susquehanna flats near Havre de Gras. Angling for these salt water migrants in this area is done by trolling a tiny, shiny bucktail, called a shad dart, on a three-way swivel. The dart is at the end of a couple of feet of leader, and the swivel also holds a two- to four-ounce sinker to bring you near the bottom, where the fish are. Below the dams on the Susquehanna and in a couple of spots on the Potomac and Patuxent rivers casters take shad on tiny bucktails and gold spinners. (You can do this up the Connecticut River too.) Although oily, shad, including the roe, are a gastronomic treat; but the season is over and gone within a few weeks.

East and south of the Chesapeake, in the bays behind the sea islands of Virginia, channel bass, or red drum, are a big spring specialty. This holds true through the Carolinas into Georgia. Mostly, spring red-drum fishing consists of anchoring at a hole or channel junction, baiting with half a small fish or clams or shedder crab, and waiting. The fish weigh about twenty-five pounds or more, so you need regular thirty-pound gear or a light surf outfit.

Weakfish and their kissing cousins, the spotted sea trout, are the most important bay fish south of the Chesapeake and all the way to Mexico. Fishing the creeks and back bays with shedder crab, chumming with shrimp, and casting small plugs, especially those with a propeller at each end, are good ways of getting a sackful of trout. (Actually, these fish aren't even obscurely related to the genuine trout species. They weren't named this by scientists, however. Some early settler knew that trout had spots, saw that these new fish had spots, so therefore they were trout. At that, this is better logic than some of today's leading public figures use.)

If you're bay fishing with bait, a No. 1 or No. 2 Sproat, Eagleclaw, or O'Shaugnessy hook will do for everything except channel bass. For them you need about a No. $^4/_0$ to handle the big baits used. The same three-way swivel rig we've been mentioning will suffice in almost all fishing except chumming, when you fish either with a bobber drifted out with the chum slick or take off even the bobber and strip the line out.

Florida

Everyone knows about Cape Kennedy and outer space, but few people know that this area had, and partially still has, some of the finest weakfishing in the world, with many "trout" up to six and seven pounds available to anglers with surface plugs and fresh water spinning or bait casting gear. Once you get down into the Florida peninsula, you can add a good many more bay species, including Spanish mackerel, ladyfish, tarpon, and snook, plus dozens of species of snapper and grunt, and the famous bonefish and permit. Bonefish country is also barracuda country; and these, along with sharks, sawfish, and sting rays, help keep life interesting on the southern flats.

Ladyfish, tarpon, and snook are caught along with the various snappers by casting lures into the mangrove-encrusted shores of Florida waterways. In this kind of fishing you never know what's going to hit your plug next, yet it's about the same as fresh water plug-casting except that you have to watch your tides carefully. (Otherwise, you could be stranded.)

Snook, a long, silvery fish with a black line running from bow to stern, are also found around bridges and docks and are often caught around Florida causeways by bait-fishermen and plug-casters at night. Live bait is the method here, and in this kind of fishing a bright lantern hung near the water attracts both bait fish and snook. (In surf-casting, a lantern frightens most of the fish away.)

Spanish mackerel run in and out of bays and are caught in exactly the same manner as small bluefish: by trolling and casting small spoons. A whipping action of the rod while reeling, called the Florida whip, is used by most of the experts. Winter through early spring is the mackerel season.

Bonefish, permit, and tarpon are found out on the flats. (Tarpon usually prefer deeper water and will run far up rivers but are found in deeper holes and channels throughout the Keys.) For this kind of fishing you need a guide both to know where to go and to handle the boat when you get there. Also, it takes a keen eye to spot a bonefish. Furthermore, running your own boat around the thousands of islands in the Bay of Florida and the Bahamas can be a good way to get lost, lose a propeller, run aground, and have a number of other mishaps that can be either funny or deadly serious, depending on the circumstances. You can catch bonefish and permit with a fresh water spinning or bait casting rod and any reel that will hold at least a hundred yards (more is better) of ten-pound test line. The better and more accurate your casting, the better your fishing will be, since you want to get your lure or bait, usually a shrimp, in front of a bonefish, but not so near that you'll alarm him.

For tarpon you'll need heavier tackle, but a fairly stiff seven- to nine-foot rod and a reel holding two hundred yards of twenty-pound line should be adequate. Tarpon fishing is especially good at night in the entire area from the Keys south to Mexico and beyond. Many anglers in the Marathon and Islamorada area fish at night with live bait or with cut mullet and blue crab. They usually use a long cable wire leader and a No. $^6/_0$ O'Shaugnessy hook. Fishing in the passes near bridges can be very good in season, with June being the best month. An especially famous tarpon area in June is at Boca Grande, where drift fishing inside the inlet is productive. Live crabs and bait fish are fished near the bottom and sometimes a rig resembling the west coast cannonball is used. Sinkers are attached with soft wire that breaks off when the hooked tarpon makes his first jump. Thus you play the fish without a lead sinker flying about.

Charter rates for this kind of are expensive in Florida and the Keys, and probably a bit less in the Bahamas. Always make certain what you'll be paying before you make final arrangements for your trip. April through June are the best months.

As you go south, bay fishing is excellent in the Chesapeake area all summer, very good in the Carolinas and Georgia in spring and fall, and excellent in Florida in the winter and spring. Winter winds are the big Florida and Bahamas curse. These are fine for sailfish offshore, but they stir up the shallow, silty bottom so that fishing is impossible.

Gulf Coast

The Gulf coast bays along Florida, Louisiana, Alabama, Mississippi, and Texas are much like the sounds of the Carolinas. Even the fish, notably sea trout and redfish (channel bass), are the same, and fishing methods are similar except for an even greater emphasis on surface plugs. A regular fresh water spinning or bait casting outfit with a ten-pound test line will do a good job on trout and redfish anywhere, especially since the Gulf variety are much smaller than their counterparts in Virginia and North Carolina.

One big specialty along the Gulf is night fishing around offshore oil rigs. Lights from flares and lanterns attract shrimp, which in turn attract the trout; and a noisy surface plug worked at a good speed will help you catch more than you know what to do with.

Another important southern surface rig is the popping cork. This is a flat- or concave-topped bobber placed about a foot ahead of the bait and worked along the surface like a fast-popping lure. Attracted to the noise, the fish sees the bait and hits. Used mostly with shrimp bait, this rig is particularly effective on sea trout. Even market fishermen use it with long cane poles.

Tarpon, which have been caught as far north as Virginia on a rod and reel, are a special attraction along the Gulf. As in Florida, they are found around river mouths and inlets (called passes on the Gulf) and will give an angler excitement. They'll hit crab bait, fish, and artificials, especially big plugs that can be either cast or trolled. Because tarpon have very hard, bony mouths and are high jumpers, they are very difficult to land; but since they really aren't edible, there isn't much point in killing them anyway. It doesn't seem possible, but this big, shiny fish is closely related to herring and anchovy and other much smaller species. Of very ancient lineage, tarpon are related to several extinct giant herrings; and one of the most famous fish fossils ever found consists of one of these with a smaller fish (its last meal) in its stomach.

Pacific Coast

There are few real bays along the Pacific coast. This is because the Pacific coast, from Alaska south to at least Chile, rises out of the sea. The Atlantic coast sinks into the sea, and former sunken valleys have become bays. As a river valley slips under water, the water rises so that what was once a brook tumbling through a meadow becomes a tidal basin contained by what were once hilltops or ridges on either side of the valley.

Starting down in Mexico, the biggest bay from Panama to Alaska is the Gulf of California, which is really an arm of the sea. This is a famous haunt of roosterfish, Sierra mackerel,

Pacific sailfish, and literally hundreds of other species, including marlin, dolphin, tuna, and albacore. Because of its size, you need a cruiser for safety; many of these are available for charter at Guaymas and other ports. Adventure-loving Arizonians trailer good-sized craft over the desert to the gulf, and it certainly looks odd to see a big cruiser trailed along through the tumbleweed and mesquite on its way to a weekend of salt water fishing.

Most fishing in the Gulf of California is trolling with spoons or cut bait; but where schools of fish can be located, you can cast plugs and spoons for maximum results. Roosterfish, which feed on the Sierra mackerel, are among the world's harder-fighting fish, and their big dorsal fin adds to their color and attraction. Bottom fishing is excellent too, but is no different from that on the Atlantic seaboard. Slices of fish fillet are the usual bait; and the standard three-way swivel rig, with about a size $^4/_0$ hook, is correct.

As you move north into California, San Francisco Bay is the first baylike body of water smaller than a tiny harbor. It's famous for striped bass, and bait fishing and casting lures for these "linesiders" is as popular here as in Chesapeake Bay. San Francisco Bay itself is only a small part of the inland waterways at the mouth of the Sacramento and San Joaquin rivers, with San Pablo Bay, Grizzly Bay, Suisun Bay, Honker Bay, and Sherman Lake all being part of this complex, which also includes a good many sloughs and connecting channels.

There are dozens of boat-launching ramps and rowboat-rental docks in this area, and fishing extends as far east as Stockton and Sacramento. Most fishing in the delta and upriver areas is with sardine and sculpin bait that is used on the bottom. Nearer the ocean there is more trolling and casting with plugs and spoons and drift fishing with live bait. This drifting is exactly the same as fishing for fluke on the east coast except that live anchovy or herring, rather than strips of fish or killies, are used.

Farther north, the next real complex of inland salt water is at Puget Sound. From there up into Alaska a broken coastline and hundreds of offshore islands and promontories provide fishing that is sheltered from the giant swells and ferocious polar winds common to most of the ocean in this area. This is primarily trolling for king and silver salmon, and with heavy tidal currents you need a sea-worthy boat and enough horsepower to make headway. Big silver spoons of various styles are the favorite lures. When the salmon get up near the surface, the fishing, especially off Vancouver Island, is excellent. Coho, or silver, salmon seem to come to the surface and feed at the change of tides and at this time can be caught on a streamer fly, fly-and-spinner combination, and small plugs and wobbling spoons.

King, or Chinook, salmon are important fish in the Northwest. Rigged herring trolled slowly with a cannonball sinker are prime lures; but the fish can be taken on spoons, spinners, plugs, and sometimes on streamer flies. These Chinooks are much bigger than the silvers and usually swim deeper, thus making them more difficult to locate. A rigged herring used with a flasher, or dodger, in front is a prime bait for trolling. This rig requires two short leaders with about two feet between the sinker and the dodger and another couple of feet between the dodger and the bait.

Bottom fishing in the Puget Sound area and farther north produces a tremendous array of rockfish. Because salmon are the glamour species, the bottom-feeding varieties of rockfish simply aren't fished for. There are literally dozens of them, and they are mostly fun to catch and good eating. The biggest problem is getting snagged in the rocky bottom. This can be overcome by using either a sinker on a breakaway piece of light line or using a tobacco sack with sand inside in lieu of a conventional sinker. Jigging just above the bottom with a heavy bucktail-type lure is seldom done but should be very successful, since the up-pointed hook won't snag.

East coast fishermen who want to fish deep turn to wire core and solid monel wire lines. West coasters seem to prefer giant cannonball sinkers. If you like to experiment, there's a likelihood that a combination of monel line and a planer (a device shaped to slant down deep in the water when it's trolled and often used by bluefish charter boats in the Atlantic) would beat the cannonballs, be easier to use, and cost less too. Whatever you use, about three feet of monofilament is tied to a swivel as a leader.

XXIII.

A Look at Salt Water Fly Fishing

There's nothing really new about salt water fly fishing . Fly rods have been used, notably for weakfish and bluefish, since before the turn of the century. During the past decade a great deal of interest has developed in fly fishing generally, and in salt water fly fishing particularly. This is due to a wide range of reasons.

First and foremost, the development of synthetic fly lines to replace silk have made salt water use of the fly rod practical. Silk fly lines rot or gum up into a solid mass unless washed off in fresh water. The improvement in synthetic fiber fly rods was another big help. These can now be made big enough and stiff enough at reasonable prices. Previously, the salt water fly-rod addict who went after big fish had to spend a relatively hefty sum for an English-style salmon rod. (This wasn't necessary so much to handle the fish as to cast the heavy flies.) And finally, the introduction of anodized aluminum reels and stainless-steel guides has made fly tackle completely rustproof.

Practically any so-called innovation in fishing is partly public relations. Salt water fly fishing is no exception. The people who went in for it can be divided into a few classes. There were dedicated trout and salmon buffs who really enjoyed fly casting and wanted to try it anywhere and everywhere. There were a few expert anglers looking for a new and more challenging method of taking bonefish and tarpon. Finally, there were (and are) a small army of publicity-hungry characters seeking a way to get their picture in sports magazines and newspapers and their names in the record books. Partly because of their value to makers of fishing tackle, and partly because there are many people hungry for fame and adulation, so-called world's records for various species of fish are almost a racket. Today, in addition to all-tackle records for the largest fish of a species, there are record fish for nearly every line-test made. If somebody has won the ten-pound test line record, you may still set a record with a smaller fish caught on a six-pound test line. That is, you can set the record provided you notify the proper authorities, submit notarized statements and a

Bonefish flies

sample piece of the line used, and so forth.

Therefore, for the past few years the publicity hounds and a few lucky and well-informed run-of-the-mill sportsmen have been very busy establishing so-called world's records on the fly rod. The only reason I call them "so-called world's records" is that they are as international as baseball's world series. Only a very few anglers outside the United States know anything about these records; and, as a matter of fact, the records themselves are well restricted to species caught by American anglers.

I'm not opposed to records. I simply think they are superfluous to what should be the objectives of any angler: recreation, relaxation, and good sportsmanship with pleasant companions. Like the fellow who refused to bet on horse races because it was quite obvious to him that one horse could run faster than another, it's quite obvious to me that one striped bass, or tuna, or bonefish, or permit can be a couple of inches longer or fatter than another. So what! In salt water all a record may prove is that you had more money for guides and more time to go traveling and fishing than most other people. Where's the glory in this?

Both in the Northeast and around the San Francisco Bay area the prime saltwater fly casting target is the striped bass. Ninety per cent of this fishing is in shallow inland waters. Either wading or in a small boat, the angler looks for signs of bass activity along the shore. Then he closes in to casting range. When no fish are rolling or rising, the only thing left to do is cast blind in areas where they should be. An electric fish finder might be a help except usually the water is four or five feet deep; and unless a fish is directly under the boat, you'd never spot it.

If bass are up on the surface chasing bait, the natural thing to do is put on a popping lure with a floating line. Cast as far as you can and work the popper in with a series of fast jerks. If this doesn't work, go a bit slower.

When the fish are down deep, most anglers shift to a sinking line and a big streamer fly on a No. 1/0 nickel-steel hook. The pattern doesn't seem too important, although there are two schools of thought here. One group likes streamers tied in a mixture of white, blue, and green with much tinsel, thus imitating a silversides or other minnow. The other group uses patterns like the Honey Blonde and Strawberry Blonde, which imitate nothing but have good results when worked fairly rapidly.

This type of fly fishing is successful from Nova Scotia and New Brunswick down to Chesapeake Bay. At both ends of this range you can get results nearly all summer. In the middle (New York, New Jersey, and Connecticut) the fish are usually in the bays and estuaries only during the spring run, which lasts about a month, approximately from mid-May to mid-June. San Francisco Bay fishing is seasonal too, with spring the best time. This is when the fish get up into the Sacramento estuary and the maze of canals during their spawning run.

Along the east coast bluefish and mackerel move into bays, and fishing for them with streamers and poppers can be very good. Flies are easily damaged, and you need a short strand of wire to keep fish teeth from your monofilament leader. This again is seasonal fishing and usually best in midsummer. In Florida the same lures work on Spanish mackerel from December through March.

There's been little fly-rod fishing from the Chesapeake Bay south to Florida except in Currituck Sound for largemouth bass, and this is really not salt water fishing at all. Weakfish and spotted sea trout and small red drum will hit a streamer or popper, but most fishing activity is with spinning or conventional tackle even in the bays. Southern salt water fishermen are basically a conservative group that see no reason to change when their current angling methods work very well. Also, except for a tiny minority of fly-rod buffs, who enjoy bass and pickerel fishing with the long rod, trout and trout tackle in the mid-South are found up in the mountains hundreds of miles from the seacoast.

Aside from San Francisco Bay, the most important salt water fly fishing area on the Pacific coast is in the Puget Sound-Vancouver Island area, where swarms of silver salmon come up

Bonefish

to the surface and feed during the turn of the tide. This is mostly streamer-fishing resembling that for striped bass except that you must locate a school of surfacing fish to get results. The Campbell River section of northern Vancouver Island is world-famous, and streamer-casting there for silver salmon from a small boat is as big a thrill as fly fishing for Atlantic salmon on east coast rivers.

The most famous new development in salt water fly fishing is casting for bonefish and tarpon in Florida Bay and throughout the Bahamas. It involves poling a small boat over the endless flats until fish are spotted and then stalking into casting range. Stiff winds, especially in early spring, are no help at all.

Bonefish are bottom feeders and generally seem to go for a pinkish or off-yellow shrimp imitation worked on the bottom so that it produces little puffs of sand when it's moved along. Tarpon go for big white, yellow, red and white, and other such gaudy streamers, especially when the streamers are tied with a divided wing that gives a kind of breathing effect when retrieved in a series of long jerks.

Because of the natural limitations of fly tackle, which is quite useless away from shallow water, catching marlin, sailfish, and tuna on a fly is a stunt more than anything else. You have to find surfacing fish, get within casting range, stop the boat, and hope for a hit; and even the most powerful fly rod is a poor tool with which to toss a hunk of hair or feathers big enough to interest a large blue-water game fish. It can be done, but lightweight conventional tackle is better suited and just as sporting. This type of stunt fishing is best left to people fishing for records and notoriety rather than enjoyment.

If you're seriously thinking of taking up fly casting in salt water, you'll be glad to know that your investment is equipment can be quite limited. Practically any bass bug-action or salmon-action fly rod from eight and a half to nine and half feet will do the job for you. Stainless-steel ring guides instead of the usual easy-rust snake guides on most fly rods are a help and will give you better casting distance. There are special salt water fly reels made today with adjustable drags. Unless you're going after big tarpon, a regular Atlantic-salmon reel big enough to hold two hundred yards of fifteen-pound test backing line in addition to your casting line is sufficient. It's a smart idea to have two reels, one with a sinking casting line and the other with a floating casting line. This lets you switch from streamer to poppers within a couple of minutes.

These are some of the preferred patterns:

Bonbright Tarpon Streamer	Coronation
Coho Special	Honey Blonde
Gibb's Striper Special	Pink Shrimp
Strawberry Blonde	

Any synthetic fly line numbered to balance your rod will do a good job in salt water. The color doesn't seem too important, especially since you'll use a long leader.

Guides in the Marathon and Bahamas areas used to buy lengths of one-hundred-pound test monofilament and then machine this down to a torpedo casting taper—now torpedo tapers are available on the mass market. They are useful for two reasons: first, they believe the line is less visible; second, they find that the monofilament slides through the guides easier and makes longer casts possible, and when you're after easily frightened bonefish that will cut and run at the shadow of a rod, the farther you can cast the better.

Leaders are just as important in salt water fly casting as in fresh water. Because they must be heavy enough to turn over a big fly or popper, they are seldom tapered down to less than ten-pound test. When fishing for big or toothy fish, add about six inches to a foot of thirty-pound test to your leader tip as a shock leader to absorb the shock of a strike and take some abrasion. For fish like blues and barracuda, you need a short strand of wire. This can have a tiny swivel for connecting to your leader, and a snap for quick changing of lures. Twenty-pound test here is ample.

As has been indicated, the well-equipped salt water fly fisher needs many less lures than his fresh water cousin. A half dozen popping lures, either wood, cork, or deer hair in all white, red and white, all yellow, and blue and white, are ample. These are about double the size used for fresh water and usually have a No. $^{4}/_{0}$ O'Shaugnessy hook.

A selection of streamers tied on stainless-steel or nickel-steel hooks in sizes ranging from No. 2 up to $^{2}/_{0}$ can run to a half dozen patterns or more. The small sizes are best in very shallow water, especially for bonefish and permit, both of which can be frightened by the splash of an oversized fly too close.

Most of these are tied with bucktail or polar-bear hair wings rather than the feather wings used in fresh water streamer flies. Those with feather wings usually have the wings split so that they have a breathing action when paused during the retrieve.

Also, the following fresh water patterns are very useful when tied on nickel-plated hooks in size $^{1}/_{0}$ and larger:

Grey Ghost	Silver Doctor
Parmachenee Belle	White Maribou

XXIV.

A Survey of Salt Water Fishing Equipment

Many years ago, during World War II, railroad stations were festooned with signs asking "Is this trip necessary?" You could really ask the same question about salt water fishing tackle.

Generally speaking, if your salt water fishing is going to be confined to shallow bays plus an occasional trip on a charter boat (with the tackle provided by the skipper) you'll get by perfectly well with a fresh water spinning or bait casting outfit. If you're going to fish in the ocean, however, you'll want one of the many types of salt water outfits available. This isn't a matter of how large the fish are but basically a question of reaching them.

A surf-caster who wants to plunk a heavy sinker 250 feet to 300 feet from the beach and against the wind can't do this with a fishing outfit designed to handle $3/8$-ounce to $5/8$-ounce lures. The party-boat customer who wants to bottom fish in eighty feet of water needs a rod and reel and line that will handle a half pound or more of lead sinker with enough reserve backbone to hook a fish. And the offshore troller and big-game angler have needs of their very own. Therefore, basically speaking, salt water fishing calls for a rod with more backbone and a reel with greater line capacity than that afforded by fresh water models.

Reels

Salt water spinning reels are—except for size and weight—almost exact duplicates of their fresh water relatives. If you expect to spend most of your salt water fishing hours surf-casting or casting from a boat to surface-feeding fish, a spinning reel is a good choice. For practical purposes it should be large enough to hold at least two hundred yards of fif-

Saltwater fly fishing reel

teen- to twenty-pound test line. You won't hook many fish that will run out that much line; but when you hook a striper, channel bass, or yellowtail at the end of a long cast, you do need reserve. Also, you can lose from a yard to twenty yards or more in a day's fishing. (This usually happens when you have no extra spool of line on hand.)

Because of a spinning reel's construction, line wound in under pressure becomes twisted as it is placed on the spool. Therefore, for trolling and for deep-water fishing, a spinning reel is no great joy to have. Simply reeling in to check your rig will twist the line enough so that when you release the bail everything explodes into a tangle of monofilament that could tempt you to use language which might impair your future salvation.

For all-around salt water fishing nothing is better than the regular multiplying reel—the winch with a geared handle that was discussed under bait casting. As with the spinning reel, a conventional reel capable of holding a couple of hundred yards of line is big enough for most purposes. If you're going after tuna, marlin, broad-bill, kingfish, amber-jack, sailfish, and other big-game species, you'll need an even bigger reel.

Multiplying reels built for surf-casting usually have extra-wide spools that are rather shallow. This is to equalize the thickness of the line-filled spool regardless of how much line is out. Since these reels usually have no level-wind device (it would be very quickly ruined by sand), the angler keeps the line level on the spool by guiding it with his left thumb as he reels with his right hand. Since surfers usually are or become very experienced anglers, the wide spool, which results in fairly constant drag pressure, is an asset.

Reels built especially for boat fishing usually have deep, narrow spools that require a minimum of thumb control of the line. These suffer from the disadvantage that a drag set for a full spool will be too tight for a relatively empty spool. This happens because an empty spool has to revolve more than a full spool to pay out an identical length of line. (A piece of string that will reach around the handle of a baseball bat won't circle the heavier tip.)

Unless you're going to do all your fishing from a boat and on bottom, I'd suggest the surf-model wide-spool reel built to take monofilament line. Monofilament builds up more pressure on a reel spool than braided or twisted line, so make sure the reel you purchase is built for this added pressure. It will say so in the manufacturer's literature.

Another thing to look for in a conventional casting reel is a lightweight spool. A generation or so ago engineers figured that because of inertia a heavy spool would continue to turn longer than a light spool. Therefore, reel spools were made very heavy on the theory that this would tend to increase casting distance. Unfortunately, these heavy-spool reels were impossible to cast. The spool tended to keep revolving after the cast ended and this over-running caused great backlashes. The makers of the Penn reels, who came out with the lightweight spool just before World War II, seemed to put most other surf-reel makers out of business for quite a while.

Any good-quality conventional salt water reel has a click device on the left side plate and a free-spool release, usually on the top right. The click dates from the days before star drags (friction drags mounted inside the handle and shaped slightly like a star) were standard equipment. About its only use today is when rigging up. Push it on and put the reel on free-spool, and you can pull off line without drag resistance and without over-running. It's also used in trolling, especially for billfish, to signal a hit when you don't want to strike the fish immediately. Using it at any other time promptly dubs you as a novice angler.

The free-spool device disconnects the handle and gears from the reel spool. This lets you cast without a backward-rotating handle as an added hazard. You'll also find that on reels with star drags the handle will only turn forward. It's now about thirty years since salt water reels were made without a star drag. Fighting a fish on the old knuckle dusters was great fun. You used either what was called a thumb stall or a leather brake attached to the reel and applied to the spool with thumb pressure to slow up a run. Then, when the fish hesitated, you could grab for the handle. This was when the click came in handy, for if things got difficult, the fish could run against the click without over-running and backlashing your line.

The biggest problem with all adjustable drags, and this includes spinning reels too, is proper adjustment. Many occasional fishermen screw the drag down tight and continue to pop lines every time they hook a decent fish. For most purposes, the best drag adjustment for salt water is about where you get considerable resistance but can still peel off line from the reel with one hand and without a big struggle. Most salt water fishing doesn't have the obstructions—such as logs, lily pads, and rocks—of fresh water angling. Therefore, you can afford to let a fish run a bit. Even areas with coral heads call for a fairly loose drag because you can't stop a bonefish or permit anyway without breaking your tackle. Because fish have a low metabolism and hence are cold-blooded, they run out of energy quickly. Many more fish are lost by anglers who try to hold them too tightly than by those who hold them with a moderate drag. If you let a fish run a bit of line out, the line itself acts as a drag and a buffer. Most lines are elastic and will absorb a shock at fifty feet that would snap them at five feet.

An important note on all salt water reels—spinning and conventional—is that they should be hosed or rinsed off in fresh water after each use in the brine. Not only is salt water very corrosive, but it evaporates and leaves behind salt crystals. These cause friction and wear out your reel. It only takes a minute after you get home or tie up at the dock to put your reel under a faucet or hose. Nothing is more frustrating than to get out fishing and find that your reel is either corroded and rusted tight or sticks and makes squeaking noises. Worst of all, salt in your reel can make the drag freeze and lose you a prize-winning fish at the vital moment. So take care of your reel. It costs nothing and results in constant angling pressure.

Conventional salt water reel sizes are marked $2/0$, $3/0$, $4/0$, and so forth. These numbers indicate how many yards of old-time linen nine-thread line testing twenty-seven pounds will fit on the reel in question. Thus a $2/0$ reel will hold two hundred yards, a $4/0$ reel four hundred yards, and so forth. Most multiplying reels for regular all-round use are $2/0$ size and will hold about three hundred yards of twenty-pound test monofilament. (Remember, the yardage on the size number is linen line.) Reels in $4/0$ to $6/0$ sizes are used for sailfish, tuna, and marlin; and sizes $9/0$ and up are for broadbills, big marlin, giant tuna, and sharks.

Rods

The prime thing to look for in a salt water rod is ability to do the job. Years ago, the main fault with many of them was that they were too stiff. Today, with artificial fibers, the trend is toward rods that are too limber. Both extremes are bad.

The nearest thing to an all-around fishing rod for salt water use is an eight- to nine-foot "steelhead" rod. This can be used for light surf and jetty work, bottom fishing in shallow water, and light trolling offshore. It's ideal for bay and inlet fishing too and will handle lures weighing from one to three ounces. For the west coast angler whose offshore fishing is mostly for yellowtail, bonito, and barracuda, it's just about perfect. In fact, he can get by

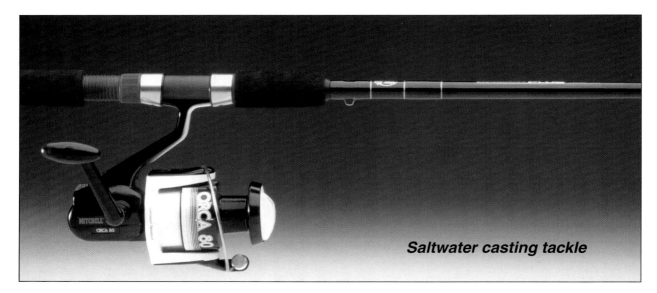

Saltwater casting tackle

with it better than his Atlantic counterpart.

The eastern seaboard has a heavy emphasis on bottom fishing, and whether for cod in Nova Scotia or red snapper in the Gulf of Mexico, bottom fishing calls for a fairly short, stiff rod. With a one-pound sinker in over a hundred feet of water, you need backbone to set a hook. You can't cast with a rod like this, but you can catch fish with it.

The real surf enthusiast won't be happy with his steelhead stick for long. To make a good long cast he must have a thirteen- or fourteen-foot surf rod fitted with either conventional or spinning guides. (Spinning guides have much bigger rings, since the line spirals from, rather than unfolds off, a spinning reel. You need the big rings to tone this spiraling down gently without killing your cast.)

The fisherman who likes trolling in deep water can be equipped for most blue-water game fish if he has a conventional thirty-pound trolling outfit. This involves a $2/0$ to $4/0$ reel that will hold three hundred to five hundred yards of thirty-pound test line, a stiff trolling rod with a slotted butt to fit in a fighting chair, and roller guides. The rod should be limber enough to have a slight bend when trolling an average lure. It should be about as stiff as a surf rod, but much shorter.

With roller guides, the line goes over sets of revolving rollers instead of passing through a ring as in most guides. You can't cast with roller guides, but they reduce friction greatly and help to eliminate cut lines. The slightest scratch on an ordinary guide will cut a line. And on a boat where rods are subject to a certain amount of wear and tear at sea, it's difficult to keep guides from scratching no matter how carefully you stow tackle. Roller guides eliminate this type of problem, and they are especially good with fairly heavy lines.

Lines

Synthetic line development has caused the same revolution in salt water that it has in fresh water. Non-absorbent, most synthetics cast like a dream and help avoid the slack that plagued users of linen lines long ago.

Linen isn't used much anymore. When a heavy, non-absorbent line is needed with no elasticity, braided dacron is the answer. Unlike nylon, dacron has very little stretch. This makes it especially suited for fast offshore trolling, when too springy a line would make it impossible to hook a striking fish.

Deep trollers on the east coast use lead-core and monel-wire line. The lead-core line with a fabric cover looks like regular braided line and handles easily; however, it is bulkier than the monel and will not sink as fast. Monel wire is very thin for its strength, offers little water resistance, and sinks like a bullet. Its one bad features is that in inexperienced hands it will kink and snap. You have to baby it a bit.

Hardware and Miscellaneous Items

Every angler needs odds and ends to fill up his tackle box, but these should be as useful as possible. The salt water fisherman needs small three-way swivels, barrel swivels of various sizes, a few connecting links, and some nickel-silver snap swivels. Another handy thing is a small cork or two. In areas filled with crabs and other bottom-feeding nuisances a cork on the leader will lift your bait enough to keep it from being bothered while you surf-cast or bottom fish from a boat. Pliers of the long-nosed style complete with wire cutters serve a hundred purposes: fixing leaders, cutting piano wire and cable, unhooking fish. Assorted eyed hooks in the Eagleclaw or O'Shaugnessy patterns from size 4 up to size $^4/_0$ will come in handy. And there's nothing like a few payroll envelopes to keep individual rigs in and to prevent tackle tangles before they happen.

Sinkers come in a wide array of shapes. The bank sinker, which is shaped like a tear drop and casts like a bullet, is probably most useful. Cone- and pyramid-shaped sinkers are for use in a sandy bottom with strong currents. They dig in and hold, whereas bank sinkers drift. Kite, or diamond-shape, sinkers are good for purposeful drifting because their flat surface rides along the bottom easily. In some areas you can get pencil-shaped sinkers that are especially good for fishing around rocks; the long, slender shape doesn't snag. A long time ago some clever gadgeteer invented a mushroom sinker like the mushroom anchor for a boat. The only problem with this sinker was that it dug in so deep you broke your line before you got it clear. Today it's extinct.

Even shallow-water trollers and casters need some weight from time to time. The best idea is to have a few trolling weights, or drails, in sizes from one to four ounces. These have bead-chain links fore and aft to help prevent twisted lines. A couple of small planers are convenient when you want to get down deep for bluefish, striped bass, or salmon.

Besides sinkers in appropriate sizes—one to four ounces for bay and surf, two to sixteen ounces for offshore bottom fishing—you should carry a small box of split buckshot for use when you chum. Sometimes the fish will hit on top, but sometimes you need a shot or two to sink and reach them. This is when a heavier sinker won't serve at all.

Few anglers carry an extra spool of line. Those who don't often wish they had. The undertackled man fishing for smaller species can be completely cleaned out of line within a split second by a shark, an albacore, or an oversized tuna. An extra spool costs little, takes up very little space, and is worth its keep, especially since you can use it for material too.

A small supply of heavy monofilament and nylon-coated cable wire for leaders is essential. If you prefer to buy ready-made rigs you should still carry monofilament and wire for emergency repairs.

The best fishing knife you can get is a long-bladed fillet knife with a wooden handle. The handle will float the knife if it's dropped overboard. Hunting knives have generally too thick a blade for fine work like cutting slices of bait and filleting flounders. A scaler of the type used in fish markets will do a much better and faster job than a sawtooth arrangement on the back of a knife blade. Such a scaler costs only a few cents.

A waterproof plastic bag can hold your lunch and keep it dry, hold your catch, and keep your car dry. You can use it to carry beer or soda on ice, protect your camera, and keep spare clothes safe from spray. A heavy-duty bag of transparent plastic complete with grommets and a closing line of light rope can be almost indispensable. If you carry fish in it, simply turn it inside out and wash it with soap to make it as good as new. The plastic won't absorb odors the way textiles do.

Another handy little item is a spool of No. 50 red thread. Use it to tie soft bait such as clams and worms to your hook and to tie on a sinker when you want it to break away when a fish hits.

Always carry a small container of lubricating oil in your tackle kit for use against corrosion. You'd be amazed at how many persons get out fishing and find that their reel has stiffened up because of salt water corrosion.

XXV.

A Quick Rundown on Salt Water Lures

The Polynesians, the Eskimos, and other primitive peoples have used artificial lures for thousands of years; but until very recently salt water artificials were a good deal cruder than those employed to fool fresh water game fish. This was natural enough, since a fish in a landlocked body of water is apt to become much more sophisticated than a blue-water game fish. "There's plenty more fish in the sea" is an old saying with some truth behind it. There are so many fish and so many thousands of square miles of ocean that an individual fish could live out its life and die of old age without ever encountering man and his works.

This is rapidly changing. The need for feeding huge human populations has forced the Japanese and Russians, among others, to thoroughly explore the world's piscine resources, so that Russian trawlers and factory ships are today found around the globe. We may think of the waters off Cape Cod and New York City as being American; but the Russians fished them very thoroughly, and tons of porgies, codfish, haddock, fluke, bluefish, whiting, and other species were caught, iced, and marketed in far-away Siberia. The Japanese are more interested in tuna, marlin, and sailfish; their long-tine techniques are severely depleting major game fish populations. This situation is becoming serious enough so that quotas have been established for bluefin tuna, striped marlin, and broadbill.

Here at home there's a conflict between the commercial fishermen and the sports fishermen. Things have reached the point where the recreational catch of salt water fish exceeds the commercial catch; and a choice is going to have to be made within the next decade or so as to whether certain species—including the Pacific salmons, striped bass, and weakfish— are more valuable as a recreational or a commercial resource. The fishery simply will not support enough fish for both purposes. This has been poignantly established in the New York City area, where fluke, a big summer flounder, were actually vanishing from overfishing; New York State has put a minimum-size limit in effect and New Jersey has established a minimum-size limit for commercial sale.

What's this got to do with lures? Only that with more people fishing than ever before—and the United States Government expects the number of salt water anglers to double within the next ten years—the fish are going to become smarter. As they become more selective, the importance of good lures well presented is going to rise. In fact, it has already.

Plugs

The real heyday of plugs (crankbaits) for salt water arrived with monofilament line and the general surge of smart anglers toward lighter tackle. The big drawbacks of plugs as lures in the brine remain the same: too much wind resistance for easy casting and too little weight for the tackle required. They have been greatly used, however, especially those made of plastic. Basically speaking, salt water plugs are either surface lures or sub-surface wobblers. Deep-diving plugs aren't used much, largely because salt water anglers aren't used to them and because other deep-working lures are available.

All surface lures make some kind of top-water disturbance. Propellers, wobbling disc tails, and concave heads are a few of the devices used. Generally, these lures are supposed to imitate a wounded or frantic bait fish and work best when whipped fairly rapidly in areas where fish are feeding on the surface. This means that you should first locate top-feeding fish and then cast into them. Don't run a boat right into the school but stay within casting distance and drift. Crowding fish too much will force them to sound and leave the area. Most sub-surface wobblers are larger cousins of the same plugs used in fresh water, and they're used in much the same way for both casting the trolling.

One new development in plugs is the metallic finish on plastics, which gives an almost perfect imitation of a bait fish. Available in both surface and sinking models, the Rebels, Mirrolures, and their relations are very good indeed. Slight variations in the color pattern are available, and some anglers insist that a silver lure with a blue back will catch fish when the same lure with a red or black back won't. This might be true, but an angler's confidence with a lure he had faith in should be more important.

Spoons

Oddly enough, spinners that work so well in fresh water fishing do nothing out at sea. Aside from a few spinners used solely for their flasher value in trolling or drifting with bait, spinners aren't used in salt water. After some experimentation in casting and trolling with various lures, I have concluded that spinners have little or no attraction for salt water fish. Wobbling spoons, on the other hand, are superb. The well-known Daredevle spoon is about as good a casting and jigging lure as you can find. More specialized salt water spoons are excellent for trolling, especially since they are designed not to revolve at high speeds. They have flash and action no plug or bait can match. Another advantage of a spoon is that many of the wobbling kind can be used with a strip of pork rind to enhance the action. With pork rind now available in yellow, red, and blue, as well as the familiar white, the spoon-and-pork-rind combination is deadly. Many salt water spoons are made rather lightweight for trolling. These aren't too good for casting, but the weighted Daredevle casting-style spoon will often out-fish plugs.

The range of sizes for these lures is large. Get the size that best approximates that of a bait fish popular with whatever species you are after. This can sometimes mean a very big lure. East coast bunker spoons, supposed to imitate menhaden, catch striped bass in extremely large sizes. No small bass would hit this spoon, as it's about sixteen inches long and about eight inches across; the hooks are in proportion, but fish that were big enough to straighten them out have sometimes been hooked.

Although plugs for salt water fishing come in all colors—including red and white, rainbow, gold, silver, orange, and even lavender, to say nothing of tiger stripes—all spoons are nickel-silver or chrome-plated. This is very puzzling, because a gold-plated or shiny brass spoon could bring startling results on sunny days, especially in shallow, clear water. One reason plugs out-fish spoons on the southern flats is that the glare of too-bright spoons may frighten the fish.

Jigs and Squids

Various types of bucktail jigs are among the best lures ever invented. They'll catch all kinds of fish when bounced or twitched along a sandy bottom. Other jigs include the Japanese feather lures, a trolling jig featuring a heavy metal head and mother-of-pearl eyes, and the old-time cedar jig. The latter is a fish-shaped piece of unpainted red cedar with a metal head and a single fixed hook. Trolled at a fair rate of speed, it has consistently caught a large number of fish over the years.

Diamond jigs are sort of intermediate between the jig and squid families. They are generally fished with an up-and-down rod motion just off the bottom. In small they take mackerel. In larger sizes weighing up to eight ounces they catch many cod, pollock, hake, and other bottom fish, plus bluefish, albacore, bonito, and other blue-water species that occasionally go deep. With a few bucktails weighing from a half ounce to two ounces and a couple of diamond jigs, you can be eating fish any place there are ocean fish to catch. These lures work in the Red Sea, the Indian Ocean, the coral reefs of the Solomon Islands, Puget Sound, and Boston Harbor.

A squid is a form of weighted spoon cleverly fashioned to wobble like a bait fish when it is cast or trolled. The difference between a squid and a jig is that a squid is designed for top-water fishing, whereas a jig is designed for bottom fishing. Squids are used mainly by surf-casters, but they also make good offshore casting lures. Designed for a relatively slow retrieve by reeling, they don't usually work too well when trolled.

Most types of squids have a keel and are made of either block tin or chrome-plated lead. The tin are best because they can be easily bent into shape and shined with sand picked up at the beach itself. They come with fixed and swinging hooks, with and without feathers or bucktail, and can be used with and without pork rind. The swinging-hook type seems to land more fish, since a fixed-hook squid gives a jumping fish a great deal of leverage.

Umbrella lures, a recent innovation, have a group of hookless attractors with a larger hooked lure trailing.

Rubber and Plastic Lures

In recent years imitations of squids and small bait fish have been molded from rubber and soft plastic. These seem to work very well at times and are extremely popular in the French West Indies. A short piece of surgical tubing trolling on a long shank hook has become a very successful type of lure too, even though it takes a drail to get it down where the fish are. With tubing now available in red and black and white as well as natural, translucent rubber, many eastern anglers are experimenting. A tube lure will never twist your line, that's for sure.

Other rather wild lures include so-called junk lures and nylon eels. The junk lures are a long conglomeration of rubber skirts, beads, and shiny metal as much as two feet long. For some reason striped bass and other fish occasionally go wild over them. Nylon eels have a painted lead head and what looks almost like a small doll's wig of colored nylon fibers trailing well behind. It looks weird, but it works nearly everywhere.

Eels and Eel-Type Lures

The eel lures are almost a monopoly of the east coast striper addict, but they'll catch fish in the most amazing places. Blue-water fish love them, and even broadbill swordfish are taken with a rigged eel.

The imitation eels currently being manufactured are threatening to put the genuine eel lure made with an authentic, smelly eel, a half-eel, or an eel skin out of business. Both anglers and wives will be glad. For one thing, it's unpleasant to have to rig eels. For another, since rigged eels represent an investment, they start many a quarrel when they're kept in the home refrigerator or freezer. The soft rubber and plastic article seems to out-fish the real eel and is certainly nicer to handle. Also, it resides happily in the tackle box or bag and causes no consternation in the household.

Eel lures are both cast and trolled. Around rocks, pilings, and other fish habitat they are cast and worked just fast enough to get them moving. When trolled, they are also worked just fast enough to get an enticing wiggle into them. You should use wire line or a drail to get your eel lure working so that it bumps the bottom from time to time. With wire line, a forty-pound monofilament leader of about ten to twenty feet is a must. Fasten it and the wire at opposite ends of a barrel swivel with or without a snap.

One unforeseen advantage of imitation eels is that they can be made in colors. Orange has been popular and seems to make stripers take notice. It's certainly more visible than the blue-green of an ordinary eel. (You may be amazed to know that when using real eels many anglers would scrape them until they assumed a blue color rather than the natural dark green of the outer skin. This was supposed to work wonders.)

XXVI.

Live Bait for Salt Water Fishing

For fun, there's nothing like lures. For fish, it's difficult to beat bait. There are many occasions in salt water fishing when bait fishing is the only way to catch fish. This is especially true of the slower-swimming bottom feeders who depend on a keen sense of smell in their feeding. The following are the different kinds of salt water baits.

Marine Worms

The less a person knows about fishing, the more apt he is to feel that worm bait is the answer to all his problems. It ain't necessarily so! In salt water this is complicated all the more because there are so many different species of worms, and some of these are much better for bait than others.

What about our old buddy, the earthworm? Well, if you ever had a course in biology, you know all about semipermeable membranes. A semipermeable membrane passes fluid through to a saltier solution. Since an earthworm is far less saline than the ocean and its skin is a semipermeable membrane, it loses fluid in salt water and becomes very washed-out and unattractive looking. Therefore, except for a bit use in flounder fishing and as a bulk factor in eel bobs, earthworms aren't very useful.

Their place is taken by a wide variety of marine-living worms that mostly burrow in the sand or mud of bays and beaches. Nearly all of them can swim fairly well and have fringes that help them wiggle or corkscrew through the water. One very important thing about most marine worms is that unlike earthworms they have strong jaws and sharp teeth. They aren't apt to draw blood, but they can make nearly anyone say "Ouch!"

The two principal types are the sandworm-clam worm-pile worm clan and the blood-worms. The sandworms and their close relatives are rather flat and dark-colored, with heavy fringes. Depending on the species, they range from dark bottle-green with scarlet fringes to pale brick-red all over, and may even range the gamut from a pale green-blue to near-yellow. These worms are usually found in mud and sand in close association with clams. Sometimes they live in holes in pilings. To see one swim is an amazing sight. They actually bore through the water like an animated corkscrew.

The bloodworms are slightly rounder, with much smaller fringes and a toothed, sucking-type mouth instead of the simple biting mouth of the sandworms. You'll know why a bloodworm got his name as soon as you try to put one on a hook. They are one of the goriest creatures for their size you ever saw.

Both bloodworms and sandworms have been the basis of a good-sized industry on the Maine coast. The extraordinary tidal range in the Gulf of Maine and Bay of Fundy uncovers thousands of acres of sand and mud flats at low water. Professional diggers armed with special digging forks get anywhere from ten- to twenty-dozen worms on a tide. It's very hard work, and since you have to be out during the few hours of daily low water, even when this is at two o'clock in the morning, a worm digger's life is no fun at all.

The digger brings his worms to a buyer who ships them to market, usually by truck, but sometimes by plane. There, the wholesalers pick up their shipments upon arrival, which can be at any hour of the day or night. They in turn deliver them to tackle shops and bait stands from Massachusetts to Maryland and beyond.

Marine worms are extremely perishable. From digging to final sale to an angler they must be kept at a temperature of about 40 degrees. Refrigeration for too long a time dehydrates and kills them. A temperature that is too cold will also kill them, as will even the least drop of fresh water. Wholesalers and bait stores have a serious financial problem with a worm inventory they must get rid of quickly. And they can't win! If they're cautious and buy only a few worms, fishing is good and their customers are screaming for more. If they plunge and buy many, a period of bad weather sets in and they're stuck with a big investment that must be sold within days or it will spoil. Most small tackle stores in fishing areas don't plan to make money on worms but simply hope the worms will bring in traffic that will buy profitable items.

When fishing for winter flounder and other small bottom species you'll use only pieces of worm, so you don't have to be overly fussy about those you buy. Simply make sure they're alive and odorless. A bad smell means dead worms and trouble.

Striped-bass anglers who know their fishing insist upon fresh, lively worms only. Fresh worms are fat and sassy with bright colors—at least for their species. If you pick up a fresh worm by the tail, he'll wiggle up and down like a yo-yo. Fat, bright-colored worms about six to eight inches long are ideal. Long, stringy ones won't catch fish if you're after striped bass. It makes sense. You wouldn't eat a sick-looking clam or oyster. Why should a fish go for sick-looking worms?

Marine worms are good bait for every bottom-feeding fish. Their only drawback is that using them becomes expensive, especially in areas where bait-stealing crabs and bergalls abound.

In nearly any area where clams can be dug, you can dig worms of one kind or another yourself. Check to be sure you don't need a special clamming license before you go out. All you need otherwise are mud or sand flats at dead low water. A garden fork and a wooden box to put the worms in are the only other requisites. (You can't keep marine worms in a metal can. The action of the sea water on the metal will very quickly kill them.) Rather than trying to keep worms in sand or mud, you should put a bit of kelp or other seaweed in the box with them to keep them moist. And the sooner you use them the better.

Along with clams and other little marine animals you may dig up a monstrous, red-colored tapeworm six feet long or longer. These worms are often an inch or more across the segments. They aren't parasites, but are one of a couple of species of free-living tapeworms that are perfectly harmless and safe to handle. Cut into pieces about six inches long they make excellent bait for striped bass, channel bass, and all other species that live along the undercut mud banks where these worms burrow.

Clams, Mussels, and Conches

Clams, either whole or in pieces, are good bait for an infinite variety of fish. For small fish, the tough foot of the clam makes a bait that porgies, sheepshead, and their friends can't steal from you. After a storm along the beachfront the big surf clams can be easily cracked and used on a size 4/0 hook for stripers, channel bass, and big weakfish. If you're a clam digger yourself, you can usually find some cracked and other inedible clams that can be put in a separate bucket and used for bait.

Because they spoil easily, most bait stores prefer to sell frozen or salted clams. These aren't quite a attractive to fish as fresh clams, but unless they smell rotten, they'll catch fish for you. Don't try to salt them down yourself; if anything goes wrong the stench is unbelievable.

Mussels make wonderful bait too. Some bait stores in various areas sell them. You can also dig them out of tidal sod banks, but you'll find it a muddy job. Generally speaking, mussels should be steamed before using as bait. This toughens them up quite a bit. It's also apt to whet your appetite; mussels from clean waters that are safe for shellfishing are good eating. (In Europe, they're more popular than clams.) You'll find them especially good for various flounders in New England and mid-Atlantic waters, and you can use them as both bait and as crushed chum, either raw or after they're been steamed.

Conches (pronounced conks) are big marine snails of several related species. They're used for codfish bait up north and for bottom fish in the tropics. I wouldn't suggest you try them unless you can buy them already shelled and prepared for bait. Conches are so tough that after being removed from the shell they have to be pounded with a wooden mallet—and I mean pounded—before they are soft enough to be hooked. They're so tough that your bait is nearly immune to pesky thievery, but they are definitely attractive to fish.

Crabs and Other Crustaceans

Humans certainly enjoy crab-meat cocktails, so it should come as no surprise that fish eat crabs at every opportunity. Along the eastern seaboard the familiar blue crab and the lady, or calico, crab of sandy beaches are wonderful bait. So are the rock and stone crabs, of which there are several species along the Pacific and a few in the Atlantic.

Aside from blackfish and other wrasses, few fish will eat a hard-shelled crab. They prefer them soft. This means buying soft crabs fresh or frozen from a bait store or food store or finding them yourself. Shedder, or peeler, crabs at the stage when the new shell has formed as a skin under the old carapace are much better. Remember, a crab sheds to grow, and he grows by soaking up sea water and expanding in his new, soft suit before it hardens into armor. Therefore, a soft crab is water-logged and extremely mushy. This isn't much of a handicap when you're using an entire crab for bait, but cutting a soft crab into pieces can be quite a mess. By using shedders you avoid this. They can be obtained at most bait stores from New Jersey southward, and you can also buy them from commercial crabbers. These men usually operate by setting up wooden stockades in shallow water. They then go out at night and "jack" for hard crabs with a big jacklight. (This takes a special license in states where it is legal.) The light attracts crabs by the bushels-full, and they are taken back and dumped in holding pens by the crabbers, who then wait for the crabs to molt.

An experienced crabber can tell when a crab is in the shedder stage by its color and a glance at the swimmer fins. Softies are generally sorted out from the hard crabs on a daily basis. Crabs are cannibals, and if the crabber left his soft crabs in a stockade with hard crabs he'd get very few to market.

With shedders, you simply crack the outer shell, peel it off carefully, and you have a supersoft crab without a large amount of excess water. If you peel the legs and swimmer fins as well as the body, a single crab will be enough for about eight baits of small size, four of medium size, or two of large size. The claws are especially good bait when peeled. Always use them.

One word of caution. Never buy dead shedder crabs or soft crabs—although softies are all right if packaged and frozen. Crabs decompose almost at once and most fish will avoid them. Besides, they turn into immediate mush.

How can you catch soft and shedder crabs for bait? You can use a small seine, where legal, and catch blue crabs in shallow, muddy bays. By pinching off the top of a claw you can tell whether the crab is ready to shed. It takes a certain amount of experience and nerve before you learn to pick up a crab safely. When held by a corner of the rear body he can't reach you.

Calico, or lady, crabs hide in the sand to shed. They can be found by raking sand bars and holes at low tide, especially around rocks and pilings. These are much smaller than the blue crabs and usually a single crab is used for bait. For kingfish (surf whiting) and other smaller species, you can use a claw or half of a crab. You can buy crab rakes, which look rather like clam rakes with a net attached, at some tackle shops. Used at low tide they're quite efficient, especially at the dark of the moon, which is the prime shedding period. All crabs don't shed at the same time, but the majority shed when the moon is dark to give the maximum protection in a very vulnerable state. A soft crab can't defend itself; it can't even move away from an attacker.

Finding soft and shedder rock and stone crabs can be a difficult job. They hide in crevices and sometimes in tiny patches of mud or sand. In areas where they are common you might get a few at low tide on mud flats near rocks.

Fiddler crabs are tiny beasts that run about sand bars and mud flats at low water waving their one big claw. They are excellent bait for blackfish and are used from New England south to New York City. You'll find them alive in bait stores, or you can chase them yourself. A sturdy butterfly net helps. Often, they won't come out and run about until after dark, so you need a flashlight too. If you don't mind getting muddy, catching fiddler crabs is good, dirty fun.

The tails of large hermit crabs are about the best bait there is. Hermit crabs live in discarded shells of snails and whelks and other mollusks. As they grow, they look for bigger and bigger shells. In most areas finding hermit crabs big enough for bait is a matter of pure luck. You can't buy them anywhere.

Many years ago, when millionaires really lived the part they used lobster tails for bait. Today, this would be like lighting a cigar with a twenty-dollar bill.

Shrimp, which are crustaceans allied to the lobster and crab, are among the most universally used bait in the world. (A crab is a big, flat shrimp with an atrophied tail that is folded under.) There are several hundred shrimp species, ranging in size from a fraction of an inch to six or eight inches in length. Depending on their size, they're used whole or only a part is used. In areas where big shrimp aren't found, you can buy shrimp in a food store, cut it into appropriately sized pieces, and catch fish. (These shrimp don't have to be cooked or veined!)

In southern waters big live shrimp are used for bait. In fact, the Gulf of Mexico is an area where almost nothing else is used. Shrimp, living or dead, will catch all shallow-water game fish and some offshore species too.

In the Northeast a seine will get you various kinds of grass and sand shrimp in any bay or estuary with eelgrass growing in it. These little shrimp are used as both bait and chum for everything from striped bass to porgies. They can be kept alive for a day if the water is drained off and they are refrigerated. As long as their gills are damp, they can breathe air. An interesting point about small shrimp species is that they work equally well as bait in fresh water. Trout, bass, sunfish, and perch of all kinds of love them dearly. The only trick is they must be alive. Once they die and turn milky and red, they don't work; however, fish-market shrimp in suitable pieces is a good, if costly, catfish bait.

Sandy beaches nearly everywhere support a little crustacean known usually as a sand bug. He's about an inch long and you can dig him in moist sand especially at low tide. In an emergency, he'll provide very good bait for most surf-feeding fish.

Sand bugs, fish-market shrimp, and pieces of crab are best fished in the surf with a couple of turns of No. 50 thread to hold them in position on the hook. Offshore or in a bay, this isn't necessary.

Salt Water Bait Fish

Literally dozens of species of small salt water fish are used for bait. Killies or mummiechogs, plus various small catfish and sculpin, are used live. Hooked through both lips or lightly through the back, they'll live a long time. Another method for hooking small bait fish without hurting them is to put the point of the hook in the mouth and out the gill. Thus they aren't really hooked at all.

Sand eels, silversides, spearing, and their relatives are always used dead. They die immediately upon being seined anyway. These long, thin fish require a special rig with a lip and tail hook, especially if they are trolled or drifted.

Small herring and young mackerel can be caught on a tiny spoon or jig and used as bait for big fish. Tuna and swordfish addicts go well offshore and catch live ling and whiting. In New England, live eels are used for striped-bass bait.

Basically, all these larger bait fish are hooked lightly through the back just behind the dorsal fin and fished with little or no sinker from a slowly drifting boat. If conditions are right and game fish are on the surface, you can use a bobber. It's a thrill to see your bobber suddenly vanish under the surface with a speed unknown to the fresh water angler.

Yellowtail fans in California use live anchovy for bait. These are kept aboard in huge tanks and usually hooked very lightly with thin wire hooks, as they are soft and easily killed.

Catching your own bait is often both fun and a good way to save money. A small seine worked along a bayshore or an umbrella net lowered from a dock will generally come up with a school of various minnow species. As a conservationist you should sort out the young game fish and return them unharmed to the water. Baiting your area with little bits of clam, worm, fish, crushed mussel shells, or even little bits of tin foil will bring regular clouds of spearing and their relatives within easy reach. The only thing to avoid in some areas is stinging jellyfish. The various killiefish and sculpin are tough and will live well in a minnow bucket of salt water if they are not overcrowded. To keep them overnight, put a small cake of ice on the bucket lid so it dips inside. The small amount of fresh water won't hurt them at all.

The most difficult time to use live bait fish is surf-casting. Your cast will either whip them off or kill them upon the impact of hitting the water. Therefore, the best place is from a slowly drifting boat where you don't have to cast. More live bait is ruined by casting than is taken by game fish!

Squid and Other Cut Bait

Many salt water species will take cut bait faster than they will take a live minnow. The reason is probably odor. A slice of fish oozes odor all over; and if it has a bit of flash, it will both attract and entice attention.

In areas where it can be obtained, squid is a very popular bait. If you've had calamari in an Italian restaurant, you know it's good. Squid should strictly be discussed along with clams, because a squid is an intelligent mollusk with a great set of eyes that behaves very much like a fish. Squid come in schools and attack shoals of bait fish, which they've probably been doing since the beginning of time when bait fish looked like tiny sharks and gars. They have a parrot-like beak and can bite; but the actual shell consists of a transparent backbone or in larger species the cuttlefish bone that canaries peck on. Another squid oddity is that like their relative the octopus they carry an ink sac and can cast a smoke screen to retreat behind.

When you take a dead squid, slit it open and pull off the head, and you will have a good-sized open cylinder of white bait. Rub off the thin skin, cut the squid into appropriate slices, and you're already to fish. The head makes a very good bait too, and an entire squid trolled backward, which is how squid swim when in a hurry, is popular with the marlin and swordfish clan offshore. The way to succeed with squid bait is to use fairly long, thin slices and pass the hook twice through one end. Balling it up will destroy any illusion of a bait fish appearance.

Nearly any kind of fish, including sea robins and other pests, can be cut up for bait. Scale, fillet, and slice the fillets into tapering pieces. With very soft fish like menhaden, slice right through the fish from top to belly. Then split these slices at the backbone. West coast salmon trollers sometimes go further; they cut off the bait's head and slice the body so that if presents a thick surface to the water like the head of a wooden bass plug.

For channel bass in the surf, many anglers cut a small spot fish diagonally behind the head. The head end makes the best bait because it is too tough to be bothered by crabs very much. The tail diagonally cut is good but much softer.

Rigging dead fish for trolling can be quite an art. The easiest and a quite effective method is to use piano wire. The hook is rigged at one end and the other end is passed up the dead fish's anal opening and out its mouth. The wire is then pulled up so that most of the hook is buried inside the bait. To keep this bait from bunching back when trolled, take the wire back from the mouth, half-hitch it around the gill covers, and bring it back through the mouth again. The only disadvantage of this is that you kink your wire unless you're careful. An alternate method uses another piece of wire around the gills and up to a swivel just ahead of the baitfish's mouth. (This method is also used with eels except a second hook through the head keeps the eel straight.)

Another idea is to use a small block-tin squid or even a small spoon with a single hook. After the wire is passed forward through the fish, the spoon or squid is hooked firmly through both lips. The protruding wire is then either wrapped on a split ring on the spoon or fastened to the eye on the squid. This is the usual method of rigging eels for striped-bass trolling, although instead of wire some experts use a long needle to pass a line through the eel. They think the flexible line gives more action. If you must use whole eels, have your bait-and-tackle man rig them for you—it's a job you can live without.

The most important thing to remember with cut bait is that you're trying to imitate a natural fish. This means that thick, square chunks aren't too good, since there aren't very many thick, square fish. Fairly long, tapered pieces coming to a thin point or cut with a forked tail will do much better as a rule. The only exception is when you're chumming for bluefish and tuna, and this is because these fish expect to see chunks of fish. The chum odor convinces them that other fish are chomping bait fish into pieces.

Chum and How to Use It

Chumming is luring fish to the dining table. If properly done, it produces excellent results. There are some who question its sportsmanship, but chumming often gives an angler the chance to use light tackle against fish that could otherwise be caught only in deep water with heavy gear. It's not what you do but the way you do it that makes a sportsman.

Bottom fishermen can chum with a little chum pot filled with crushed clams, mussels, or crabs. (You can use hard crabs of any kind for this.) If you have no chum pot, put a couple of rocks along with your chum in an onion or orange sack and lower it to the bottom. If you want to be modern and you live in the Northeast, you can buy a chum log of frozen mossbunker chum and use it on the bottom in your pot or onion sack.

Chumming with fresh or frozen mossbunker and other oily fish is a standard method in the mid-Atlantic region. Fresh chum is preferred because it sinks, whereas frozen chum floats. Either way, a small quantity of this ground-up, oily mess (formed by putting fish through a meat grinder) is mixed in a bucket with a small amount of sea water and ladled overboard. In bay and river fishing you can put a quantity of chum in an onion sack, tie this on the stern of your boat, and shake it once in a while. The tide will do your chumming for you.

From the Chesapeake Bay region south, chumming with live shrimp is popular. Contrary to what you might suppose, very light chumming with a couple of shrimp at a time is better than a wholesale effort. Quite obviously, overdoing the shrimp gives the fish enough to eat without bothering your bait.

On the west coast, especially around Santa Barbara and down to San Diego, live bait fish are used for chum. Even the commercial tuna clippers use them to get the fish up on top and hold them there. Usually, the skipper looks for surfacing fish and puts out enough anchovy to hold their interest. Slightly injured anchovy that flutter around on top are the best chum of all.

Aside from clams and mussels, about the only way to get chum is to buy it through regular bait shops and other commercial channels. Even with shrimp, it would take you an extremely long time to catch enough to make chumming worthwhile. Even at a dribble, you can use a gallon of grass shrimp in a day without half trying.

If you've never seen chumming done, it would be wise to take a ride on a party or charter boat and observe the operation before trying it yourself. Especially with mossbunker chum, it can be so messy you might not want to get involved with it at all. You have no odor or mess with shrimp; but you need a live-box to keep them in, and the same, of course, holds true for anchovy and other fish.

Can you use salt water chum in fresh water fishing? Yes, and no. For one thing, in a stream you have too much current, and in a lake you don't have enough. Then, of course, you don't want to be accused of polluting the water. Grass shrimp are probably the best fresh water chum and will definitely attract fish from a limited area. By and large, fresh water chumming isn't worthwhile; it is worthwhile, however, to bait the fishing grounds with oatmeal and cornmeal when you're after carp and catfish.

If you want to experiment with salt water chumming and can't buy chum, there are alternatives that work quite well. A can of sardines, punched at both ends so the oil escapes, is one idea. You can do the same thing with dog and cat food. And if you have a small quantity of shrimp or other chum and want to stretch it, a little oatmeal will help it go further.

Chum selection in a nutshell:

Bottom species: chum with clams, mussels, crabs, mossbunker log, or dog food.

Bluefish, bonito, yellowtail, and tuna: chum with mossbunker on east coast and anchovy on west coast.

Bay species: chum with shrimp or other small live bait. Mossbunker sometimes works.

XXVII.

Women in Fishing

Historically, fishing has been perceived by most as a 'male' sport—included wholeheartedly in every real man's macho repertoire. Thanks, however, to the efforts of women anglers all over the United States and Canada, the fishing world is starting to recognize women as competitive, viable participants in this continuously-growing sport. Since the 1970s, organizations aimed at female anglers have sprung up all over the US and Canada: clubs, fishing schools, competitive leagues, and guide services dedicated solely to getting women out fishing.

The first writings on fishing known to western civilization are attributed to one of fishing's original pioneers: Dame Juliana Berners. She was an English noblewoman/nun, who wrote her "Treatyse on Fysshynge wyth an Angle" from the Sopwell Nunnery near St. Albans in 1496. Dame Juliana has become somewhat of a figurehead for women anglers everywhere, but she is not the only woman who has made an impact on fishing. Cornelia Crosby was a nationwide sports personality by 1900, renowned for her daring behavior and adventurous spirit, as well as her unparalleled knack for catching huge Atlantic salmon. Kay Brodney, former librarian at the Library of Congress explored uncharted waters in the depths of the South American jungle in search of dorado and peacock bass in the 1950's. Eugenie Marron caught a world-record swordfish

Cecilia "Pudge" Kleinkauf helps a young angler get her start at Women's Flyfishing in Alaska

(772 pounds) in 1954, while dedicating her life to critical studies in marine science. More recently, women continue to break ground in all aspects of fishing; Joan Wulff continues to write, run the Wulff School and oversee the Royal Wulff product lines with tenacity and leadership. In 1995, Pacific Northwesterner Lyla Foggia published the definitive text on women who fish: *Reel Women: The World of Women who Fish,* and has since founded the first-ever magazine for female anglers: Reel Women. Chris Houston, Penny Berryman, Linda England and Fredda Lee break new records in competitive bass fishing each year, while at the same time increasing the popularity, awareness and financial backing of the sport in leaps and bounds.

Besides the individual women who are making an impact on the fishing world, there are also a variety of clubs, schools and guide services that are aimed primarily at women. While the focus is clearly on fishing, women's guide services and fishing schools often include philosophical and social agendas in their adventures. Women's fishing organizations are concerned with providing positive role models for young girls. They seek to create a framework for women to interact with one another and with nature in a non-competitive, single-sex environment; as well as help women find ways to challenge themselves physically in the outdoors. And, of course, the first priority is to simply have fun with fishing. There are fishing organizations for women in almost every state and every category of fishing—here are a few to get you started.

NATIONAL ORGANIZATIONS

Bass n'Gal
P.O. Box 13925
Arlington, TX 76013
(817) 265-6214

"Becoming an Outdoors Woman"
Check your state department of natural resources for information on these increasingly popular weekend workshops.

International Women's Fishing Association
P.O. Box 3125
Palm Beach, FL 33480

ALASKA

Women's Flyfishing
Cecilia "Pudge" Kleinkauf
P.O. Box 243-963
Anchorage, AK 99524
ckleinkauf@micronet.net

ARIZONA

Dame Juliana Anglers
510 W. Willetta Street
Phoenix, AZ 85003
avilez@aol.com

CALIFORNIA

Golden West Women Flyfishers
790 27th Ave
San Francisco, CA 94121

The Irresistibles
2042 Alexander Dr.
Escondido, CA 92025

COLORADO

Colorado Women Flyfishers
c/o 945 Cook St.
Denver, CO 80206

Flyfisher Ladies Angling Club
252 Clayton St.
Denver, CO 80206

CONNECTICUT

The Better Half Bass Club
c/o Amy Perry
44 Parker Hill Road Ext.
Killingworth, CT 06419
(203) 663-3330

DELAWARE

Delaware Valley Women's Fly Fishing Association
711 Fairview Ave.
Wilmington, DE 19809
oreflyfish@aol.com

FLORIDA

International Women's Fishing Association
P.O. Box 3125
Palm Beach, FL 33480

Tampa Bay Fly Fishing Club
10424 Raffia Dr.
Port Richey, FL 34668

MARYLAND

Chesapeake Outdoor Women
735 Thayer Ave.
Silver Spring, MD 20910

MASSACHUSSETTS

Orvis Cape Cod School
(They have a women-only section in their coursebook)

MICHIGAN

Fly Girls
P.O. Box 828
Pentwater, MI 49449
jdschramm@oceana.net

MINNESOTA

Women Anglers of Minnesota
P.O. Box 580653
Minneapolis, MN 55468

Women For Fishing
6127 Birchwood Hills
Lakeshore, MN 56468

MONTANA

Missoula Fly Fishers
650 Big Flat Rd.
Missoula, MT 59801

NEW JERSEY

Fish 'N Chicks
P.O. Box 923
Far Hills, NJ 07931

NEW MEXICO

She Fishes!
3214 Mathews N.E.
Albuquerque, NM 87501
shadowbot@aol.com

NEW YORK

Juliana Berner's Anglers
25 East 86th St.
New York, NY 10028

OHIO

Buckeye Lady Anglers
2143 Melrose Ave.
Columbus, OH 43224

Walleye Mamas Fishing Club
1102 Buckingham
Sandusky, OH 44870
(419) 627-1333

OKLAHOMA

Oklahoma Lady Anglers
218 Cherokee
Wagoner, OK 74467

OREGON

The Damsel Flies
3800 N. Delta Highway
Eugene, OR 97408

The Lady Anglers, High Desert Chapter
P.O. Box 12253
Umatilla, OR 97882

The Lady Anglers, Portland Chapter
17084 S. Monroe
Mulino, OR 97042

The Tomboy Club
P.O. Box 846
Dallas, OR 97338

PENNSYLVANIA

SEE DELAWARE;
**Delaware Valley Women's Fly Fishing
  Association**

RHODE ISLAND

Ladies of the Long Rod
203 Sterling Ave
Providence, RI 02909

UTAH

The Lady Anglers, Utah Chapter
992 Halcyon Dr.
Murray, UT 84123

VIRGINIA

Virginia Women in the Outdoors
5806 Mooretown Road
Williamsburg, VA 23188
lnorris@dgif.state.va.us

WASHINGTON

Northwest Women Flyfishers
P.O. Box 31020
Seattle, WA 98103
steltsfish@aol.com

WISCONSIN

Wisconsin Sportswomen Club
W237 N. 1480 Busse Rd.
Waukesha, WI 53188

XXVIII.

Conservation & Restoration

The challenge to protect our environment while at the same time encouraging people to get out into nature and enjoy themselves is an important issue in the sport fishing world. In the last century, we have seen fish populations and water quality fluctuate considerably with the changing realities of commerce and recreation. Although great strides have been taken to educate the public and secure a commitment to environmentalism in both the private and the public sectors, it is still a continuing effort. It's especially important that those of us who value recreation in the outdoors to be aware of not only our impact on the environment, but the impact that conservation programs and legislation have on the condition of our fish and their habitat.

The combination of responsible individual choices and support of positive changes in environmental policies can only help improve fishing, both commercially and recreationally. Obey licensing regulations, practice Catch-and-Release (or eat what you catch within the legal limits), be aware of your impact on the environment when you are out fishing, and pay attention to environmental issues in your area.

Protection Agencies & The Sportfish Restoration Cycle

There are a variety of agencies in North America that exist to encourage conservation and restoration of aquatic resources: the U.S. Fish & Wildlife Service, which is divided into 7 separate regions throughout the U.S., the Environmental Protection Agency, The Nature Conservancy, the National Marine Fisheries Service, the Bureau of Land Management, the U.S. Geological Service's Biological Resources Division, the National Parks Service and the International Association of Fish & Wildlife Agencies. Basically, all of these organizations (and others) address different functions in the web of issues surrounding the preservation of natural

TIPS FOR LOW-IMPACT FISHING

Be Kind to Your Waters...

• Use designated trails for water-access—making your own encourages erosion and destroys riparian zones (the grasses, trees and plants growing around a lake, stream or river) which are vital to maintaining fish habitats.

• Make sure your boat engine is running properly—any leaks or smoke can be extremely damaging to water quality.

• Be aware of your impact on a campsite when cooking & cleaning near water. Use biodegradable soap and keep it at least 50 yards from the water (it seeps through soil and poisons water for fish).

• Pick up after yourself—don't leave spent leader or hooks in the water or on the ground. Take all of your equipment with you, whether it's still in use or not.

• Pick up any trash you see—have an extra pocket in your vest. Fish don't like cigarette butts, soda cans or plastic bags, and neither do anglers that care about protecting good fishing.

• NEVER leave garbage or waste behind—if you brought it in, take it with you when you go.

Be kind to the fish...

• Catch and release! Only keep what you plan to eat, within the legal limits.

• Return the fish to the water as soon as possible. Every second out of water renders a fish more disoriented and injured, so get him off of your hook and send him back—gently.

• Release the fish by hand in gentle water. Make sure that it is facing upstream and hold it underwater until it has a chance to catch its breath—it will take off as soon as it's ready.

• Never, ever throw a fish back. The shock of being out of water is enough without having to be returned to the water in an abrupt and painful way.

• Make sure that you use barbless hooks. You may have to take the barb off yourself with a pair of pliers, but the hook will still be just as effective and kinder to the fish.

• Never handle a fish with dry hands. If your hands are dry when you take a fish out of the water, it causes a reaction with the membranes around the fish's skin and puts the fish into a state of shock.

populations and habitats, usually through federal and state resources.

There are also agencies that specialize in the concerns of sport fishing enthusiasts. In the 1980's, the International Association of Fish & Wildlife Agencies and the American League of Anglers and Boaters were instrumental in the enhancement and implementation of the Sport Fish Restoration Act, passed originally in 1950. Essentially, the improved Sport Fish Restoration Act provides the structure for the highly effective "user-pays, user benefits" system program, whereby anglers and boaters, through licensing fees, pay for fisheries management, boating access and other state-organized restoration programs. Although this legislation has been highly successful, the funds apportioned for future use are expected to be less than enough. Legislators and environmental protection agencies are constantly working to improve the situation, but Congressional support of the Sport Fish Restoration Act is vital to its continuing success. Find out how your Representatives stand on this issue—let them know that the improvement of water quality and fish populations matters to their constituents.

XXIX.

It Pays to Be a Well-Equipped Angler

Tennis players wear shorts and sneakers, and skiers wear a variety of high-tech outfits; but anglers don't have to be quite so fussy. Nearly any clothes that can pass the following short test will suffice: You need protection, comfort, low visibility, and washability.

Protection

Any place you fish is going to have sun and water, and clothes can make the difference between painful burns and a good time. Unless you're already well tanned, you should start out cautiously, especially in southern waters. Long-sleeved shirts, a pair of pants, and topsider or similar sneakers with gripping soles (bare feet can get sunburned too) will keep the sun off you quite well. You also need a hat or cap of some kind. All you want is something that will keep the direct rays of the sun off your head. The long-billed caps so popular with surf-

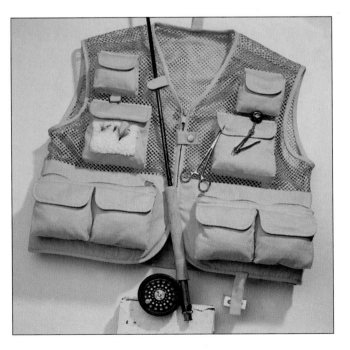

A well-organized vest can make fishing easier and more efficient.

casters and swordfishers are quite good except that they do nothing for the back of your neck. A sombrero or ten-gallon hat of some sort is ideal.

Bugs are another problem. They're so bad in some places that anglers wear mosquito netting draped from their hats. With modern insect repellents, you'll have no real bug problem. The greasy kinds seem to last longest. Be sure to put plenty around your wrists and ankles to discourage mosquitoes and flies from getting up inside your clothes. Certain dark colors, notably navy blue, are supposed to attract flies and mosquitoes.

If you do a great deal of fishing, you'll be caught in a rainstorm sooner or later, so you should have a light two-piece rain suit. The gore-tex ones (or any number of competitors) weigh nearly nothing and will pack in a tackle bag or a lunch box with no trouble. Rain isn't the only time you'll wear your rain gear; in a cold wind a rain suit makes a good windbreaker. A combination of a headwind and a small boat can get you soaked with spray at any time of day or night.

Comfort

A fashionable fisherman is a comfortable fisherman. This is one sport where clothes are cut for comfort first, last, and always. Loose clothes are better to fish in, give you room to sit down, and protect you better against insects. If you must look sharp at all times, a variety of high-end outdoor stores can outfit you to appear like a millionaire sportsman. If you're less fussy, the basics will do the job. If you're going to handle the boat and bait, clean the fish, and do other chores, you'll feel better in inexpensive clothes, since you won't have to worry about making a mess out of expensive ones. If, on the other hand, you have a guide or captain to do the work, or if you're a fly caster first, last, and always, you won't get dirty enough to ruin a stylish outfit.

For comfortable fishing, it is advisable to wear too much rather than too little. You can always take clothes off—some clothes anyway—but there's nothing worse than being caught offshore in a stiff breeze with no sweater. And in most areas things cool off markedly when the sun goes down. A fleece pullover is technology's greatest gift to those who love the outdoors: a variety of thickness for different warmth levels, easily washed, quick to dry. With rain gear, it can keep you comfortable in temperatures down in the forties or even lower.

Low Visibility

As we've noted, fish can see. Therefore, you shouldn't stand out as a menace. White, ivory, and cream are poor colors to wear fishing except maybe for trolling from a big cruiser. These colors reflect much light and are thus highly visible. Practically any shade that is neutral from an angling point of view is fine. All the buffs, tans, blues, and greens—even reds—will do a good job, since they absorb more light than they reflect.

Washability

Until you've cut bait, handled greasy outboards, and cleaned fish, you haven't ever been really dirty. There's very little point in wearing anything fishing that you can't take off and toss in the washing machine. Of course, in Alaska you'll want to wear wool at all times, but you'll probably be wearing boots over your wool slacks. It always makes sense to get fishing clothes that can take a bath in soap regularly. And if you're not wearing boots or waders, a set of denim overalls or even a carpenter's apron can be a good thing to wear over your regular attire. Down in the bass country of the Ozarks many traveling salesmen carry a fishing rod and a tackle box in the trunk of the car along with their denim overalls. This lets them do some fishing between calls without making a lot of clothing changes.

Sooner or later most fishermen accumulate quite a collection of tackle. Tossing all this stuff into a closet and forgetting it isn't going to do much for your investment. It won't do much for your disposition either when you mash a rod in a closet door, step on a reel, or get out in a boat before you discover that the bottom of your tackle box is a great big rat's nest of plugs, leaders, hooks, and other hardware. So before you do anything else, find a place in your home or apartment where you can hang up your tackle.

A basement corner—if dry—is ideal, as is an empty closet (but who has one?). Even a garage corner will do in a pinch, although it's not recommended because of grit and dust.

For most of us, a basement corner and an empty chest of drawers such as most people have in an attic will do a good job. An old glass-front bookcase is efficient too.

Fishing rods should be hung up when not in use. The trouble with putting them back in the aluminum case they came in is that the least dampness will cause sweating and damage to wrappings, reel seats, and so

Keep your flies and lures as dry as you can when in storage—they can rust easily if neglected.

forth. A few little brass hooks screwed into a molding will take care of hanging your rods properly. You can use larger hooks for hanging boots, waders, gaffs, landing nets, raid suits, and other paraphernalia.

Put your reels in the old bureau. This gets them out of air-borne dust and dirt. Additionally, it gets monofilament lines away from sunlight, which rots them. Assuming you can put your reels in a single drawer with room to spare, put the reel oil and graphite and little wrenches in with them. Then use the rest of your old chest for lures.

There are two ways to easily store such items as plugs and spoons. You can keep the original box the lure came in and put the lure back into this box when you're finished using it, or you can get some light plywood and build yourself a honeycomb affair for lures inside a bureau drawer. Unless you do one or the other, every time you open and shut a drawer you'll slide all your lures into a heap, and chaos will reign.

Fly casters are quite lucky. They simply put their flies away in a flybook and more or less forget them. A few camphor balls in the bureau drawer may be added for peace of mind. If you have a collection of colorful steelhead and Atlantic-salmon flies, you can either buy or make shadow boxes to display them on a wall of your den. By using small magnets you can make the flies hang on the black velvet background of the box without hooking them into the material.

Tackle bags and boxes are excellent equipment, but after a trip you should go over them thoroughly, take everything out, and clean and repack them. By doing this you'll avoid accumulating old, rusty hooks and other debris.

Anyone who fishes on foot needs a vest. Equipped with a multitude of pockets, pouches and loops, most vests are capable of carrying everything that an angler might need, hands free. Just like most other recreational acoutrements, you can spend a fortune on the newest, most high-tech version or you can achieve virtually the same level of convenience and function at a much lower price at your local sporting goods store. If you are lucky, you might inherit one from a family member, complete with the good karma that is intrinsic to such historic items.

In a boat nothing beats a box, the bigger the better. The most expensive tackle boxes today are made of wood, usually mahogany, and will never rust. Plastic boxes are excellent, especially if you can get them with brass, instead of steel, hinges. Aluminum is all right for fresh water and so is painted steel. For salt water fishing you'd be foolish to have anything except a wood, or possibly a fiberglass, tackle box.

The advantage of a tackle box over a bag is that it opens wide, and you can see at a glance everything you have aboard. A bag requires more feeling around and more memory on your part. A box is better protection too, especially for reels and plugs.

What about boots and waders? A pair of lightweight hip boots is useful for any angler. But if you're going to be wading sizeable rivers or surf-casting from a beach, it would pay you to spend the extra money for chest-high waders. Waders are safer, if you either use a rubber safety strap or wear a tight belt, they will float you in an emergency. People wearing waders have actually dived into fast water and swum around fairly easily. You can't keep water out of boots, so be sure you can take them off in the water. Whether you use boots or waders, wear a lightweight life jacket if you expect trouble. Some of the new types that inflate with carbon dioxide in an emergency weigh nearly nothing, and you shouldn't face a brawling river without one.

Waders come in two styles: sock-foot and boot-foot. Fly fishing enthusiasts tend to wear stocking foot waders with felt soled or hobnailed boots, while most other anglers use the less expensive boot-footed waders. On slippery rocks (which most are, when wet) you definitely need either felt soles or hobnails. One way of adding hobnails is to have a shoe-maker sand off the waders' corrugated rubber soles and cement golf shoe soles onto smooth rubber. My personal feeling is that hob-nails wear better, are more easily replaced, and probably cut through slime better than felt soles.

You need an emergency patch kit for both boots and waders. You can buy a tube repair kit at any automotive store or service station for repairs in the field. For permanent fixing, it pays to go to a tire-repair service, and depending on the type of rubber or synthetic in your waders, they'll put a permanent patch over the damage.

Boots and waders made of today's synthetic rubbers last much longer than they used to. Natural rubber used to oxidize, and I'll never forget pulling on a pair of boots and having them split down the seam from old age (theirs, not mine). You can keep boots and waders in shape when not in use by hanging them from the feet on wire boot hangers.

In addition to all of the above, you'll need a few odds and ends to carry about in your box or bag pockets. Every angler needs a knife, and except for the surfer, who needs a sheath blade, a folding pocket knife will do a good job for the most part. For the angler who expects to catch and clean a lot of fish, nothing beats a long, thin-bladed fillet knife and a separate scaler.

Another handy accessory is a small pair of long-nosed, side-cutting pliers. These come in handy in working with wire and monofilament. They're also good for unhooking pike, pickerel, and salt water fish—most of whom have teeth.

The fresh water angler needs a set of little scissors or snips. The little two dollar manicure snippers sold everywhere are as good as anything. If you want to make a bigger investment, get one of those Swiss Army knives with a small scissors. Made of stainless steel, these multi-purpose pocket knives will last forever and do an excellent job. The biggest problem with these is in sharpening the cutting blade. The type of stainless steel used is difficult to hone to a really sharp edge.

Under the heading of nice-but-not-essential you could put ferrule cement, a candle stub, strong plastic tape, and a set of small screwdrivers and wrenches for reel repair.

Ferrules, which are what join a rod at its joints, often come loose. Ferrule cement, a relative of sealing wax, is melted with the candle and dripped on. Then the loose ferrule is pushed back over the cement. The tip-top, or top guide, on a fishing rod is put on the same way, so that if you catch a rod tip in a car door and mash an inch or so, you simply heat the tip-top and remove it, whittle the remaining rod tip down to size, apply some ferrule cement, and replace the tip-top. Your rod will be shorter and stiffer, but useable anyway.

The plastic tape is used to put on loose guides and make other repairs. You can even repair a hollow fiberglass rod with it. Take any handy scrap of wood a few inches long and whittle it down to fit into the two ends at the break; apply ferrule cement; force the broken ends down over the stick until they meet and wrap with tape. (If you're near a tackle store and break your rod you can sometimes avoid buying a new one by getting ferrules of the right size and turning the break into a ferrule joint.)

The most frequent reel repair is usually simple lubrication. A reel that is kept oiled causes little trouble. Screws do loosen, however, and you'll need a small screwdriver to keep them tight. Sand and sea water in a reel cause trouble too.

There's only one thing to do with a reel that has broken parts or is in need of other major repair: Ship it back to the factory for an overhaul. You will get a guaranteed job, and usually the cost is much less than what you would pay locally. On the other hand, if you lose a screw, snap a spinning-reel bail, or otherwise break a simple part, you can probably pick up a replacement at a bait and tackle store in your area. An ounce of prevention is a pound of cure along these lines. Clean all reels in fresh water after fishing, oil them at least once every few months, tighten screws a couple of times a year, and you'll save yourself aggravation and expense.

Years ago, every angler carried a tiny stone for sharpening hooks and keeping his knife keen, and it's still a good idea. Now, with monofilament line and eyed hooks, costly snelled hooks aren't used much, and it's probably easier to toss out dull or rusty eyed hooks than to try and sharpen them. Hooks on lures get dull and even rusty, however, and should either be cleaned and sharpened or replaced. A piece of emery cloth or waterproof sandpaper will help too. If you ever try to cut bait or clean fish with a dull knife, you'll never go forth again without a sharpening stone. Of course, you'll find modern steels harder to sharpen than the soft carbon steel of yesteryear, but it's necessary to sharpen them just the same.

We've already talked about using thread to tie on soft bait in connection with salt water fishing. A spool of sewing thread can also be used to repair flies and for various other chores.

Every angler has his or her own way of organizing their gear, so experiment, explore your local fly shop or sporting goods store and design the gear system that works best for you. Part of the fun of becoming an angler is creating your own set-up, and having your vest or tackle box set up so perfectly that it seems like an extension of yourself.

XXX.

Tying Essential Knots

A long with yachtsmen and Boy Scouts, anglers have to know something about knots. As a matter of fact, today's monofilament lines and light tackle call for a more intelligent use of knots than ever before.

Back in the days when fishing was usually done with very heavy lines, the type of knot used to connect the line to the leader or lure didn't make much difference. You had enough reserve strength in the line so that even a poor knot would be strong enough. With the introduction of spinning tackle and lightweight monofilament line for most kinds of fishing came the realization that certain types of knots will cut the line strength by nearly half. Other knots that will hold well with a braided or twisted line slip with monofilament because of its nearly frictionless surface.

You need three basic knots for fishing: a blood knot for tying two lines together, a clinch knot for tying lures and hooks to the end of a line or leader, and an end loop for putting a loop in the end of a line.

These three knots are sufficient for about 90 per cent of all fishing. You may also want to learn a Turle knot for attaching flies in trout and salmon fishing. And a fly caster should also learn the nail knot for attaching the leader to the line.

There are many other knots, of course, but most of them, especially those which involve a jammed slipknot of some sort, seriously weaken monofilament. With a few minutes of practice, you can learn to tie any knot you're going to want. Any person with normal coordination can learn to tie fishing knots quickly and easily. There's no secret involved. And since the knot is the weakest link between you and fish, it's also the most important.

One important factor in knots is the manner in which they are tied. Pulling a knot up slowly and tightly is essential for best results. The leading cause of knot failure with any knot is too short a tail. An eighth-inch tail won't frighten a fish, and it will guarantee that your knot will hold.

Knots used to connect the line or the leader with a lure or a fly should be checked regularly during fishing. If the knot or the last inch or so of the line shows abrasion, cut your line and tie your lure on again. The same thing applies if you get hung up and have to pull very hard on a knot. This can get it tight enough to seriously weaken your line at that point, and it's better to tie a fresh knot than to have one let go when you hook a fish.

BLOOD KNOT: Usage: Tying leaders together or leader to line.

Step 1: Lay ends of lines across one another in an x, with approximately 6 inches of line on each end.

Step 2: Grasp the two lines at the crossing point and wrap the tag end of one of the lines around the other 6 or 7 times.

Step 3: Bring the tag end of the same line back through the x and pass it between both lines.

Step 4: Change hands and repeat Step 2 on the other side, while holding the x.

Step 5. Repeat Step 4 on the opposite side.

Step 6. Let go of the tag end, pull both lines SLOWLY (long ends) away from each other to tighten the knot.

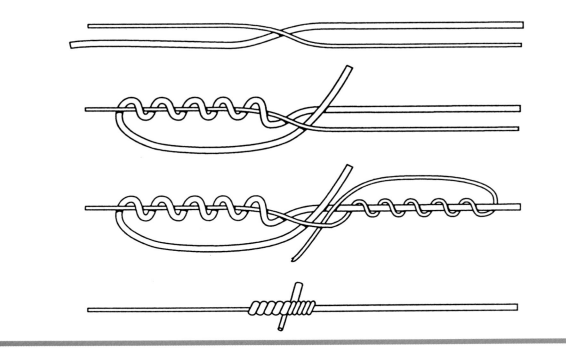

CLINCH KNOT

Usage: Connecting tackle to lines or leader.

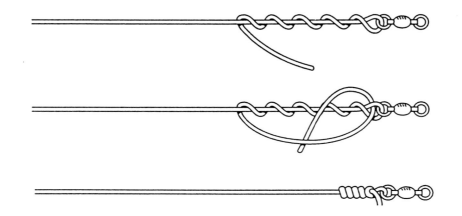

Step 1: Pass the line through the eye of the hook, swivel or lure. Double back and make five turns around the standing line.

Step 2: Holding the coils in place, thread the tag end of the first loop above the eye , then through the big loop.

Step 3: Hold the tag end and pull slowly on the standing line to tighten the knot. Make sure that the coils are in a spiral, not overlapping each other. Slide up tight against the eye.

Step 4: Clip the tag end, making sure not to nick the knot or clip too much off.

END LOOP KNOT

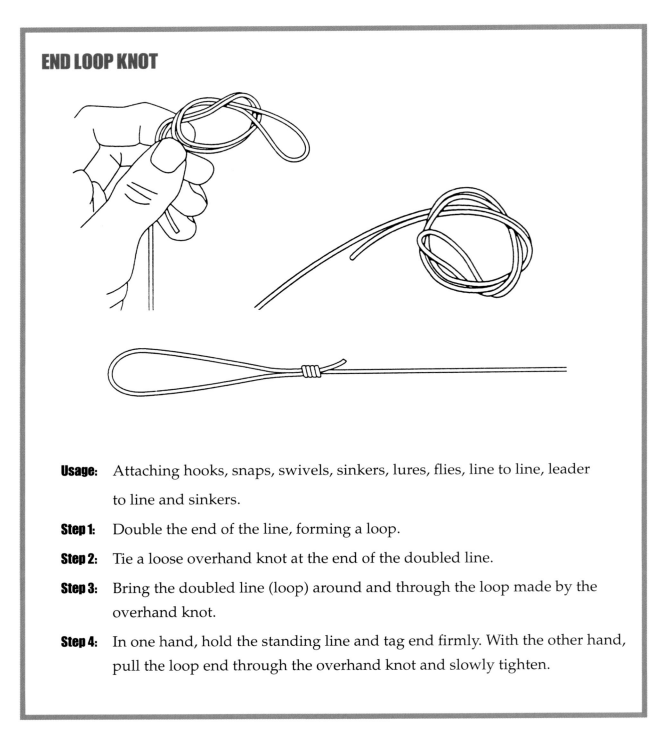

Usage: Attaching hooks, snaps, swivels, sinkers, lures, flies, line to line, leader to line and sinkers.

Step 1: Double the end of the line, forming a loop.

Step 2: Tie a loose overhand knot at the end of the doubled line.

Step 3: Bring the doubled line (loop) around and through the loop made by the overhand knot.

Step 4: In one hand, hold the standing line and tag end firmly. With the other hand, pull the loop end through the overhand knot and slowly tighten.

TIPS FOR KNOT TYING (& UNTYING!)

- Go slowly—until you have mastered the knot, tying too quickly will only end up in tangles.

- When clipping off loose ends, be extra careful not to trim too much. If the clipped end is too close to the actual knot, it can slip and compromise the strength of your knot.

- Carry a pocket-sized knot book in your vest—preferably a waterproof one. They can be very useful as a reminder and a source for a different knot, if the one you know isn't working.

- Carry a knot pick in your vest—they can be invaluable. Use your knot pick (sometimes found on clippers) to untangle your line in the event of a snag or knot or to undo a knot that you've tied.

XXXI.

Fishhooks

Hooks for catching fish are one of man's most ancient inventions. Relics of the Bronze Age are very much like the hooks in use today. You really don't need to know the history of hooks in order to catch fish however. Much more important is that you know something about the different styles and types of hooks and the size you'll need. To confuse matters, unfortunately, there is no such thing as standard sizes for fishhooks. Some patterns, such as Cincinnati Bass, have numbers like 22, 36, and so forth. More normally, fishhooks get smaller in size as their number gets bigger: A No. 18 hook is smaller than a No. 12 hook. And they increase in size as the number is followed by a slash and a zero: A $5/0$ hook is bigger than a $4/0$ hook.

Although hooks come in literally hundreds of styles, the average angler can get by with very few. The most useful of the older types are the Sproat, O'Shaugnessy, and Carlisle, to which might be added the Limerick. In recent years a few new styles, including the Eagle-claw, have been developed and become extremely popular. What's the difference between these? Sproat and O'Shaugnessy are almost identical except that O'Shaugnessy has flat

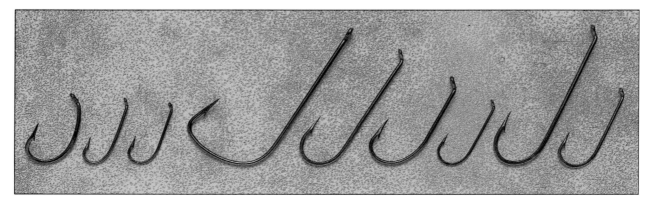

sides because it is forged. It is also very strong for this same reason. Carlisle hooks have very long shanks and are well-suited for members of the pike family and sharp-toothed fish in salt water. Limerick and Aberdeen hooks are made from very fine wire and therefore are good for use with delicate, small bait fish as bait and with small flies.

A good many fishing books go into great detail on sizes and styles of hooks. Yet, in years of buying fishing tackle and hanging around bait and tackle stores, I've never yet seen a customer ask for a 1/0 Sproat or a 3/0 Carlisle. Instead, he'll saunter in and say, "Give me a half dozen fluke hooks and a couple of hooks for school stripers." Or he'll ask for "those little hooks with a barb-like up the shank to hold the bait with."

Therefore, the following table of approximate hook sizes for bait fishing is only a generalization:

Species and Size of Fish	Size of Hook
Small trout and panfish (a half pound or less)	8 or 6
White perch, rock bass, and other large panfish	4 or 2
Carp and suckers	8 or 6
Largemouth bass	2 through $^2/_0$
Smallmouth bass	2 or 1
Pike and pickerel	1 through $^3/_0$
Porgies, surf whiting, and other small salt water bottom feeders	4 through 2
Striped bass, channel bass, and Pacific white bass	2 through $^6/_0$
Weakfish, sea trout, and bluefish	2 through $^2/_0$
Mackerel—all species	4 or 2
Tuna, bonito, and albacore	$^4/_0$ through $^6/_0$
Sailfish, marlin	$^4/_0$ through $^6/_0$
Broadbill swordfish, giant sharks, and tuna	$^6/_0$ through $^{11}/_0$

As you can see from this simplified table, if you carry hooks in sizes 6, 4, 2, $^2/_0$, and $^4/_0$, you are equipped for about 90 per cent of all fishing anywhere. You're ready for everything except very large game fish offshore and very tiny minnows. (To get minnows for bait you need a No. 12 hook or smaller.)

You can tell quality fishhooks by their appearance and finish. The cheapest hooks have a Japanned or blued finish. This is all right in fresh water. For salt water fishing you want nickel-plated, bronzed, solid nickel steel, or stainless-steel hooks. Gold-plated hooks are good also, and in salt water fishing a shiny hook seems to attract attention rather than frighten the fish.

Snelled hooks usually have no eyes and are attached to a snell or a leader that is usually six inches long but may run to eighteen inches or more with a loop at the end. These are still popular in salt water fishing because the loop can be passed through the eye of a swivel and the hook pulled through the loop and tightened to make a foolproof attachment.

The trend today, especially in fresh water fishing, is to buy eyed hooks and tie these directly to the monofilament line or leader. This is much less expensive, and there is no loop or other connection to pick up weeds or attract piscine attention. Another advantage of eyed hooks is that they are easy to store in small plastic boxes. Snelled hooks are a storage and housekeeping problem.

Eyed hooks can be found with a turned-up and a turned-down eye; one doesn't seem to be any better than the other. Straight-eyed, or ringed, hooks are usually very cheap but not very dependable. The offset eye has a definite function in keeping clinch knots from slipping.

XXXII.

What in the World Will You Do with All Those Fish?

ere in the twentieth century we've come to the realization that numbers of fish are limited, even in the sea. We know that over-harvesting of this natural resource will eventually ruin fishing. This is why every state and Canadian province has regulated sport and commercial fishing in fresh water and some states are beginning to regulate salt water fishing as well.

In any dispute between commercial fishermen and sportsmen, the sports-fishing interests generally have won in the long run. The reason is that sports fishermen bring much more money into an area than commercial fishermen do. In Norway, a small country with world-famed salmon fishing, an army of wealthy anglers carrying foreign exchange into the country and willing to pay hotel bills, guide fees, and so forth is much more valuable than a few commercial fishermen selling salmon wholesale at a few cents a pound. Thus, river netting and traps have been abolished, and even in the open fjords, where Norwegian farmers have netting rights going back to the days of the Vikings, netting has been discouraged. Additionally, the Norwegian government and others have made such strong protests to Denmark about salmon netting off the coast of Greenland that this has been greatly curtailed.

With fish a valuable resource everywhere, a real sportsman isn't going to keep more than he can use. Photos of anglers posing with several sailfish or giant tuna is considered extremely poor form. Years ago, sports fishermen, especially in salt water, thought nothing of leaving a catch of two hundred bluefish to rot on the dock. Today, this is no longer true, and with the development of home freezers there is no excuse for anyone selfishly wasting fish. If you are not going to take it home an eat it, throw it back.

Despite the fact that fish are a limited natural resource, it's been proved almost impossible to fish out a lake by hook and line. Trout in a stream can be picked off one by one, but bass are another story. Overfishing in any body of water can throw off nature's balance, however. If enough big predatory fish are removed, the smaller species multiply to fill up the gap. This eventually results in an overpopulation of stunted panfish, and for this reason many areas have no size or bag limits on panfish. Without commercial netting, they multiply faster than their food supply if the larger species that keep them in check aren't numerous enough.

The obvious thing to do with surplus fish is to return them alive to the water to bite again. With lightly hooked fish this is no problem at all. You simply unhook them and toss them back with as little splash as possible. With deeply hooked fish the best idea is to sacrifice a five-cent hook by cutting the line or leader at the fish's mouth and then put him back in the water. A fish's digestive system will handle any hook in short order. Fish can take a lot more punishment than humans, and I've often returned deeply hooked bass by cutting my monofilament line, only to come back a day or so later and catch the same fish with the stub of line still in his mouth. So just because a fish is hooked in the throat or stomach is no excuse for not putting him back. You'll just have to return him with your hook in him. Tearing out the hook is what kills him.

Of course, small fish that are deeply hooked with a treble-hooked lure are poor prospects for survival, and you'll probably want to keep the lure anyway. Yet, if the fish isn't hooked in the gills, so he bleeds to death, a little care on your part will enable him to survive. Up in Ontario I once caught a northern pike that had evidently been landed the year before by someone who simply yanked his spinner loose and tossed the fish back. This fish's gills were loose and floating around in his mouth, but he had healed up and was feeding actively. Thinking he deserved a break, I carefully returned him to the lake.

If you catch fish you're going to keep, the best idea is to keep them either alive or on ice until you can clean them. If you use a stringer, the fish should be hooked through both lips. In the days of wooden boats many of these were built with live wells in which live fish could be kept. Then, when you returned to the dock, you could sort out your catch and return those you didn't want to the water. All bass boats are fully equipped for this sort of thing—some even have little motors to keep water circulating. Marine boats can be fitted with circulating water in bait tanks. You can also buy chemical additives for your tanks to help keep the fish alive.

If neither a stringer nor a live well is used, the best idea is to kill a fish with a smart rap on the head and then keep him as cold as possible. Ice is usually preferred, but a wet sack of any kind will keep fish cool by evaporation. A well-iced Coleman cooler is a good place for keeping fish, as is an old-fashioned galvanized tub with a cake of ice. Any shade, even that of a boat seat, is much better than the blazing sun. On the beach you can bury fish in wet sand, with the tails sticking out so you can find them. One thing you can be certain of is that fish left lying in the sun are going to dry out, making scaling and skinning a chore. Another and more important thing is that they'll spoil and become inedible.

How to Clean and Fillet Fish

Cleaning fish is fairly simple and not as messy as you might think. If you have the proper tools, it's a fast-moving operation. To start, you need running water if possible, otherwise, a bucket of water. You also need a sharp, thin-bladed knife, a pair of pliers, and a scaler. Some people like a small pair of shears to trim the fins with.

The first step in this operation is to decide whether your catch should be scaled or skinned. Scaling is easier. All you do is pull the scaler up against the grain of the scales while using the fish's head as a handle to hold him with. With sharp-finned fish, take care you don't run a spine into your finger; it's a good way to pick up a nasty infection. Nearly all fish, except catfish of all kinds and eels, can be scaled; however, fresh water fish from muddy and algae-filled ponds and lakes as well as slimy salt water fish are usually better skinned. Soft fish, such as mackerel, herring, bluefish, and members of the tuna and bonito family, are impractical to skin because the skin is what holds the fish together. Basically, therefore, you should scale your fish unless they are catfish or eels or you are bothered about a muddy taste from the water.

After a fish is scaled, the easiest and usually best thing to do is cut off the head. Start just behind the skull and make a diagonal slice behind the pectoral fins. This eliminates most of the ribs and muscles. If you do this correctly, you can give the head a pull when you're nearly finished severing it, and most of the insides will come along with it and can be tossed in the garbage can in a single piece. Wash out the inside with cold water, and your fish is ready for icebox or freezer.

It's a good idea to wrap fish in waxed paper, covering all seams with masking tape, before placing them in a refrigerator or a freezer. Fresh fish is odorless but will dry out if

Skinning bass and other fish is a bit more complex. Here's how you go about it:

1. Take a sharp knife and cut down on each side of the dorsal and anal fins (the longitudinal fins).
2. Take a pair of pliers and pull these fins completely out of the fish.
3. Score through the skin behind the pectoral fins and along the full length of the fish on top and bottom.
4. Using the head as a handle in your left hand, take the pliers and strip the skin separately from both sides of the fish.
5. Behead the fish, throw the head and the insides away, wash off, and you're finished.

left unwrapped. The length of time fish will stay fresh in a freezer depends on the species. Oily fish, including shad, mackerel, bluefish, and bonito, don't freeze well. They should be eaten within a few weeks. On the other hand, flounder, codfish, and other bottom species will be in good condition after a year.

Skinning isn't much more complicated. With catfish and eels, cut the skin with a very sharp knife completely around the body just behind the head (and behind the spiny pectoral fins on a catfish) and work it loose enough so you can grip it with your pliers. Then grab the skin with the pliers in your right hand, hold the head firmly in your left hand, using the catfish spines to aid your grip, and pull. The skin will come off over the tail inside out. At this point you behead the fish, taking out the insides along with the head. Then you wash it out, and you're finished.

It's a good idea to fillet good-sized fish, especially flatfish. With flatfish, lay the fish dark side up and make a cut the full length down the middle of the dark side and all the way to the spine, with secondary cuts to the fringe fins at both sides of the head. Starting at the cut down the middle, work off two fillets from this side. Then turn the fish over and repeat the same process on the white side. With the skin side down, you can then slide your knife along between the skin and the flesh and emerge with skinned, boneless fillets. The easiest fillet method for regularly shaped fish is to split the fish open from head to tail, remove the insides, and split down along both sides of the spine. The ribs can then be pulled out to give boneless fillets.

Fish of twenty pounds and over can be steaked after they are cleaned and scaled. Lay the fish on its stomach after washing it and cut through the backbone for the desired thickness of the steaks. Instead of ruining your knife on this backbone cutting, use a butcher cleaver or a hatchet. You can make precise cuts with a hatchet by laying it on the spot you want to cut and hitting the hatchet with a hammer.

There's really nothing to cleaning fish—when you're finished take a hot shower with plenty of soap and put all your smelly clothes in the wash! Seriously, it would probably be worthwhile, if you do a great deal of fishing, to get an apron especially for this job. With a rubber apron and cotton work gloves, you can clean a very large number of fish with very little mess on yourself.

Always remember that cleaning fish is best not postponed. The sooner you can start, the easier it is and the less odor there will be. As soon as you've stopped fishing is the best time to start. The fisherman who arrives homes with his catch scaled or skinned, cleaned, washed out, and packed in ice gets his money's worth from his catch and a happy welcome from his family.

Fish Mounts—A Brief Introduction to Taxidermy

Ever since a cave man put the head of an enemy on a post to impress the passersby, men have been interested in trophies of the chase. With birds and animals this is no real problem. Horns are permanent, and hides and feathers are easily preserved. Fish mounts are much more difficult to make.

The earliest fish mounts were simply preserved skins stretched over a wooden form or tacked on a board. There was no attempt to insert artificial eyes and, of course, no attempt at painting. The result wasn't lifelike, and the unprotected fins frayed away within a few years.

Today, fish taxidermy is quite an art. First, a plaster-of-Paris mold is made of the fish in the desired position. Then the fish is carefully skinned, and the skin is tanned. Meanwhile, the plaster-of-Paris mold is used to make a positive form of papier-mâché or plastic. The skin is put back over this positive form, the fins are reinforced with plastic or sheet metal, and finally, with an artist's touch, the entire fish is painted to look as it did when alive. The quality of the painting, as much as anything else, determines the success of a fish mount. Most specialists in this field are true artists. They start by coating the fish with a silver metallic finish and then paint over this with transparent colors. The result is a vibrant-looking mount that is colored to look almost alive.

If you want a professional taxidermy job, you should look around and choose a taxidermist before you catch your prize. Where do you find taxidermists? The yellow pages of the telephone book, satisfied customers among your friends, and suggestions from the curator of a natural history museum are all good for leads. Before making a final decision, visit the man's shop and look at what he's turning out. The advantages of seeing a taxidermist in advance are several. For one thing, you can look over his finished product and decide whether you like it. For another, you can discuss prices. Equally important, he can tell you how to get the fish back to him ready to be worked on.

You don't have to do any of this. You can arrange to have a charter boat captain or a fishing-camp operator handle your fish mount for you. In most cases they'll be delighted. They usually have a business arrangement with a taxidermist and get paid for referrals. There's nothing the matter with this ethically. A broker or go-between is entitled to a commission. You will have a professional job done, but whether or not you'll like it is something else again. In some areas there are mass-production taxidermy studios from which each fish emerges looking like every other fish. Even different species are painted in the same color tones. If you want only something to hang on the wall, you won't mind this. If you're fussy, and especially if you know something about fish, you won't always be overjoyed at what you get.

There is a shortage of top taxidermists today. It's a growing field too, because with more anglers and hunters the demand for fish and game mounts will increase. A young man with a keen color sense, good manual dexterity, an interest in animals, and a love of the outdoors can go far toward financial security by choosing taxidermy as a career.

Generally speaking, the sooner you get your fish to the taxidermist the better. If it's fresh, he can skin it immediately after making a mold, and you can eat it too. If you can't get it to him right from the water, freeze it and bring it in frozen solid.

If you're really out in the wilds, don't give up. After weighing the fish and taking its length and girth measurements, select the side you want to show on the finished mount, cut the skin longitudinally on the opposite side, and completely skin the fish. Cut the head off short without cutting through the skin on the side that will show. Remove the gills and the eyes too. Cut off all fins underneath the skin. Then remove as much flesh as possible by scraping the inside of the skin with a dull knife. Finally, heavily salt the flesh side of the skin, roll it up, and put it in a waterproof, air-tight container. Even a coffee can will serve for lack of anything else. Next day, drain the container and add more salt. This salted skin will keep for quite a while, and your taxidermist can construct a mold from your measurements.

If you have the do-it-yourself bug, you may want to try mounting fish yourself. The easiest and simplest method is to soap the fish well, bury it halfway in sand, and pour plaster-of-Paris to make a mold. Always pour the plaster over the fish; forcing the fish down in the plaster will distort it. Then, oil the mold carefully or use more soap, and pour in plaster. Setting a bit of hardware cloth with bolts through it in this mold before hardening will help you attach the finished cast to a board. This final "positive" is painted, and you've mounted a fish both cheaply and conveniently. If you really want to do a professional job using the skin and fins of the fish, you need Edward Migdalski's book, How to Make Fish Mounts; or you can buy small do-it-yourself taxidermy kits complete with instructions. Several mail-order merchants, including Herters, Inc., Waseca, Wisconsin, and the Orvis Company in Vermont, sell these.

No matter what you do, the biggest problem will be the painting. Get a color a picture of the species of fish you are working on and try to copy the picture as closely as possible. A color close-up that someone has taken of your own fish can be an immense help. If you're painting a plaster cast, watercolors will do a good job. They're easy to thin down and blend together smoothly. After they thoroughly dry, a coat of spar varnish or even shellac will protect them and add a gloss to your finished product. More advanced painting on real fish skin requires transparent oils and a real artist's technique. Fred Huber, a now retired taxidermist who worked for museums all over the world, used fine brushes and painted each scale individually. It would take him over a year to complete one mount, but it looked like a fish that had just been caught.

So, if you "mess around" with mounting fish, and "mess around" is what you'll find it is—don't expect perfection immediately. Practice makes perfect, and by the time you've made a few mistakes, you'll either give up or improve. There's no middle ground here.

XXXIII.

How to Plan Successful Fishing Trips

I n fishing, as in warfare, being in the right place at the right time makes all the difference. A really successful angler is a person with imagination. Because of his knowledge of fish habits under varying conditions of season, wind, and weather, he knows how to fit his fishing to the circumstances.

The "hot spots" where everybody goes aren't always the best by any means. Just by simple common sense you know that over-all fishing success is going to vary inversely with the fishing pressure. This means that small, overlooked ponds, stretches of river that can't be reached from a road, and brooks that require a good hike back into the hills to reach can be better than a big, well-known resort lake with concrete launching ramps.

Even in built-up areas there are often good fishing spots going unnoticed. Sometimes these are just off main highways. More often, you may have to ask a farmer's permission to walk in and fish. How, therefore, do you find good fishing spots? The answer, for most of us, is with maps.

Everybody is familiar with the road maps available at gasoline stations. Not everybody knows that many of these are filled with minor errors. Furthermore, a road map omits a great many things that a fisherman would like to know. The inexpensive answer to these problems is to write to Office of Outreach, U.S. Geological Survey, 119 National Center, Reston, VA 20192, and request the master map for the state you want to fish in. (For Canada write to the Map Distribution Office, Department of Mines and Technical Surveys, Ottawa, Ontario, Canada.) Most United States Geological Survey maps are published at a scale of one inch to each two thousand feet. In a few western states the scale is slightly different. These maps show cities, towns, highways, railroads, and many individual buildings, including churches, farmhouses, barns, and schools. They also show water features printed

in blue and including all ponds, streams, and rivers. Even more important, these maps have brown contour lines showing elevations and a green overprinting that shows woods. Thus, when you look at a Geological Survey map, you can tell whether a stream is cutting through a steep canyon in the woods or idling along by an open meadow. Swamps and marshes and dams are also shown. All in all, a few Geological Survey maps for the areas you expect to fish will give you planning material you simply can't duplicate, and the cost is very reasonable. They're so complete, you'll be amazed.

Also available free from most state fish and game bureaus are sets of maps, sometimes for the entire state and sometimes for specific fishing areas. These are handy too, especially as they often show docking sites and specific good fishing areas.

When going fishing locally, you should have good maps of your area plus additional information on where to go. Today, more local newspapers than ever before have a hunting and fishing columnist, whose column is usually found on the sports pages. This is a man who is being paid to find out where the fishing is good so that he can tell you about it. If you don't use him, you should. Read what he has to say and then call him at the paper for more information. If you join a sportsmen's group, have the local writer speak at a meeting. Most newspapers are congenial and glad to share their information. The same is true of radio commentators on fishing. Letters and postcards aren't nearly as effective as a telephone call.

Another good source of information is your local conservation office or game warden. This is another person part of whose job is to help you catch more fish. Go and meet him and you'll usually find that he's full of useful information for you that can help make your fishing trips more productive.

At one time or another nearly everybody goes out fishing and leaves at home his bait, his fishing reel, the oars for the boat, the gas tank for the motor, his flies, or you name it. Aside from jumping up and down and making frustrated noises, your only recourse is to go back home and fetch what you've forgotten. This forgetfulness usually means that you miss the evening rise of fish or the best hour of the entire day. The answer is to have a check list posted in the garage or someplace handy, even in your wallet, and refer to it item by item before you leave. It takes only a moment to do this, and the result is highly worthwhile. Nothing is so exasperating as to forget some important piece of equipment. A check list will keep your blood pressure down, your temper under control, and your enjoyment of angling at an all-time high. Be sure it's complete, and then use it. Even some little item can make a big difference. Leaving a rowboat anchor home nearly cost me my life once.

Fishing Guides

In some Canadian provinces the use of a guide is required by law. In many other areas a guide is an excellent investment. What is a guide anyway, and what will he do for you?

A guide is usually a man with a first-rate knowledge of the outdoors. He makes his living by taking people fishing in the summer and by working in lumber camps or other outdoor

Getting there can often be just as exciting as the destination—guides often use small planes to take clients to remote spots.

There are many advantages in using a guide; these are only a few of them:

1. In a strange area—to you—a guide brings you the experience of a lifetime on where and how to fish.

2. Guides are a safety factor. A guide will keep you out of serious trouble in dangerous waters.

3. A guide is a great convenience factor. He or she can arrange for bait, boat, motor, and anything else you need for a successful trip.

4. A guide will make your fishing more pleasant by taking care of rowing, cleaning fish, and other tasks, leaving you free to fish while he or she looks after other things.

---

activities at other times of the year. In the North he knows all about handling small boats and canoes. In the Florida keys he knows the Gulf like the palm of his hand.

Generally, a guide provides a boat and motor or a canoe, as required. This may either be his personal property or belong to the fishing lodge or resort. He takes you fishing, baits your hook—if bait is used, and ties on lures and flies for you. He'll point out where to cast, will net or gaff your fish, and take care of them for you. In most northern areas a guide prides himself on his skill as an outdoor chef and will serve up shore dinners and other fancy repasts at the drop of a skillet. In the Deep South and on charter boats the angler is expected to provide lunch for himself and his guide.

Areas that require guides also require that they be licensed. This means that they must pass examination on their knowledge of the outdoors, on cooking, and on boat-handling ability. Resorts in areas that do not license guides still want the best guides possible, because a good guide can build much business for them. Most of the time, therefore, any guide that is assigned you or that you hire will be a man who knows his job well. People are different, however, and you may get a guide you simply do not get along with. Sometimes it is possible to change, but usually you will have to make the best of things.

If you find the guide assigned to you by a resort operator or outfitter is drunken, incompetent, or extremely lazy, complain. If you have a good case, you'll have a sympathetic audience and will probably be assigned a different guide.

At a camp or a fishing lodge you'll be assigned a guide. If you're going out fishing only by the day as part of a family vacation, you should get a guide if possible. The way to do this in regions without a list of registered guides is to write ahead to the local chamber of commerce and ask them for suggestions. Otherwise, you may get recommendations from a sporting-goods store, a bait and tackle dealer, or even the local garage.

Even if you consider yourself an experienced angler, you owe it to yourself to hire a guide when you first encounter new waters or a totally different type of fishing. For example, if you've never been fly fishing, you should have a guide when trying for salmon even in Nova Scotia, which doesn't require one.

These are a few ideas that will enable you to get the most from the vast majority of guides:

1. Remember that he (or she) is the local expert. Ask how to rig up, what lures to use, what baits to buy, and where to look for fish.

2. Don't try to impress with your income, your position, or your great ability as an angler. He'll get to know you much faster than you'll get to know him. Although uneducated by conventional standards, guides become very astute at understanding people and their foibles. If a customer is a good sport, they'll go out of their way to please.

3. Liquor and guides are a bad combination. It's best not to offer a guide alcohol until the fishing day is over. It's also better not to take it along for yourself. On a hot day you can bring a few cold beers for yourself and the guide, but keep the stronger stuff back in your room or cabin until after fishing hours.

4. To tip or not to tip is a good question. If you're at a resort, ask the owner what is customary. Usually a twenty-dollar bill is an ample tip for a week's work.

5. If you have great success with a lure that's new to the area, give your guide a sample or two. This is a gift he'll really appreciate. If you expect to come back and ask for him again, send him a Christmas card.

XXXIV.

Where to Obtain Reliable Fishing Information

Whether you're going near or far for your fishing, you'll find a great deal of information available from the various states and Canadian provinces as well as from Bermuda. This information includes complete descriptions of fisheries, laws, and license fees. It's impossible to list the laws or the fees here because both are frequently changed. Generally, however, a non-resident fishing license is about five dollars, and some states have a one-day or one-week license that is less expensive. Resident licenses usually run from one dollar up to four dollars. The cost of a fishing license is a tiny segment of the outlay necessary for fishing. You can buy one at most fishing camps and certainly at a town hall. In some areas they are sold in sporting-goods stores as well.

The following breakdown of each of the fifty states includes a brief description of the types of fishing to be found in each along with the published information that is available. Most of the publications are free unless otherwise indicated.

Alabama

Write to the Game & Fish Division, Alabama Department of Conservation, Montgomery, Alabama 36104. A thirty-page booklet, "Public Fishing and Boating Areas of Alabama," will help you locate all fishing waters in the state. It lists all fishing camps in the state, directions for reaching them, the name of the operator, and his telephone number. You can also ask for a copy of "Fishing in Alabama" by I.B. Byrd, Chief Fisheries Biologist. Be sure to request a copy of "Alabama Regulations Relating to Game, Fish and Fur Bearing Animals." If you live in Alabama, subscribe to Alabama Conservation, a magazine. Except for Alabama Conservation, all of these publications are free.

Alaska

Ask the Alaska Department of Fish & Game, Subport Building, Juneau, Alaska 99801, for a copy of "Roadside Sport Fishing Guide." This eighty-page booklet includes maps of all the easily accessible fishing areas, describes the fish found at each, gives details on parking and boat launching facilities, and even tells you what times of year are best for fishing at specific locations. Although some of these spots require a sixty-eight mile boat ride each way, they are all nearby by Alaskan standards. Also get a copy of "Alaska Sport Fishing Seasons and Bag Limits Summary."

Arizona

Although this state is usually looked upon as being mostly desert, "Arizona Fishing Holes" lists nearly two hundred lakes and rivers. This guide to fishing waters and facilities is available free from the Arizona Game & Fish Department, I & E Division, State Building, Phoenix, Arizona 85007. It tells you whether boats or motors are available to rent, whether there are launching and parking areas, what type of access roads exist, and what kind of camping, lodging, and shopping facilities are in the area. You also need a copy of "Arizona Fishing Regulations."

Arkansas

Contact the Game & Fish Commission, Game & Fish Building, Little Rock, Arkansas 72201, and ask for detailed fishing information. In the heart of the Ozarks, Arkansas offers excellent sports fishing, with float trips down the White and Buffalo rivers a specialty.

California

The State of California Resources Agency, Department of Fish & Game, 1416 Ninth Street, Sacramento, California 95814, will provide you with "California Sport Fishing Regulations," "Salmon and Steelhead Fishing Map," "Striped Bass Fishing Map," and "Salt Water Fishing Map." All these maps include a great deal of additional information, including the fact that California is a state requiring a salt water license. If you're a real Alpinist, you'll want a little brochure entitled "Where to Find California's Golden Trout." Since this fish is found only at about the eight thousand-foot level, getting there is probably much of the fun.

Colorado

A note to the Department of Fish & Game & Parks, 6060 Broadway, Denver, Colorado 80216, will get you a copy of "Colorado Fishing, Boating, Parks Information" for a beginning. Also available free are the "Fishes of Colorado," published by the state, and "How to Catch

Trout in Colorado," printed by the Great West Savings & Loan Association, Boulder, Colorado. You'll also want the "Colorado Highway Map," available from the State Highway Department, 4201 East Arkansas Avenue, Denver, Colorado 80222; and the "United States Forest Service and Primitive Area Maps," available from the Denver Federal Center, Building 85, Denver, Colorado 80225. The state also publishes (at a one-dollar annual subscription rate) Colorado Outdoors, and residents should certainly subscribe. The address is 6060 Broadway, Denver, Colorado 80216.

Connecticut

Fishing information on Connecticut comes from the State Board of Fisheries & Game State Office Building, Hartford, Connecticut 06115. In addition to "Hunting, Trapping and Sport Fishing Laws and Regulations," you can obtain "A Guide to Public Access to Connecticut Fishing Waters." This booklet lists every fishing area in the state, both fresh- and salt water, tells how to reach them, what fishing exists, and whether launching sites are available. Another folder, "Salt Water Fishing Information," goes into greater detail on boat-launching sites and fishing possibilities on the Long Island Sound shoreline of the state. Few people realize that Connecticut offers a broad range of angling opportunity, ranging from small-mouth bass and trout to mackerel and bluefish, plus probably the best hook-and-line shad fishing in the East.

Delaware

A small state areawise, but a big one fishwise, Delaware offers both fresh- and salt water angling. Write to the Board of Game and Fish Commissioners, Dover, Delaware 19901, for a copy of "Game, Fish and Dog Laws and Regulations." Some of the best fresh water fishing is in the Chesapeake and Delaware Canal, which crosses the state. Salt water action is found in Delaware Bay and the Atlantic Ocean.

Florida

Send for "Florida's Fresh Water Fishing and Hunting Regulations," published by the Game and Fresh Water Fish Commission, Tallahassee, Florida 32304. Also ask for "Facts about Florida Bass." The Commission also publishes a magazine, Florida Wildlife; a year's subscription is $2.50. For salt water fishing information, your best source is to write a letter to the chamber of commerce of the towns(s) you expect to visit.

Georgia

Write to the Georgia Game & Fish Commission, State Capital Building, Atlanta, Georgia 30302, for "Georgia Fishing Regulations and Trout Schedule" and "Georgia Fish and

Fishing." The latter is a brief guide to lakes, rivers, and streams. A big state, running from mountains to the sea, Georgia has quite a variety of fish life, ranging from rainbow trout in the hills to speckled trout and stripers in the salt water reaches, Maps of the seven U.S. Army Corps of Engineers reservoirs in Georgia, including Allatoona, Lanier, Hartwell, Clark Hill, Fort Gaines, and Savannah Bluff, are available free from the U.S. Army Corps of Engineers, South Atlantic Division, Lawyer's Title Building, Atlanta, Georgia 30302.

Hawaii

This is probably the only state with fishing regulations for octopus. The Division of Fish & Game, 400 South Beretania Street, Honolulu, Hawaii 96813, will send you a schedule of license fees, a booklet, "Freshwater Fishing in Hawaii," a directory of local and common names of fish in Hawaiian waters, and a "Digest of Salt Water Fishing Laws and Regulations." Along with limited fresh water fishing, Hawaii offers excellent surf-casting and some of the finest offshore game fishing in the world. The Kona coast is especially famous for large marlin and dolphins plus yellowfin tuna.

Idaho

High in the Rocky Mountains, Idaho is a salmon and steelhead state per excellence. Write to the Fish & Game Department, P.O. Box 25, Boise, Idaho 83707, for "Idaho Fishing Seasons and Regulations," "Hunting and Fishing in Idaho," and "Salmon and Steelhead in Idaho." Pend Oreille Lake is especially noted as the home of huge Kamloops rainbow trout of thirty pounds and more. Additionally, there is some good but little known bass fishing and the mountain equivalent of big-game fishing, with sturgeon weighing over four hundred pounds. These sturgeon are caught in the Snake River on heavy surf-casting gear, and only those between three feet and six feet in length are legal. (If you get a seven-footer you must put him back.)

Illinois

This state goes to a great deal of effort to keep anglers happy. Write to the Department of Conservation, 400 South Spring Street, Springfield, Illinois 62706, for "Illinois Fishing Regulations." Two other excellent publications are "Illinois Fishing Guide" and "What Fish is This?" The "Fishing Guide" lists waters by county, detailing all facilities, including boat rental and camping, plus the major species of fish. "What Fish is This?" is a very useful pocket-sized booklet showing exactly how to identify thirty-six species of fresh water fish. This would be handy tackle box addition for fishermen anywhere in the Northeast as well as the Middle West.

Indiana

Write to the Division of Fish & Game, State Office Building, Indianapolis, Indiana 46204, for detailed information. Much of the best fishing is on private farm ponds.

Iowa

Out where the tall corn grows you get fishing information from the State Conservation Commission, East 7th and Court, Des Moines, Iowa 50308. In addition to "Iowa Fishing Seasons and Limits," they will send you "Iowa Trout Fishing," which details the areas in the northeastern part of the state where beautiful streams—including the Turkey, Upper Iowa, Yellow, and Wapsipinicon rivers—flow through narrow valleys bounded by heavily timbered bluffs to create some of the Midwest's finest scenery. Another pamphlet, "The Fish Factories," gives interesting details on the raising of wall-eyes and northern pike in state hatcheries. In addition to these free publications, you can subscribe to The Iowa Conservationist for one dollar yearly. It's published monthly by the State Conservation Commission.

Kansas

Who would think of Kansas as a fishing state? Yet fourteen federal reservoirs now dot the countryside, and five more are nearly finished. In addition, more than forty state-owned lakes are open to fishing; and there are thousands of farm ponds, creeks, and rivers. The larger rivers offer catfish up to seventy pounds, and the smaller watercourses, including the Elk, Fall, Delaware, Caney, Wakarusa, Whitewater, and Pawnee rivers, have numerous bass, crappie, and other game fish.

"Kansas Fishing Regulations," "Where to Fish in Kansas," and "What Have I Caught?" are all available free of charge. "Where to Fish in Kansas" lists every public water in the state, with full details on the fish to be found and the availability of camping, picnicking, bait, and boats. "What Have I Caught?" is a good identification manual that is especially excellent on the various buffalo fish and suckers not included in most pocket guides of this type. "Four Seasons of Fun in Kansas," a small folder, includes location maps for the prime fishing waters of the state, and "Guide to Strip Pit Fishing and Hunting" details the fishing opportunities in the strip-pit areas of Crawford and Cherokee counties in southeastern Kansas. Write to the Forestry, Fish and Game Commission, Box 1028, Pratt, Kansas 67124, for all this material.

Kentucky

The biggest problem in Kentucky fishing has long been pollution, which has ruined several of the best bass rivers in the state. For full details on Kentucky fishing write to the

Department of Fish and Wildlife Resources, State Office Building Annex, Frankfort, Kentucky 40601.

Louisiana

The bayou area along the Gulf coast has long been famed for excellent bass fishing. Louisiana also offers excellent salt water bay and offshore fishing for a wide variety of species. The place to write for information is the Wildlife and Fisheries Commission, 400 Royal Street, New Orleans, Louisiana 70130.

Maine

Among the top fishing in the nation, Maine is extremely eager to attract and please anglers. The Inland Fisheries and Game Department, Augusta, Maine 04330, is the place to write. In addition to "Maine Fishing Laws Summary," you'll want two interesting folders, "Maine Inland Fishing" and "Maine Salt Water Fishing." The latter publication offers a complete list of all the salt water sports-fishing captains in the state and includes name, address, and telephone number for each, information on size and capacity of his boat, and what equipment is carried aboard. Information on where to stay for Maine fresh water fishing can be obtained from the Maine Publicity Bureau, Gateway Circle, Portland, Maine 04111. They offer a complete list of hotels, motels, camps, and tourist homes and can also furnish a list of licensed guides.

Maryland

This is another superb fishing state. Write to the Department of Game and Inland Fish, State Office Building, Annapolis, Maryland 21404, for their "Angler's Guide." This contains details on trout streams, lakes, and ponds open to public fishing and boat-launching ramps on inland waters. You'll also want "Maryland Tidewater Fishing Guide." This is a huge map that shows access roads, marine facilities, and fishing grounds throughout the famed Chesapeake Bay area. For one dollar a year you can subscribe to The Maryland Conservationist, a bi-monthly magazine filled with information on fresh- and salt water angling and wildlife. It's published by the Department of Game and Inland Fish.

Massachusetts

Write to the Division of Fisheries and Game, 73 Tremont Street, Boston, Massachusetts 02108, for complete details. Noted especially for striped-bass fishing around Cape Cod, Cuttyhunk, and the Elizabeth Islands, Massachusetts has some excellent fresh water fishing as well. The giant Quabbin Reservoir nearly in the center of the state is especially good, and there are many other smaller lakes and ponds, including a few with trout bass in the middle of sandy Cape Cod.

Michigan

Noted as a state for outdoorsmen, Michigan over the years has invested a fortune to produce and continue good fishing. Along with other states on the Great Lakes, Michigan was dealt a severe blow when the sea lampreys invaded these lakes and proceeded to nearly exterminate trout and whitefish. Today, after years of research, the lamprey has been brought almost under control, and the state is now looking for ways of controlling threadfin shad and other minnows that eat quantities of lake-trout spawn. Pacific salmon, including Cohoes and kokanees, have been introduced successfully, and fishing for Cohoes is expected to become even better than that on the Pacific coast. Some thought has also been given to introducing striped bass, but this has been postponed pending a review of the success with various salmon species.

The Department of Conservation, Lansing, Michigan 48926, publishes "Rules for Fishing in Michigan," "Directory of Lakes and Ponds Planted with Trout," "Michigan Water Access Sites," "Sport Fishing Guide to Grand Traverse Bay," "Handbook for Ice Fishermen," and an educational booklet, "Fish for More Fishermen." In addition, a small folder, "Michigan Fish," describes the various game-fish species and gives details on how to catch them throughout the state. (All booklets mentioned are free.)

Minnesota

Another outstanding fishing state, Minnesota has many aids for the angler. Contact the Department of Conservation, Division of Fish & Game, St. Paul, Minnesota 55101, for "Fishing Law Synopsis" and "Let's Go Fishing in Minnesota." Also free is "Recreation News, Official Guide to Minnesota Waters." Along with these free publications, Minnesota has produced some very worthwhile maps and guidebooks for sale at moderate prices. These include three regional books collectively covering south, north, and central Minnesota, with two-color depth-sounding maps of Minnesota lakes. Each regional book is two dollars and contains maps for twenty-five lakes. Additionally, for three dollars you can purchase "Guide to Fun in Minnesota," a 132-page listing of canoe trails, trout streams and lakes, county maps, camp grounds and access sites, and much more. These priced publications are sold by the State of Minnesota, Documents Section, 140 Centennial Office Building, St. Paul, Minnesota 55101.

Mississippi

This self-termed Hospitality State certainly offers both native and visiting anglers a wide variety of fishing to choose from. The State Game & Fish Commission, P.O. Box 451, Jackson, Mississippi 39205, is the place to write for full details. You'll want "Digest of Sport Fishing Laws and Regulations," "Fishing in Mississippi," and "Mississippi Game and Fish

Commission Owned Lakes" from the Commission. Individual maps of Enid Lake, Sardis Lake, and Askabutla Lake are available free from the Mississippi River Commission, United States Army Engineer District, Vicksburg, Corps of Engineers, Vicksburg, Mississippi 39180. Also free from the state is a map of the Ross Barnett Reservoir, a giant body of water stretching forty-three miles from the outskirts of Jackson nearly all the way upstream to Carthage on the Pearl River. Largemouth bass, several species of sunfish, and catfish are the prime target of Mississippi anglers; and there is good fishing for redfish, spotted sea trout, king mackerel, and other species in the Gulf off Biloxi, Gulfport, and Pascagoula. Despite a turbulent recent history of civil-rights disturbances, the sportsman visiting Mississippi can count on receiving a good welcome and good fishing unless he goes out of his way to look for trouble.

Missouri

Noted for very good bass fishing in the Ozarks down near the Arkansas border, Missouri plays host to many visiting fishermen every year. Contact the Conversation Commission, Box 180, Jefferson City, Missouri 65102, for detailed data. Table Rock Lake and Lake Taneycomo are especially highly regarded.

Montana

Some of the material you can get from the Department of Fish & Game, Helena, Montana 59601, includes "Montana Hunting and Fishing," "Montana Fishing Map," "A Classification of Montana Fishing Streams," "A Guide to Boating in Montana," and "Montana Camping and Picnic Areas." You also need "Montana Fishing Regulations." This state is especially noted for its trout fishing, with such nationally famous streams as the Big Hole River, Flathead River, Madison River, Rock Creek, and the Yellowstone River; however, there are walleyes, northern pike, catfish, and bass in the larger rivers and reservoirs in the eastern and central parts of the state. Both the "Guide to Boating" and "Montana Hunting and Fishing" list fishing access sites open to the public. A list of licensed guides, most of whom specialize in summertime horseback pack trips into high mountain country that sees very few anglers, is available through the Department of Fish & Game in Helena.

Nebraska

Although probably few people would think of traveling to Nebraska on a fishing trip, it offers a broad variety of very good fishing for bass, pike, panfish, catfish, and carp. Write to the Game, Forestation and Parks Commission, Lincoln, Nebraska 68509, and ask for "Nebraskaland Fishing Guide" and "Where to Fish in Nebraska." The latter thirty-five-page booklet gives complete maps and details for lakes and streams in every area of this big state. A resident should subscribe to the Commission magazine, Nebraskaland, which is probably the most colorful, best illustrated, and most interesting of any of the state magazines; the three-dollar annual subscription is a bargain.

Nebraska is where the world's record sauger was caught; and it has produced ten-pound largemouth bass, twenty-eight-pound northern pike, twelve-pound rainbow trout, and a two-pound-eight-ounce bluegill sunfish. This isn't bad for the heart of the Great Plains!

Nevada

Better known for gambling than fishing, Nevada has some wonderful trout areas. Write to the Nevada Fish & Game Department, Box 678 Reno, Nevada 89504, for "Fishing Seasons and Regulations," "Angler's Guide to Lake Tahoe," and "Angler's Guide to Northeast Nevada." These publications emphasize a good many uncrowded waters that can be reached only on foot or by horse. The angler willing to walk or ride a pack horse can find numerous Nevada waters suffering from too little fishing pressure. The Ruby area, including Boulder, Kleckner, Long Canyon, Pearl, Soldier, Secret, and North Furlong creeks, is very good and includes some out-of-the-way mountain lakes in spectacular scenery.

New Hampshire

Combining mountains and seashore, this is another first-rate fishing state. You can rate it well at the top of your list. The Fish & Game Department, 34 Bridge Street, Concord, New Hampshire 03301, will supply you with "Fishing Rules and Regulations," "New Hampshire Fishing and Hunting," "Recommended Bass Waters," and "Angler's Guide to Trout and Salmon." ("Salmon" here refers to landlocked salmon and not to Atlantic or Pacific species.) Lake Sunapee trout, also known as aureolus or golden trout, are a species found in only a few lakes. They are not related to the golden trout of California, but are considered a landlocked subspecies of Arctic char by some scientists and a distinct species by others. You'll find them very difficult to catch. New Hampshire also has special pamphlets available on salt water fishing, striped-bass fishing, and smelt fishing. Ask for them if you're interested.

New Jersey

Write to the New Jersey State Division of Fish & Game, Box 1809, Trenton, New Jersey 08607, for information. You'll want "Compendium of New Jersey Fish Laws." This includes a listing of all waters stocked with trout, plus a listing of tidal waters for which no license is required. New Jersey Outdoors, published by the Division of Fish & Game at two dollars a year, is an excellent small magazine devoted to local fishing and hunting. The F. &. M. Schaefer Brewing Company, 430 Kent Avenue, Brooklyn, New York 11211, also publishes a free pocket booklet, "Fresh Water Fishing in New Jersey." The state has published very little on its excellent salt water fishing. Information on this may be obtained from the Cape May

County Chamber of Commerce, Cape May Courthouse, New Jersey 08210; the Asbury Park Press, Press Plaza, Asbury Park, New Jersey 07712; and the Long Branch Daily Record, 192 Broadway, Long Branch, New Jersey 07740.

New Mexico

As is true in neighboring Arizona, New Mexico fishing has been greatly improved by the big increase in dam building that started in the 1930's. Along with white and black bass, crappie, bluegill, and catfish in the lakes, New Mexico offers first-rate trout fishing in its high mountain country. Write to the New Mexico Department of Game & Fish, State Capitol, Santa Fe, New Mexico 81501, for "New Mexico Fishing Regulations" and "Fishing in New Mexico." For complete information year-round, subscribe to New Mexico Wildlife at one dollar for six bi-monthly issues. It's published by the Game & Fish Department. In addition, you may want free copies of "Fishing Waters of New Mexico," a keyed map showing trout and warm water streams and lakes, and "Hunting and Fishing Map of New Mexico," which emphasizes the fourteen million acres of public domain within the state.

New York

Despite a huge human population, the Empire State need take a back seat to none when it comes to fishing. The Conservation Department, Division of Conservation Education, Albany, New York 12226, will provide you with "Hunting-Trapping-Fishing Guide." You'll also want "1,001 Top New York Fishing Waters," a free publication that includes a list of wilderness ponds accessible only to hikers, public fishing streams, and fifty top trout streams. All these waters are arranged by major species of fish. One of the top publications of its kind, The New York State Conservationist is a beautiful magazine selling for just two dollars per year through the Division of Conservation Education. Special reprints from this magazine are available and include "Baits for the Marine Fisherman" and "Some Panfishes of New York." Available free from Newsday, 550 Stewart Avenue, Garden City, New York 11530, is "The Long Island Fisherman." This booklet covers salt water fishing and includes some where-to-go information.

North Carolina

For fishing information on the Tarheel State write to the Wildlife Resources Commission, Raleigh, North Carolina 27602, and ask for "Fishing Regulations" and a copy of the illustrated booklet, "Fishing and Hunting in North Carolina." This free guidebook takes you all the way from the Gulf Stream off Cape Hatteras up into the mountains and lists many other additional maps and guides with instructions on how to obtain them.

Something very unique with North Carolina is their college course to instruct sportsmen and their families in the fine art of angling. Each June the College Extension Division of

North Carolina State University offers a six-day short course in sports fishing at Hatteras. The "lab work" includes boats, piers, and salt and fresh waters in Dare County. The fee covers board, lodging, boats, bait, and instruction. For details and application blanks write to the Extension Division, North Carolina State University, P.O. Box 5125, College Station, Raleigh, North Carolina. Even if you've had a great deal of fishing experience, this course is an exceptional bargain and gives you an opportunity to do a large amount of varied fishing at nominal cost.

North Dakota

Write to the Game & Fish Department, Bismarck, North Dakota 58501, for a current copy of "Fish and Game Code." Until quite recently North Dakota fishing was not especially good. A major problem was that most lakes and streams were shallow and froze so thickly in the severe winters that fish could not survive. In recent years big dams on the Missouri River have created better fish habitat, especially for northern pike.

Ohio

The Ohio Division of Wildlife, 1500 Dublin Road, Columbus, Ohio 43212, will send you "Fishing Law Digest," "Travel Ohio for Fun," "Ohio State Parks Camping Guide," and "The Wonderful World of Ohio State Parks." Another small pamphlet, "Fish and Hunt in Ohio," lists, locates, and shows on a handy map all public fishing grounds in the state. With over one hundred thousand acres of inland lake, seven thousand miles of streams, and a large section of Lake Erie, there's certainly enough water. Lake Erie, however, is so badly polluted that fishing has fallen off badly and will continue to be poor until this situation is corrected, probably sometime in the 1970's. One of the few states with all of the North American members of the pike family, Ohio contains northern pike, muskellunge, chain pickerel, and the smaller pickerels too. It is particularly noted for its bass and catfish.

Oklahoma

For information on fishing in Oklahoma contact the Department of Wildlife Conservation, 1801 North Lincoln, Oklahoma City, Oklahoma 73105. This is another state that had very little dependable water until recent years, but has since developed some fairly good fishing in man-made reservoirs. Among the folders available are "Digest of Oklahoma Fishing and Hunting Laws," "Public Recreation Areas of Oklahoma," and "Game Fishes of Oklahoma."

Oregon

The Oregon State Game Commission, Box 3503, Portland, Oregon 97208, will send you "Synopsis of Oregon Angling Regulations" and their handy booklet, "Fishing in Oregon."

The latter guidebook divides the state into ten angling zones and discusses each separately. Unlike eastern states, most Oregon beaches are publicly owned, and about a quarter of the state is part of the National Forest lands. This means that camping is relatively simple. Along the seacoast, there's good fishing for striped bass in the Coos Bay area and for various salmon species from California to Washington. Inland, there are steelhead and trout streams everywhere, plus quite a few lakes containing largemouth and smallmouth bass and panfish. Various shore-caught fish, including greenling and ling cod, are found in astronomical numbers. In short, fishing in Oregon is mostly a pleasure.

Pennsylvania

A note to the Pennsylvania Fish Commission, Harrisburg, Pennsylvania 17120, will bring you "Fishing Regulations and Summary of Fish Laws." The "Fisherman's Guide to Pennsylvania Waters and Access Areas" is about the best-organized little book of its kind. Lakes and streams are arranged both alphabetically and by county, with a listing of fish species and access routes. There's also a chart of Fish Commission access areas that shows launching ramps and other facilities. Another good thing to have is the Atlantic Refining Company's "Atlantic Fishing Map of Pennsylvania." You may be able to get one from the Fish Commission; otherwise see an Atlantic Oil dealer. If you are seriously interested in Pennsylvania, you should subscribe to The Pennsylvania Angler. This publication of the Pennsylvania Fish Commission is two dollars a year.

Some of the best trout streams in North America are found in Pennsylvania, and there is good fishing for everything from bass and muskies to carp and catfish. Among its special delights are some of the finest fly fishing -only areas of any state. And it offers three unusual "Fish for Fun" projects in which fishing is allowed year-round, but all fish caught must be returned unharmed to the water.

Rhode Island

Good things come in small packages, and the nation's smallest state offers some of its finest fishing. Write to the Division of Fish & Game, Veterans' Memorial Building, 83 Park Street, Providence, Rhode Island 02903. You need a copy of "Rhode Island Fishing Laws," and you might also like a small release entitled "Rhode Island Fish You Might Catch." Primarily famed for striped bass and bluefish, little Rhode Island also offers trout, yellow and white perch, largemouth and smallmouth bass, and chain pickerel in more than thirty lakes and ponds.

South Carolina

"From the Mountains to the Sea . . . Fishing in South Carolina" is published by the South Carolina Wildlife Resources Department, Box 167, Columbia, South Carolina 29202. Here, amid many maps and illustrations, you'll get the complete picture on where to go, where to launch, and how to fish. Included are complete maps of lakes Marion and Moultrie, which are known for their well-established populations of fresh water striped bass; the finest lake fishing in the world for these marine game fish is found here. Lake Murray, near Columbia, is noted as one of the best largemouth-bass lakes in the world, so South Carolina is good in more than one department. Angling here varies from catching trout in miles of streams up in the hills to fishing for more than fifteen major salt water species, ranging from sheepshead on bottom to tarpon on top. "Fishing Regulations for the State of South Carolina" is essential and is automatically given to every license buyer. If you're interested in fresh water, read these rules carefully because extra permits are required on some bodies of water.

South Dakota

The Department of Game, Fish & Parks, Pierre, South Dakota 57501, will send you "Fishing Regulations" and "Fishing the Great Lakes of South Dakota." These impoundments on the Missouri River are quite big. Oahe Reservoir is 250 miles long and 210 feet deep; Lake Sharpe is 80 miles long; Lake Francis Case is 110 miles long; and Lewis and Clark Lake is 37 mile long. These large lakes have created excellent fishing for walleyes, northern pike, catfish, and bass. Some of the strings of fish taken here are really eye-openers. Also available is a little booklet, "Know Your South Dakota Fishes." It has good pictures of thirty-three species.

Tennessee

Northern and southern species meet here in the twenty-two lakes created by the TVA and the United States Army Corps of Engineers. The smallest of these has 900 acres of surface water, the largest over 2,800 miles of shoreline. The Tennessee Game & Fish Commission, Doctors Building, 706 Church Street, Nashville, Tennessee 37203, will gladly send you "Guide to Tennessee Fishing," "Tennessee Fish and Where to Catch Them," and "Fishing Guide to the Twenty-two Great Lakes of Tennessee." This last folder lists the facilities available at 324 fishing docks along with the name and address of each operator. It also has pictures of some of the record fish taken in these lakes, including a twenty-six-pound brown trout, a twelve-pound smallmouth bass, and twenty-one-pound walleye. The giant lakes are only one part of the fishing picture in a state with over fifteen thousand farm ponds and dozens of mountain trout streams. There are also many excellent smallmouth bass streams, especially the Powell and Clinch rivers, Little River, Elk River, and a variety of others.

Texas

There's so much fishing in Texas, you'd be best off checking out "Game Fishes of the

Texas Coast." "Let's Go Fishing in Texas" is a complete guide to finding and catching the various fresh water species in the state, with special emphasis on catfish and carp, but including information on white bass, largemouth bass, and crappie. "Food and Game Fishes of the Texas Coast" is a beautifully illustrated guide covering seventy Gulf of Mexico species. This is probably the most complete guide to southern salt water fish available. It's free, so don't miss it.

Utah

This is still another naturally arid state that has developed some very fine fishing. Request the Department of Fish & Game, 1596 West North Temple, Salt Lake City, Utah 84116, to send you their "Angling Regulations" and "Utah Fishing and Hunting Guide." There are literally dozens of first-rate trout streams in Utah, hundreds of productive brooks, and a number of lakes and reservoirs, including 186-mile-long Lake Powell in the Glen Canyon National Recreation area. The guidebook gives you exact directions to many of the better fishing areas.

Vermont

Much like New Hampshire, Vermont is basically a region of trout streams and small ponds. Its one really big lake is Lake Champlain, which it shares with New York all the way up to Canada. Smallmouth bass, northern pike, yellow perch, and pickerel round out the fishing picture, although the smelt shanties on Lake Champlain during the winter are famous. For information contact the Fish & Game Department, Montpelier, Vermont 05601.

Virginia

Fishing in the old Dominion much resembles that in North Carolina. There is excellent salt water fishing in Chesapeake Bay and in the ocean. Most of the rest of the state is large-mouth-bass country, with trout and smallmouths found along the West Virginia border high in the Appalachians. A letter to the Commission of Game & Inland Fisheries, Box 1642, Richmond, Virginia 23213, will bring your complete details.

Washington

The Department of Fisheries, General Administration Building, Olympia, Washington 98501, is the place to go for facts on Washington State fishing. Ask for "Sport Fishing Regulations," "Tips for the Salmon Salt Water Angler," and "Guide to Salmon Lures," As you might guess, Chinook and Cohoe salmon are the most important sports fish along the coast. Inland, there are steelhead in the rivers, trout in the mountains, and bass and panfish in the lakes and reservoirs. This is one state with definite bag limits on many kinds of salt water fish, as well as on clams and crabs. Even if you expect to fish only in fresh water, you'll be smart to get a copy of the regulations.

West Virginia

Despite the fact that some people still think that West Virginia refers to the western part of the mother state, Mountaineer Land is not only independent, but is blessed with numerous creeks and rivers. Write to the Department of Natural Resources, Charleston, West Virginia 25321, for "West Virginia Fishing Regulations." You'll also want "A Guide to Year-Round Trout Fishing in West Virginia," and you can ask for a fishing map of the state. The Department also publishes a magazine, West Virginia Conservation.

In addition to trout, West Virginia is noted for smallmouth bass, with particularly good fishing in the Potomac and Greenbrier river systems. There are largemouth bass in creeks draining into the Ohio River and also some muskellunge. The state is probably most noted for its West Virginia Centennial golden trout. Actually a partial albino rainbow, this beautiful yellow fish was developed to become an important part of the state's Centennial Celebration in 1963. Since that time, it's been purchased by other states for stocking in their own waters. It is not related closely to either the golden trout of California or the Sunapee golden trout of New Hampshire.

Wisconsin

Noted as a state well-stocked with muskies, walleyes, and northern pike, Wisconsin also has a large number of largemouth and smallmouth bass, and yellow perch by the barrelful. Contact the Conservation Department, Box 450, Madison, Wisconsin 53701, for full information.

Wyoming

Write to the Wyoming Fish & Game Commission, Box 378, Cheyenne, Wyoming 82001, and ask for "Wyoming Fishing Orders" and "Wyoming Fishing Guide," The Guide describes all waters in the state arranged by area, with comments on accessibility and fishing quality. This is primarily a trout state, with rainbows predominating, but there are also some excellent cutthroat streams. A few high mountain streams and ponds have greyling and true golden trout. The Powder, Yellowstone, Sweetwater, and Buffalo rivers have as good fly fishing as you'll find anywhere. One note of caution: Before you go wandering around unpaved roads, ask locally whether you need a four-wheel drive vehicle to get out again. Most of the best Wyoming trout waters are a good distance from highways, and some must be reached either by hiking or on horseback.

In addition to the fifty divisions of the United States, excellent fishing is also found in Bermuda and the various Canadian provinces. Here's a brief rundown on these.

Bermuda

This beautiful island lies right in the Gulf Stream and offers varied fishing for everything from bonefish and barracuda to marlin, tuna of several species, and a huge variety of reef fish. For fishing information write to Bermuda Fishing Information Bureau, 50 Front Street, Hamilton, Bermuda. They will send you a beautiful booklet, "Bermuda—Island of Great Fishing," which contains a rundown on all available species of fish and types of fishing and a complete list of the members of the Bermuda Game fishing Guides Association and their telephone numbers. The Association is an
organization of captains and boat owners that protects the public by setting standards for equipment and crew and establishing prices.

Canada

If you're looking for a quick review of Canadian fishing, the Canadian Government Travel Bureau, Ottawa, Ontario, Canada, has a booklet, "Where to Fish in Canada." This will give you a superficial idea as to what the thirteen individual provinces and territories have to offer. Bear in mind that Canada is larger than the continental United States and you can't really cover the country in a thirty-two-page handbook.

The Canadian Government Travel Bureau does provide a free travel-counseling service to help you get the most from a Canadian vacation. You can either contact them at Ottawa or at the following addresses in the United States: Canadian Government Travel Bureau, 680 Fifty Avenue, New York, New York 10019; Canadian Government Travel Bureau, 102 West Monroe Street, Chicago, Illinois 60603; Canadian Government Travel Bureau, 1 Second Street, San Francisco, California 94101.

Taking the Canadian provinces and territories separately, the following lists some of the literature available to you (without charge, unless otherwise indicated).

Alberta

The place to write is the Department of Lands and Forests, Fish and Wildlife Division, Edmonton, Alberta. They'll send you a "Summary of Angling Regulations" and "Angler's Guide to Alberta Fishes," an illustrated booklet that indicates where to fish for each species. Running west from the Great Plains way up into the Rockies, most of Alberta is high, cold water trout country.

British Columbia

Lying just north of the state of Washington, British Columbia has superb salmon fishing, especially along the eastern shore of Vancouver Island. Inland, you'll find the world's finest fishing, plus cutthroat and Dolly Varden trout. Contact the Department of Recreation and Conservation, Victoria, British Columbia, Canada, and tell them the kind of fishing that interests you. "Sports Fishing in British Columbia" offers a road map of the province and information on season, species, and areas.

Manitoba

Contact the Tourist Development Branch, Department of Industry and Commerce, Winnipeg 1, Manitoba, Canada, for a copy of "Fish Manitoba!" If you want special personal attention on planning the details of a fishing trip, write to Mr. Wilf Organ, Director of Tourist Development, 511 Norquay Building, Winnipeg 1, Manitoba, Canada. The leading species here are eastern brook trout, Arctic chair, lake trout, walleye, northern pike, small-mouth bass, and northern pike. A booklet, "Where to Stay in Manitoba," lists hunting and fishing lodges and licensed outfitters. The Canadian National Railroad also runs Manitoba fishing tours on a package-deal basis.

New Brunswick

The Premier of this province recently described it as differing from the United States in that "We have pockets of prosperity." This is not a region of rich industry or agriculture, but when it comes to fishing, there are few places like it in the entire world. For one thing, the Restigouche and Miramichi rivers are probably the two finest salmon rivers in North America. Smallmouth-bass fishing is sensational in the St. Croix River area, and brook trout are all over the place. Salt water fishing is first-rate also, but few tourists take advantage of it. There is almost untapped stripped-bass action in the St. John River and the Bay of Fundy; codfish, flounder, and other bottom species are a drug on the market.

Available from the Fish & Wildlife Branch, Department of Lands and Mines, Fredericton, New Brunswick, Canada, are "Summary of Fishery Laws," "Where to Stay in New Brunswick," and "Fish and Hunt in New Brunswick." This last publication lists every licensed fishing camp and outfitter in the province, his name, address, accommodations, and type of fishing offered. They'll also send you a free tour map and a list of tenting, trailer, and picnic sites.

Newfoundland

For the salmon and trout fisherman, Newfoundland and Labrador stand nearly alone. There is also excellent fishing for giant tuna, some of it in the immediate vicinity of St.

John's. Send to the Newfoundland Tourist Development Office, St. John's, Newfoundland, Canada, for a copy of "Fishing in Newfoundland and Labrador." Also ask them for their list of licensed guides and outfitters. One note of caution: Most roads in Newfoundland are not paved, making driving difficult. Airline rates are low enough in Canada so that it would probably be best to fly from Sidney or even from Halifax, Nova Scotia, to Corner Brook or Gander and arrange to be met at the airport.

Northwest Territories

Feel adventurous? Write to the Northwest Territories, Tourist Office, 400 Laurier Avenue, West, Ottawa 4, Ontario, Canada. They'll send you a copy of "Travel North" and "Inn and Igloo." The latter publication is their accommodation guide and explains that you can travel by dog sled and your Eskimo guide will build you a snow igloo. They suggest that igloos are only suitable in winter and early spring (too damp in warm weather).

One brand new idea just begun by the Hudson's Bay Company is a "U-Paddle Canoe Rental Service." The company rents aluminum canoes to experienced canoe-trip fans throughout the North at such places as Yellowknife, Ile à la Cross, La Ronge, and Norway House. The charges are twenty-five dollars a week, which is the minimum rental period, and as with car rental, canoes may be picked up at one company post and turned in at another. If you're interested, contact the Northern Stores Department, Hudson's Bay Company, Hudson's Bay House, Winnipeg 1, Canada.

What can you catch up there? Arctic char, Arctic grayling, plus northern pike up to forty pounds. Very big lake trout and the Inconnu, a member of the whitefish family weighing up to seventy pounds, will also keep you busy. Ask for the pamphlet, "Angling in the Arctic."

Nova Scotia

Along the 4,600 miles of coastline here you'll find some of the finest salt water fishing in the world. The world's record bluefin tuna, 977 pounds, was caught off Cape Breton. You'll also find pollock, cod, haddock, mackerel, flounder, and striped bass in ample supply. Combine this with exciting fishing for Atlantic salmon, brook trout, and small-mouth bass, and you really have an angler's paradise, with beautiful scenery thrown in for good measure.

Write to the Nova Scotia Travel Bureau, Provincial Building, Halifax, Nova Scotia, Canada, for "Salt Water Sport Fishing." "Outdoors in Nova Scotia," and a list of licensed guides and outfitters. Also available is a list of inns, hotels, and motels that have been government inspected and approved.

Ontario

Several times the size of Texas, this province has such varied fishing that they publish separate guides for the various divisions. The Department of Lands and Forests, Parliament Buildings, Toronto 5, Ontario, Canada, will provide you with "Where to Fish in Northeastern Ontario." "Where to Fish in Southern Ontario," and "Where to Fish in Northwestern Ontario." You'll also want an official road map to which these booklets are coded. You'll need "Summary of Ontario Fishery Regulations" as well. Ontario fishing covers a wide variety, but the province is especially noted for smallmouth bass, northern pike, walleyes, and muskellunge. Some of the Rideau lakes and Gananoque Lake near the St. Lawrence River have excellent largemouth-bass fishing too.

Prince Edward Island

Totally unlike the other Maritimes, Prince Edward Island is probably best explained if you imagine the state of Delaware moved several hundred miles north and dropped into the Gulf of St. Lawrence. Trout fishing is good, and deep-sea fishing is excellent, especially because the sheltered waters of the gulf prevent the formation of big ocean swells that cause seasickness.

Write to the Department of Fisheries, Charlottetown, Prince Edward Island, Canada, for "Summary of Angling Regulations," "Where to Fish on Prince Edward Island," "Prince Edward Island Trout Fishery," and "Fishing Fun for Everyone in Prince Edward Island." This last publication gives a complete list of deep-sea fishing boats and their captains, complete with addresses and telephone numbers. Cod, haddock, hake, and mackerel are in huge supply up here, and fishing is good enough to satisfy anybody.

Quebec

With Atlantic salmon both on the Gaspé Peninsula and in rivers running into the north shore of the St. Lawrence River, plus lake and brook trout, pike, bass, walleyes, muskellunge, landlocked salmon, whitefish, and sturgeon, Quebec has a wide range of angling activity. While few visitors try it, salt water fishing is excellent for cold water species, including cod, haddock, halibut, and mackerel.

Write to the Department of Tourism, Fish and Game Branch, Hotel du Government, Quebec, P.Q., Canada, and ask for the booklet of the Quebec Outfitters Association. This lists, in both French and English, every fishing camp and registered outfitter in the province, provides maps for each region (in general form), and details which species of fish are found in each location. Additionally, you'll want "Summary of the Fishing Regulations for Quebec" and "Provincial Parks of the Province of Quebec." In beautiful full color, this last booklet describes and provides maps of the six provincial parks and explains their facilities, which include camp grounds, inns, and much more.

Saskatchewan

A letter to the Tourist Development Branch, Power Building, Regina, Saskatchewan, will bring you. "The Fish of Saskatchewan," "Saskatchewan Tourist Accommodations," "Saskatchewan Campers' Guides," "Saskatchewan Fishing Guide," and "Saskatchewan Invites the Angler." These will help you get organized for a trip to an area with some of the finest fishing on the North American continent. At the present time new roads have opened lakes formerly reached only by trails or by aircraft, and the fishing is extremely good.

With more than 100,000 lakes, Saskatchewan offers everything from grayling to northern pike. Lake trout weighing over one hundred pounds have been taken. And you have a choice of either camping out yourself or going to a regular fishing camp with complete accommodations and guide service. Saskatchewan is putting a great deal of money and effort into research both to maintain and improve sports fishing and to discover whether or not commercial and sports fishing need be mutually exclusive. This type of praiseworthy foresight is going to insure that fishing will continue to be excellent for a long time to come.

Yukon Territory

This is the area made famous by Jack London and Robert Service and is the site of the original "Shooting of Dan McGrew." Today, much of the Yukon is accessible via the Alaska Highway. As you might suppose, fishing is excellent for grayling, several species of trout, northern pike, and introduced Cohoe and kokanee salmon. The place to write is the Department of Fisheries, Box 2410, Whitehorse, Yukon Territory, Canada. They'll send you "A General Fishing Guide for Yukon Territory," "Fishing Guides and Camps" (complete with full addresses), "Campgrounds and Lunch Stops," and "Alaska Highway, Road to Yukon Adventure." This gives you full information on everything, including a complete list of motels and other accommodations along the route. One big advantage of a Yukon fishing trip is the cost of a non-resident fishing license—two dollars.

XXXV.

How to Decide Where You Should Go

Decisions, decisions, decisions! Nobody can make them for you. Deciding where and when to go on a fishing trip to distant waters is a real chore. The best idea is to get as much information as you can before making a final decision. Additionally, wherever you go, be sure that the timing of your trip coincides with the usual best time of year for fishing in that area.

Where to stay is less of a problem. If you're in doubt about a fishing camp, ask the camp for references, preferably from people who live near you. Then check with them and be sure to ask not only about the fishing, but whether the buildings were comfortable and the food satisfactory. You won't find many highly skilled chefs at fishing camps, but neither do you want to subsist on canned beans.

As with local fishing, it is often advantageous to get in touch with the man who writes the hunting and fishing column for your newspaper. He probably has some information on nearly any area that you might want to visit. Additionally, he may know other outdoor writers who can give you first-hand facts from their own experience.

Magazine articles in sports publications are a good source of ideas. But remember that most of these articles were bought for their pictures as much as for their story. Also keep in mind that an angler whose trip was a failure isn't going to write a magazine piece about it.

Advertisements in the "Where to Go" columns of outdoor magazines are good to browse through. These ads are expensive, and you can be quite certain that anyone investing in this kind of advertising wouldn't spend the money unless he could back it up with the kind of fishing that brings repeat business and referrals. Incidentally most of the best resorts will want a small deposit with your reservation. This is because fishing camps generally have limited accommodations, and if you fail to show after making a reservation, the operator has empty space he could have rented to somebody else. Any fishing camp owner has only a few weeks or months of the year to make a profit, and he simply can't afford the luxury of empty quarters.

What about travel agents? Frankly, unless they are anglers themselves, they could give you an unfortunate experience without meaning to. If you are looking primarily for a family vacation with fishing as an afterthought, a travel agent can be of help. But if you are seriously interested in a fishing trip and want the help of an agent, be sure to consult one of the half dozen or so agencies that specialize in hunting and fishing vacations. These also advertise in outdoor magazines and can provide you with just about everything from a Canadian or Florida trip to a jaunt to Norway for salmon or to New Zealand for marlin.

Once again, it all depends on what you want to do and when you can get away. Winter is the time to visit much of Latin America, New Zealand and Australia, plus South Africa. (It's summer there when it's winter here.) Early spring is especially good for most Florida fishing. By May fresh water fishing is good right up to Canada, with June even better in the northern states. July and August are the time to go far north either in North America or to Norway, Sweden, and the British Isles. This is also salmon time in the Northwest. The fall months are good almost everywhere, with September an excellent striped-bass period in the Northeast. By November winter has pretty much set in again in the Northern Hemisphere, but December is a top Florida sailfish month and is good in lower California as well.

Photography Credits

Tony Stone Images: p. 10/Hanson Carroll, p. 14/Terry Vine, p. 19/Dan Ham, p. 126/Brian Bailey, p. 188/David J. Sams

J. Faircloth/Transparencies, Inc. : p. 100

Photo Researchers, Inc.: p. 103/William H. Mullins, p. 165/Will & Deni McIntyre

Brown Brothers: p. 134

Photodisc: All cover images, unless otherwise credited below

Grateful Acknowledgement is made to the following for their kind permission to reproduce the photographs listed below:

Arthur & Joan Cone: p. 221

Bass Pro Shops®: p. 49, p. 50, p. 53, p. 54, p. 56, p. 57, p. 63, p. 89, p.219, p. 23, jacket product shots

Nathan C.S. Frerichs: top right cover (courtesy of Marley Hodgson)

Hadley Fly Company: p. 93

Cecilia Kleinkauf/Women's Flyfishing: p.196, p. 240, bottom left back cover

Jessica MacMurray: p. 67, top center cover

Ross Reels: p.123, p. 193, bottom right back cover

Sassy Sara's: p. 139

Stren®: p. 226, p. 227, p. 228

U.S. Fish and Wildlife Service: p. 35, p. 44, p. 76, p. 104

All fish drawings © 1999 Vineyard Books

Icons appeariung in page corners and chapter heads © 1999 Dennis Cunnnigham

Index

Numbers in blue indicate illustrations